From Comparison to World Literature

SUNY series in Chinese Philosophy and Culture

Roger T. Ames, editor

From Comparison to World Literature

ZHANG LONGXI

SUNY
PRESS

Published by State University of New York Press, Albany

Printed in the United States of America

For information, contact State University of New York Press, Albany, NY
www.sunypress.edu

Production, Jenn Bennett
Marketing, Anne M. Valentine

Library of Congress Cataloging-in-Publication Data

Zhang, Longxi, date.
From comparison to world literature / Longxi Zhang.
pages cm. — (SUNY series in Chinese Philosophy and Culture)
Includes bibliographical references and index.
ISBN 978-1-4384-5471-9 (hc : alk. paper)—978-1-4384-5470-2 (pb : alk. paper)
ISBN 978-1-4384-5472-6 (ebook)
1. Comparative literature—Oriental and Western. 2. Comparative literature—Western and Oriental. I. Title.

PJ312.Z525 2015
809—dc23 2014007255

10 9 8 7 6 5 4 3 2 1

Contents

Introduction

The most noticeable development in literary studies in the last decade or so is undoubtedly a renewed interest in world literature, and this is happening not only in the United States and Europe, but also in China, India, Japan, and many other countries in Asia as well as in Latin America and other parts of the world. The term *Weltliteratur* was first made prominent by Johann Wolfgang von Goethe in the early 1820s, but Goethe's cosmopolitan vision of world literature as the coming together of very different literary traditions—he spoke of an imminent age of *Weltliteratur* in his conversation with Johann Peter Eckermann when he was reading a Chinese novel in translation—did not materialize in comparative literature that emerged in Europe in the late nineteenth century and was dominated by a positivistic emphasis on *rapport de fait* within the sphere of European history and culture. Comparative literature as a discipline remained largely a Eurocentric affair, by which I do not just mean self-centeredness, parochial interests, and hegemonic norms in a negative sense, but also in a descriptive sense: serious and influential scholarship that has mainly been concerned with comparing literary works in the European or Western tradition only. From Goethe to Erich Auerbach, from Leo Spitzer to René Wellek, from Franco Moretti to Pascale Casanova, all distinguished scholars who have made significant contributions to, and thus made their names well-known in, comparative literature are all Western or have made their career in the West. That is now changing, however, and the rise of world literature today has definitely a tendency to go beyond Eurocentric and any other ethnocentric enclosure to reach a truly global perspective, and a study in world literature would typically be expected to discuss important non-European poets, writers, and critics in addition to well-known European ones. Perhaps the time is now for world literature finally to engage literatures of the entire world rather than just one particular dominant region, and to give us a truly global view of human creativity in the various forms of literary manifestations.

The expansion of horizon in literary studies is exciting, and it surely has its basis in economic and political changes in our time, in an age of globalization. More specifically, it occurs at a time when the world is witnessing the rise of Asian and South American economies and concurrently a financial crisis and economic downturn in the United States and the European Union. We find the world today a very different one from merely twenty years ago. At the same time, however, we must also realize that literary and cultural relations are different from economic and political ones, and that they are not just reflections of patterns of political economy. As Pascale Casanova argues forcefully, "there exists a 'literature-world,' a literary universe relatively independent of the everyday world and its political divisions, whose boundaries and operational laws are not reducible to those of ordinary political space," even though the forms of literary relations may in many respects depend on "the forms of political dominion."[1] Despite the leveling effect of globalization in the production and distribution of material goods as commodities, the emphasis in the creation and appreciation of literary and artistic works lies precisely on diversity, specificity, and local identities, on the features of a particular tradition that are nonetheless accessible to a global audience or reading public. World literature is by no means a simple by-product of economic globalization; it can and must be studied within its own "literature-world" on issues that are specific to certain cultural and historical circumstances, to some aesthetic or formal characteristics, while they can, and in many cases must, be put in the larger context of social and political interactions among nations and national traditions. The social and the cultural, the political and the literary, the local and the global—these are not mutually exclusive claims in the study of human experiences and human expressions, and world literature thus offers us not just the occasion to appreciate works from different traditions for their aesthetic appeal and broadly human interest, but also the glimpse into the specific conditions in which those works are created and circulated, the opportunity to understand different cultural and historical circumstances that necessarily deepen our appreciation.

From the very beginning, comparative literature as an academic discipline has for very good reason put linguistic proficiency high on the priority list of required expertise, and it is understandably difficult to cross over the huge

1. Pascale Casanova, *The World Republic of Letters*, trans. M. B. DeBevoise (Cambridge, MA: Harvard University Press, 2004), p. xii.

gaps of language groups, particularly between East Asian and European languages. Linguistic rigor, however, cannot be an excuse for denying large-scale comparisons, and for world literature to develop beyond the usual East-West divide, it is absolutely necessary to bridge linguistic and cultural gaps, and also to take adequate translation into consideration. The possibility of cross-cultural understanding and the question of translatability are still major issues that challenge comparative studies and world literature. Many influential thinkers and scholars in both the West and the East tend to argue for the fundamental difference between Asia and Europe, particularly ancient China and ancient Greece as originating sources of difference; and they insist on the untranslatability of different languages and cultures, particularly between East Asian and European languages. Indeed, China is often thought to be the opposite of Europe, inhabiting an improbable space of a Foucaultian *heterotopia*, with its non-phonetic scripts representing the irreducible writing of a Derridean *différance*, symbolizing the ultimate non-European Other. Such dichotomous views create a major obstacle for cross-cultural comparisons and world literature, and I take it to be the task of the present volume to examine such claims to cultural incommensurability and fundamental differences between China and the West, and to argue not only for the possibility, but also the necessity of cross-cultural understanding against all odds, despite all the differences.

The first three chapters in this book deal with the theoretical and methodological issues of comparative studies across linguistic and cultural differences. Chapter 1 lays the ground for comparative studies by presenting comparison as ontologically given in thinking and in all human actions, as we always need to make decisions in life and act upon our decisions, and all decision-making or choices are based on comparison. In that basic sense, then, comparison is something we always do, and it is pointless to talk about whether we should or should not compare. The question is not whether, but how, and what consequences our comparisons, choices, and decisions will have in our own lives as well as those of others. Such questions constitute the ethics and politics of comparison. Facing a crossroads is a conceptual metaphor of making comparisons and difficult choices, and the nineteenth-century motif of *tuer le mandarin* in European literature is another metaphor for thinking about ethics as a moral choice, as extending one's moral responsibilities to outsiders and strangers as compared with one's relatives and inner groups. Translation is inherently comparative, as it is all about finding comparable or equivalent expressions in one language for those in another, and the issue of translatability on a conceptual level is crucial for any effort at cross-cultural understanding. By looking at the conceptual metaphors of crossroads and distant killing, and by discussing the problem of translatability, the first chapter deals with the moral and political implications of choices and decisions, and argues for the absolute necessity of comparison.

Chapter 2 takes difference seriously and examines differences on three distinct levels—individual, cultural, and cross-cultural. The tendency toward East-West dichotomy usually ignores internal, individual differences within the same culture so as to put an overemphasis on collective or cross-cultural differences. Ethnography as a discipline is often trapped by the ethnographer's presumption of a "surplus of difference" in the exotic tribe's allegedly different ways of living, and Thomas Kuhn's concept of incommensurability has the same problem of assuming fundamental differences between paradigms that deny the possibility of understanding and communication. By looking at some of the dichotomous arguments and their critique, and by discussing Geoffrey Lloyd's more balanced view of China and Greece as both different and comparable, this chapter shows how the universalist's denial of any difference and the relativist's insistence on all difference without affinities are both mistaken, and that differences exist everywhere, within the same culture as well as between or among cultures. Chapter 3 continues the discussion and revisits the question of difference and affinity as a methodological issue in comparative studies. From a hermeneutic point of view, any comparative study, indeed any scholarly argument, could be understood as proposing an answer to a specific question as its context, and therefore it is pointless to ask, without a particular context, whether one should put emphasis on difference or on affinity in comparative studies. In ancient times, both Chinese and Greek philosophers realized that harmony is not the effect of one or uniformity, but the combination of diverse elements. More importantly today, it is necessary for us to realize that affinity does not mean sameness without diversity, and difference does not mean incommensurability that denies the very possibility of comparison and communication.

The next three chapters discuss in more specific terms the issue of understanding China from a cross-cultural perspective. Chapter 4 launches a critique of a distorted view of "heaven and man merging into one" in the Chinese tradition, which presents an "Eastern holistic view" of man and nature as forming a perfectly harmonious relationship, while depicting an aggressive "Western analytic outlook" that sets out to conquer nature and creates all the problems we face in our world today. By going back to the classic articulation of "heaven and man" in the works of Dong Zhongshu (179–104 BCE) of the Han dynasty, I demonstrate how such a distortion has little to do with the traditional Chinese idea, which aimed at setting up a cosmological and political hierarchy for legitimizing the imperial rule, and how that Chinese concept was in fact highly comparable with the European idea of correspondences between nature and man as macrocosm and microcosm, and with the idea of the body politic in Western political theory. Distortions by Chinese scholars in the interest of a narrow-minded nationalism and the ethnocentric sense of the superiority of Eastern culture are just as untenable and detrimental to cross-cultural understanding as the East-West divide set up in a relativist paradigm in the West.

Chapter 5 examines the debate about different models in understanding Chinese history in American China studies, particularly Paul Cohen's critique of West-centered American Sinology and his counterproposal of a "China-centered" approach, one that tries to reconstruct Chinese history through empathetic understanding as the Chinese themselves had experienced it. While I admire Cohen's effort to go beyond Western-centrism, I question whether assuming a Chinese insider's view would necessarily guarantee a better understanding of Chinese history as a whole. Individual views are all limited, whether from the inside or the outside, and how to reach a comprehensive view of history from such limited and finite individual experiences is a challenge that needs to be answered by the historian in proposing a method in historical studies. Drawing on a great Chinese poet Su Shi's (1037–1101) famous lines on Mount Lu, I argue that neither the insider nor the outsider has the monopolistic access to knowledge and truth, as the true face of Mount Lu is multiple, not singular, the combination or integration of all the different views from different vantage points, "high or low, or far or nearby," from the inside or the outside. That also means to integrate knowledge and understanding between Sinology and native Chinese scholarship. Chapter 6 discusses the structural similarities and important differences between historical and literary narratives and argues against the extreme view that sees history as no different from literary fiction. By drawing on examples from both Western and Chinese historiographies, I maintain that historical writing is indeed similar with literary narrative in many ways and has often been appreciated for its literary quality as much as for its fidelity to historical facts, but in the West and particularly in China, important differences between history and literary fiction are always recognized and properly acknowledged. The Chinese concept of *shi de* or the historian's virtue, the historian's commitment to telling the truth as a moral choice and responsibility, is crucial for understanding such differences. History and fiction are indeed comparable, but the certitude of historiography lays a solid ground for moral and political action that cannot be neglected in irresponsibly erasing the difference between the two forms of narratives.

The last four chapters move from comparison toward world literature. Chapter 7 discusses utopia and its double—dystopia—as an important genre in world literature, and by drawing on utopian elements not only in the European tradition, but also from Chinese and Islamic cultures, this chapter shows how the pursuit of a land of happiness is a basic and universal human desire; but the delicate balance between individual happiness and the collective interests of a social order has always been a difficult problem with all utopias, also the reason why it has the nasty tendency to turn into its dystopian opposite. We are now perhaps living in a post-utopian age of disillusionment of all social hopefulness, but it is impossible for the human dream of a better society to die down completely and forever, and therefore utopia, or at least some form of a better version of the utopian construction, is still to come in our literary and social imagination. Chapter 8 is an attempt to present an erudite modern Chinese scholar, Qian Zhongshu, as an important model in the study of world literature. Intellectual encounters between China and Europe can be dated back to the late seventeenth century, when Jesuit missionaries came to China and started to interact with Chinese literati-officials, whereas Western ideas and cultural values presented a much greater challenge to the age-old Chinese tradition during the twentieth century. Given his background and upbringing, Qian Zhongshu may arguably be the most learned and the best representative of modern Chinese scholars in integrating great traditions of both China and the West. He is extremely knowledgeable in the tradition of Chinese culture and Chinese classics, and he also has a profound understanding of Western culture and its intellectual tradition. His scholarly works are textually based, typically with a wealth of quotations not only from classical Chinese texts, but also from texts in English, French, German, Italian, Spanish, and Latin. The intertextuality of his writing always presents his ideas with strong textual evidence and makes his point valid and significant across linguistic and cultural boundaries. I am confident that Qian Zhongshu will become as important as any of the more familiar names in the Western scholarly tradition when more and more people come to read his works and realize what an eminent and exemplary comparatist he is, and in so doing benefit from his works for acquiring a truly global perspective in the study of world literature.

Chapter 9 is an attempt at conceptualizing a poetics of world literature. In its literal sense world literature means all the literary works produced in the world, but that would include such an impossibly huge amount of literary works that the word would become meaningless, because no one can read even a tiny portion of the world's literature. What world literature really means is those literary works that are read and appreciated, most likely in adequate translations, by readers the world over, far beyond the original environment of a particular language and a particular national tradition in which the works are produced. Likewise, the poetics of world literature does not mean the juxtaposition of all the critical concepts and ideas from the world's different literary traditions, but a set of fundamental questions concerning the nature, origin, qualities, values, techniques, and components of literature, questions that poetics or critical theories are dealing with in different cultures and traditions. True to its name, the poetics of world literature must include critical views coming not only from different traditions, but from different regions or continents of the world. In this chapter, therefore, in addition to discussions of the Western tradition and its most celebrated work, Aristotle's *Poetics*, there are also discussions of commentaries and critical theories from the Arabic, the Indian, and the Chinese traditions. Although there can be many more ideas of poetics from other traditions, I maintain that what matters for poetics is not so much comprehensiveness as relevance and representativeness, that is to say, the poetics of world literature must be comparative, encompassing more than one national or regional tradition, and should lead us to a better understanding of world literature with depth and appreciation. What is important in the poetics of world literature, and indeed in world literature itself, is the integration of different literary and cultural perspectives, a truly global and cosmopolitan vision that helps making cross-cultural understanding possible among the world's different peoples and their communities.

By revisiting world literature as a changing concept, Chapter 10 sums up the points made in much of this volume. For East-West comparative studies, the Chinese connection of Goethe's concept of *Weltliteratur* certainly has a particular relevancy, for he related his experience of reading a Chinese novel with the idea of world literature, finding himself completely capable of entering the world of a foreign work, both strange and familiar. The cosmopolitan vision of world literature has the potential of reading and evaluating literary works of really very different traditions, but some of the influential models in the study of world literature we have today still pose a problem of Eurocentric limitations. Drawing on Immanuel Wallerstein's "world-systems" theory, which is in itself based on European historical experience, Franco Moretti argues that the modern novel develops from European centers of metropolitan culture to non-European peripheries, a kind of a radiation of influence from European centers to non-European receptacles. Such a model largely ignores the local tradition and its resilience, the counter-influence of a local form that often plays a significant role in the transformation of the traditional novel into a new and modern incarnation. Similarly, Casanova's concept of the "world republic of letters" has its capital in Paris, and this Paris-centered view of world literature is blissfully oblivious of the existence of other literatures, literature of other regions and time periods, indeed any other part of the world outside Europe and its former colonies. If we are serious about the "world" in world literature, we must transcend such Eurocentric limitations and embrace the world as we know it in its marvelous richness and diversity. That is the reason why we need to emphasize the inclusiveness of our approach to the study of world literature, the integration of different views and insights, and the possibility of new and more expansive horizons. The conceptual openness or flexibility of world literature, the dynamic mix of new works from previously neglected regions into the canon of well-known major works, all these make world literature a vital and vibrating new field with new possibilities for literary studies.

By definition world literature is a global notion, but it is necessarily localized whenever it appears in a real context. No work of literature is created as a work of "world literature" for the simple reason that it is always inextricably linked with a particular language and a particular tradition. Despite the anxiety of losing distinct linguistic and cultural traits in what Stephen Owen has criticized as "world poetry," no significant work of world literature is produced originally in a "universal language" like Esperanto or written in such a way as to be translated for global transmission and consumption.[2] It is true that a global tendency is emerging that some internationally well-known contemporary writers have produced works in one language but have given permission to translation of their works into other languages to be released simultaneously, sometimes even before the original version is available. These are often internationally best-selling novelists such as Salman Rushdie, Don DeLillo, Paul Auster, and Gabriel García Márquez, not to mention the hugely popular *Harry Potter* series. Contemporary success as international best sellers, however, may not guarantee the status of a canonical work in world literature, while the success of these very works depends in a significant measure on the special local features of a tradition that situates the narrative in a humanly meaningful manner.

If we look at the several successful world literature anthologies currently available in the book market, most of the selections are canonical works in various traditions in addition to the usual European classics. David Damrosch's influential book, *What Is World Literature?* discusses the earliest literary works like *Gilgamesh* and the unfamiliar works in Mesoamerica and ancient

2. See Stephen Owen, "The Anxiety of Global Influence: What Is World Poetry?" *New Republic* (Nov. 19, 1990): 28–32.

Egypt, and he argues that even for very well-known canonical European works, world literature provides a new perspective for quite different possibilities of understanding. "Major canonical masterpieces are worthy of sustained attention both for aesthetic and for cultural reasons," says Damrosch, "but they persist so strongly, after all, not because they float forever in some eternal realm but because they adapt so effectively to the changing needs of different times and places, and the transformation now occurring in the shape of world literature is having a major impact on the ways we read even the greatest of great books."[3] World literature with its global context changes the way a particular work is read, and the local and the global have an interesting relationship in the transformation of a work from its original national milieu to the context of world literature. "Works of world literature are best read with an awareness of the work's original cultural context," Damrosch continues, "but they typically wear this context rather lightly. Read as a work of Italian literature, Dante's *Commedia* is naturally seen in close connection to a host of medieval poets, theologians, and political thinkers, most of whose works are likely to be entirely unknown outside Italy except to specialists."[4] Many canonical works of Western literature, like Dante's *Commedia*, have a global impact because they have already been read as works meaningful not only in their local environment, but globally as works of world literature. For works from non-Western traditions, world literature now provides an excellent opportunity to move beyond their local, national environment to a much larger context in which they can be understood and appreciated by readers they never anticipated to reach, readers with very different background, cultural values, reading habits, and expectations. This is indeed a great opportunity for scholars working in non-Western literary traditions, but it is also a great challenge to make non-Western works that are canonical in a local environment adequately understood and appreciated in a global context, and in my view, this is where comparative literature and cross-cultural studies can help make a difference.

In putting together this volume, I have made various degrees of revision for all the chapters that have either been previously published or to be published in a different form. Chapter 1 was written as a chapter in *Comparison: Theories, Approaches, Uses*, edited by Rita Felski and Susan Friedman and published by the Johns Hopkins University Press in 2013; Chapter 2 was published in *Interdisciplinary Science Review* (Dec. 2010), in a special issue in response to G. E. R. Lloyd's contribution to that journal; Chapter 3 was published in

3. David Damrosch, *What Is World Literature?* (Princeton, NJ: Princeton University Press, 2003), p. 135.

4. Ibid., pp. 139–40.

Revue de littérature comparée (Jan.–March 2011); Chapter 4 was included in *Comparative Political Theory and Cross-Cultural Philosophy: Essays in Honor of Hwa Yol Jung*, edited by Jin Y. Park and published by Lexington Books in 2009; Chapter 5 first appeared in *History and Theory* (Feb. 2010); Chapter 6 was published in *Rethinking History* (Sept. 2004); Chapter 7 was written at the invitation of Professor Piero Boitani of the University of Rome "Sapienza" and presented at the international conference "Dall'antico al moderno" held in Rome in September 2012; Chapter 8 was published in *Revue de littérature comparée* (June 2013); Chapter 9 was published in *The Routledge Companion to World Literature*, edited by Theo D'haen, David Damrosch, and Djelal Kadir and published by Routledge in 2012; and finally Chapter 10 was the concluding essay written at the invitation of Professor David Damrosch of Harvard University for the volume *World Literature in Theory* which he edited and was published by Wiley-Blackwell in 2014. I am grateful to my many friends and colleagues who have invited me to contribute to the various books and journals or to give lectures or conference presentations, and have given me much inspiration, encouragement, and moral support over the years of my academic career. There are too many I would like to thank to be fully listed here, but their friendship and collegiality are deeply appreciated; all the mistakes and imperfections that remain in these pages are, of course, my own responsibility.

Zhang LONGXI
Cherry Crest, Hong Kong
March 2014

1

Crossroads, Distant Killing, and Translation

On the Ethics and Politics of Comparison

> The way (*tao*) of Heaven, isn't it comparable to pulling a bow?
> That which is too high is lowered down; that which is too low is lifted up.
> That which is too much is reduced; that which is not enough is compensated.
> The way of Heaven is to reduce what is too much and compensate what is not enough.
> The way of man is not like this:
> It takes from those who have not enough and gives it to those who already have too much.
> Who can take the too much and give it to all under heaven?
> Only the one who is in possession of the *tao*.
>
> —*Laozi*, chapter 77[1]

To compare or not to compare, unlike to be, or not to be: that is *not* the question. On a most basic level, ontologically speaking, we cannot but compare, and we compare all the time in order to differentiate, recognize, understand, make judgments or decisions, and act upon our decisions. All our actions in cognitive and physical terms depend on making comparisons, and we have no other alternative but to compare, because as human beings we all rush into existence *in medias res*, with our living conditions and social environment,

1. Wang Bi (226–249), *Laozi zhu* [*Laozi with Annotations*], in *Zhuzi jicheng* [*Collection of Masters Writings*], 8 vols. (Beijing: Zhonghua, 1954), 3:45. All translations from Chinese are mine. The *Laozi* or *Tao te ching* has dozens of English translations; interested readers may look at *Tao te ching*, trans. D. C. Lau (Harmondsworth: Penguin, 1963), or *The Classic of the Way and Virtue: A New Translation of the Tao-te ching of Laozi as Interpreted by Wang Bi*, trans. Richard John Lynn (New York: Columbia University Press, 1999).

including language and culture, already in place, and our life is always caught in between what is given and what is yet possible, external reality and our dreams, desires, and choices. High or low, superfluity or destitution, all these are impossible to conceive without comparison, and it is impossible to achieve the appropriate equilibrium between having too much and having not enough without making the right choice in comparison. It is one of life's little ironies that we have no choice but to choose, and when we choose, we must compare. The contrast between the self-plenitude of identity and the multiple-dependence of difference is an illusion, because the very concept of identity is established through comparison and differentiation, as Sigmund Freud has argued in psychoanalysis and Ferdinand de Saussure in linguistics.

Freud describes the ego as developing according to the "reality principle" by constantly comparing and interacting between the desires and impulses of the id on the one hand, and what is available in the external world on the other. For my purposes here, I cite a short piece by Freud that deals with the problem of identity and difference with direct reference to language in a way that reminds us of Saussure's linguistic understanding. "Our conceptions arise through comparison," says Freud in a review of Karl Abel's *Über den Gegensinn der Urworte*. "Were it always light we should not distinguish between light and dark, and accordingly could not have either the conception of, nor the word for, light," Freud reminds us with Abel. "'It is clear that everything on this planet is relative and has independent existence only in so far as it is distinguished in its relations to and from other things' . . . 'Man has not been able to acquire even his oldest and simplest conceptions otherwise than in contrast with their opposites; he only gradually learnt to separate the two sides of the antithesis and think of the one without conscious comparison with the other.'"[2] In psychoanalytic understanding, nothing exists without comparison with, and in contradistinction to, its opposite. The naive belief in one's own plenitude is mere "narcissism," typical of children and "primitive man," which Freud sees as gradually dismantled by the progress of science: "the self-love of humanity suffered its first blow, the *cosmological* one," when the Copernican heliocentric theory was generally accepted; Darwinian evolution dealt "the second, *biological* blow to human narcissism"; and Freud's own psychoanalysis constitutes the third blow, "the *psychological* one."[3] The human self is fundamentally and dynamically constructed in comparison and

2. Sigmund Freud, "The Antithetical Sense of Primal Words," trans. M. N. Searl, in *Collected Papers*, 5 vols. (New York: Basic Books, 1959), 4:187

3. Freud, "One of the Difficulties of Psycho-Analysis," trans. Joan Riviere, ibid., 4:351, 352.

differentiation, and its development a process of *Bildung* that proceeds through a constant cycle of alienation and return, an endless process of learning from what is different and alien.

We find an eminently comparable formulation of identity and difference in Saussure's structural linguistics. "The linguistic mechanism is geared to differences and identities," says Saussure, "the former being only the counterpart of the latter." He considers language as a system of mutually defining terms, in which the value of each sign is determined in comparison with those of other signs, and what is seen as identical is actually equivalent, that is, of equal values in comparison. He illustrates this characteristic of linguistic signs by drawing comparisons with non-linguistic examples. "For instance, we speak of the identity of two '8:25 p.m. Geneva-to-Paris' trains that leave at twenty-four hour intervals. We feel that it is the same train each day, yet everything—the locomotive, coaches, personnel—is probably different. Or if a street is demolished, then rebuilt, we say that it is the same street even though in a material sense, perhaps nothing of the old one remains."[4] The examples bring out the point that what we consider to be the same or the identical may in fact be quite different, and what counts as same or different is determined by an entire network of signs in mutual differentiation. "In language there are only differences," says Saussure. "Even more important: a difference generally implies positive terms between which the difference is set up; but in language there are only differences *without positive terms*."[5] The point is that identity is not self-sufficient but is defined by what it is not more than what it is. In other words, identity is established in and through comparisons. Human existence is one of relations, and the necessity of comparison is a given in life, which presents both a good opportunity and a serious challenge.

Crossroads and Parallelism

The difficulty of comparing and making choices is well-illustrated by the story about an ancient Chinese philosopher Yang Zhu, who "wept at a crossroads, for it could lead to the south or to the north."[6] This may sound odd, but it

4. Ferdinand de Saussure, *Course in General Linguistics*, trans. Wade Baskin (New York: Philosophical Library, 1959), p. 108.

5. Ibid., p. 120.

6. Liu An (?–122 BC), *Huainanzi* [*Master Huainan*], in *Zhuzi jicheng* [*Collection of Masters Writings*], 7:302. A slightly different version of this story can be found in an even earlier text, *Xunzi*, and we can learn about the life and thoughts of Yang Zhu in several other texts, notably *Liezi*.

takes a philosopher to weep at the juncture of uncertain possibilities, where the philosophical *Angst* is as much about making comparison as it is literally about choosing the right road. Facing a crossroads is of course a conceptual metaphor for facing the dilemma of uncertain possibilities and difficult choices. As George Lakoff and Mark Turner argue, "metaphor resides in thought, not just in words."[7] Conceptual metaphors reveal the deep-seated metaphoricity of the mind that constantly puts things in comparison and maps them over one another. It would be sheer stupidity to take a road that may lead to the south or to the north without considering what may lie ahead, but it is the figurative or metaphorical meaning of a crossroads that enables us to understand Yang Zhu's anxiety—not that he was perplexed by roads going in different directions, but that he feared the consequences of making a wrong move.

In facing roads that diverged in a wood, Robert Frost may have shown, in comparison with the Chinese philosopher, a more robust sense of determination in simply saying that "I— / I took the one less traveled by, /And that has made all the difference."[8] The last line seems to make a factual statement about the consequences of the road taken or the choice made, but what about the road not taken (which is, after all, the title of this famous poem)? Isn't the statement made "with a sigh"? Isn't there the suggestion of a sense of loss or regret, a tinge of sadness perhaps in those words? As another American poet, John Whittier, puts it, "For all sad words of tongue or pen, / The saddest are these: 'it might have been!' "[9] It is in comparison with what "might have been," the lost opportunity of an imagined better condition, that sadness sets in. Happiness or sadness is of course a matter of perception in comparison. "All happy families resemble one another, each unhappy family is unhappy in its own way," so begins Leo Tolstoy's great novel, *Anna Karenina*, in a neat parallelism.[10] The Chinese novel *Romance of the Three Kingdoms* starts likewise

---

7. George Lakoff and Mark Turner, *More than Cool Reason: A Field Guide to Poetic Metaphor* (Chicago: University of Chicago Press, 1989), p. 2. The concept of identity is not "autonomous," Lakoff and Turner insist, and they present their argument against the "autonomy claim" of language, i.e., the view that conventional language is semantically autonomous and not metaphoric. Instead, they maintain that "conventional language and our conventional conceptual system are fundamentally and ineradicably metaphoric," and that "there are general mappings across both poetic and everyday conventional language." Quoting Robert Frost's lines about roads taken and not taken, they argue that if the metaphor is not fundamentally conceptual, "there would be no way to explain either why we understand this passage to be about life or why we reason about it as we do" (p. 116).

8. Robert Frost, "The Road Not Taken," *Selected Poems* (New York: Gramercy Books, 1992), p. 163.

9. John Greenleaf Whittier, "Maud Muller," in Percy H. Boynton (ed.), *American Poetry* (New York: Charles Scribner's Sons, 1918), p. 254.

10. Leo Tolstoy, *Anna Karenina*, trans. Louise Maude and Aylmer Maude (Oxford: Oxford University Press, 1998), p. 1.

with a comparison, a cyclical notion of history, which presents unity and division as the two choices alternately made in the unfolding of dynastic history: "Speaking of the overall condition of all under heaven, it tends toward unity after prolonged division, and division after prolonged unity."[11]

It could be instructive to see how many memorable beginnings of great novels tell us about the world, real or fictional, by way of comparison. Here is one of the most well-known, the beginning of Charles Dickens's *A Tale of Two Cities*:

> It was the best of times, it was the worst of times, it was the age of wisdom, it was the age of foolishness, it was the epoch of belief, it was the epoch of incredulity, it was the season of Light, it was the season of Darkness, it was the spring of hope, it was the winter of despair, we had everything before us, we had nothing before us, we were all going direct to Heaven, we were all going direct the other way—in short, the period was so far like the present period, that some of its noisiest authorities insisted on its being received, for good or for evil, in the superlative degree of comparison only.[12]

The parallel structure of this passage is fundamentally comparative, and comparison is, as noted above, not just a structural given in language, but in the mind itself. "In giving shapes to human beings, nature always makes their bodies in symmetry with limbs in pairs. Through the use of divine principles, nothing is left in isolation," says Liu Xie (465?–522), a fifth-century Chinese critic, as he traces parallelism in language and thinking to a natural, even divine origin. "The mind creates literary expressions, and puts a hundred thoughts in the right design. The high and the low are mutually dependent, thus one-to-one parallels are naturally formed."[13] Liu Xie's words seem perfectly suited to what we experience in reading the passage from Dickens. The rhetorical juxtaposition, antithesis, and parallelism are all predicated on the mental work

11. Luo Guanzhong (1330?–1400?), *San guo yanyi* [*The Romance of the Three Kingdoms*] (Beijing: Renmin wenxue, 1985), p. 1. For an available English translation, see *Three Kingdoms: A Historical Novel,* attributed to Luo Guanzhong, trans. Moss Roberts (Berkeley: University of California Press, 1991).

12. Charles Dickens, *A Tale of Two Cities* (New York: The Modern Library, 1996), p. 3.

13. Liu Xie (465?–522), *Wenxin diaolong zhu* [*The Literary Mind or the Carving of Dragons with Annotations*], 2 vols., annotated by Fan Wenlan (Beijing: Renmin wenxue, 1958), 2:588. For an available English translation, see Liu Hsieh, *The Literary Mind and the Carving of Dragons: A Study of Thought and Pattern in Chinese Literature*, trans. Vincent Yu-chung Shih (New York: Columbia University Press, 1959).

of thinking in comparisons, and in reading Dickens's depiction of an age full of contradictions, we seem to detect a strong rhythmic impulse that reveals a natural tendency toward comparison.

For Roman Jakobson, parallelism embodies Saussure's legacy, his "radical distinction between the 'syntagmatic' and 'associative' planes of language," a "fundamental dichotomy."[14] Jakobson further develops that dichotomy into the two axes of "positional (namely, syntactic) contiguity" represented by metonymy and "semantic similarity" represented by metaphor, the interaction of which can be seen everywhere in language, but is particularly pronounced in literary parallelism. "Rich material for the study of this relationship is to be found in verse patterns which require a compulsory parallelism between adjacent lines," says Jakobson, and he mentions examples "in Biblical poetry or in the West Finnic and, to some extent, the Russian oral traditions."[15] If he knew Chinese, he would probably have added Chinese poetry as the most exemplary, for the second and third couplets in a Chinese *lü shi* or regulated verse, also known as "recent-style poetry," require the parallel structure of an antithesis far more strict than most other prosodies. A famous poem by the great Tang poet Du Fu (712–770) is unusual in having parallelism in every couplet, which may give us some idea of the strict prosodic rules for making a regulated verse in classical Chinese poetry:

> The wind is strong, the sky high, sadly the gibbons are crying,
> The islets are clear, the sands white, in circles the birds are flying.
> Boundless forests shed their leaves swirling and rustling down,
> The endless river flows with waves rolling and running near.
> Ten thousand miles, in sorrowful autumn, often as a wanderer I sigh,
> A hundred years, old and sick, alone up the high terrace I climb.
> In misery and hardships, I hate to see my hair turning all white,
> Out of ill fortune and poor health, I've lately abstained from wine.[16]

In my translation above, I try to keep the word order as close to the original as possible so that the parallelism of each couplet can be seen clearly. Each word in the adjacent lines of a couplet is put in comparison with its

14. Roman Jakobson and Morris Halle, *Fundamentals of Language* (The Hague: Mouton & Co., 1956), p. vi.

15. Ibid., p. 77.

16. Du Fu, "Climbing Up the Terrace," in Qiu Zhao'ao (fl. 1685), *Du shi xiangzhu* [*Du Fu's Poems with Detailed Annotations*], 5 vols. (Beijing: Zhonghua, 1979), 4:1766–67.

counterpart—thus "the wind is strong" and "the islets are clear," "the sky high" and "the sands white," "the gibbons are crying" and "the birds are flying," "boundless forests" and "the endless river," "ten thousand miles" and "a hundred years,"—all these are strictly parallel and must contrast to one another in meaning, grammatical category, and particularly tone, as Chinese has four tones and the tonal pattern forms the basis of the musical quality of the language. As Yu-kung Kao and Tsu-lin Mei note, "Jakobson's theory can account for the facts of [Chinese] Recent Style poetry with greater ease than for those of Western poetry—for which the theory was originally intended."[17] In discussing the formation of Chinese phrases and the required antithetical structure of regulated verse, James J. Y. Liu claims that "there is a natural tendency in Chinese towards antithesis." He makes a distinction between antithesis in Chinese poetry and parallelism in other literatures and argues that "antithesis, known as *tuei* in Chinese, differs from 'parallelism,' such as in Hebrew poetry. Antithesis consists of strict antonyms, allowing no repetition of the same words, as parallelism does."[18] It is true that Chinese poetry requires a more strictly antithetical structure than biblical parallelism, but the principle of its structure is comparative, and in that sense, antithesis can be seen as a subspecies of parallelism, not something entirely different in kind. Indeed, whether it is identity through differentiation in a psychological or a linguistic sense, crossroads as a conceptual metaphor or contradictions juxtaposed at the beginning of a novel, the antithesis in a Chinese regulated verse or parallelism in biblical poetry, all these are fundamentally related to comparison, which proves to be the *modus operandi* of thinking and language.

In the postmodern critique of fundamentals, we are told not to essentialize anything and not to hold things in a metaphysical hierarchy, as though any kind of comparison or differentiation, any value judgment, or any order of things would result in a repressive regime that privileges one and, of necessity, excludes all other alternatives. That may explain why some feel uneasy about comparison and question its validity, but if we do not compare and prioritize at all among a number of possibilities, we cannot move, and there would be no action, no narrative, no literature, and no history. Weeping at a crossroads as the philosopher Yang Zhu did may be in itself a temporary choice, but

---

17. Yu-kung Kao and Tsu-lin Mei, "Meaning, Metaphor, and Allusion in T'ang Poetry," *Harvard Journal of Asiatic Studies* 38:2 (1978): 287.

18. James J. Y. Liu, *The Art of Chinese Poetry* (Chicago: University of Chicago Press, 1962), p. 146. For a classic study of parallelism in biblical poetry, see James L. Kugel, *The Idea of Biblical Poetry: Parallelism and Its History* (New Haven, CT: Yale University Press, 1981).

eventually you need to choose a road and move on. Otherwise, you may shed a lot of tears, but your life remains an empty possibility, not a lived experience. The point is, again, not that we can choose to compare or not to compare, but that we need to make reasonable comparisons and good choices rather than bad ones: good and bad in a profoundly ethical and political sense, as the comparison and the choice we make have consequences affecting our own lives as well as the lives of others. Since comparison is something we always do anyway, all the talk about whether to compare is but idle talk. The question is not whether, but how;—it is a matter of the relevance or reasonableness of the comparison we make, and of its consequences and implications.

Killing a Chinese Mandarin

Kwame Anthony Appiah presents cosmopolitanism as a moral choice, the idea that "no local loyalty can ever justify forgetting that each human being has responsibilities to every other."[19] Here local closeness is compared with, or contrasted to, the distance of the "other," whose fate and condition may seem far from one's immediate concerns. Distance in time and space is a matter of comparison: How far does one's obligation or responsibility extend to a stranger as compared to one's relatives or close friends? How does one treat someone unseen or even unknown in comparison with one's own group or community? In this context, Appiah recalls a scene in Balzac's novel, *Le Père Goriot*, where Eugène Rastignac talks to a friend and poses a question he attributes, erroneously, to Jacques Rousseau. "Have you read Rousseau?" asks Rastignac. "Do you recall the passage where he asks the reader what he'd do if he could make himself rich by killing an old mandarin in China merely by willing it, without budging from Paris?"[20] The killing of a Chinese mandarin far from France by mere volition, without ever getting close and dirtying one's hands, and therefore without the danger of being found out and punished, is presumably something a Frenchman might fancy in view of getting the mandarin's wealth in return. Like Yang Zhu weeping at a crossroads, wondering whether to kill a mandarin in China may serve as another conceptual metaphor with philosophical implications. "Rastignac's question is splendidly philosophical,"

19. Kwame Anthony Appiah, *Cosmopolitanism: Ethics in a World of Strangers* (New York: W. W. Norton, 2006), p. xvi.

20. Honoré de Balzac, *Le Père Goriot* (Paris: Éditions Garniers Frères, 1961), p. 154; quoted in Appiah, *Cosmopolitanism*, p. 155.

Appiah notes. "Who but a philosopher would place magical murder in one pan of the scales and a million gold louis in the other?"[21] Weighing a stranger's life on a balance against "a million gold louis" vividly evokes the point of moral choice and challenges one to consider the ethical and political implications of comparison, and also the core idea of cosmopolitanism as extending one's moral responsibilities to distant outsiders and strangers.

Rastignac's question, however, does not come from Rousseau, but more likely from Adam Smith in a passage in *The Theory of Moral Sentiments* (1760). In discussing the limitations of moral imagination, Smith speculates how a European might react to the news of an imagined earthquake that suddenly wiped out "the great empire of China." Though a decent European might feel sorry for "the misfortune of that unhappy people" and reflect on "the precariousness of human life," eventually he would go back to his daily routine, "with the same ease and tranquility, as if no such accident had happened." The death of millions of Chinese would seem insignificant in comparison with the smallest pain that might happen to his own person. "If he is to lose his little finger to-morrow," writes Smith, "he would not sleep to-night; but, provided he never saw them, he will snore with the most profound security over the ruin of a hundred millions of his brethren, and the destruction of that immense multitude seems plainly an object less interesting to him, than this paltry misfortune of his own."[22]

Appiah sees both Smith and Balzac posing a question about the moral implications of physical and psychological distance, responsibility, and emotional involvement, all based on the comparison of gain and loss: "If we were to apportion our efforts to the strength of our feelings, we would sacrifice a hundred millions to save our little finger (Smith's inference); and if we would do that (this is Rastignac's corollary), we would surely sacrifice a single faraway life to gain a great fortune."[23] Ethics is all about making the right moral choice, and what constitutes the right choice is based on the comparison of the good and the bad, and sometimes the bad and the less bad. For Appiah, cosmopolitanism implies giving up killing a mandarin in China, even if it also means giving up the opportunity to get rich without much effort or risk. It is a moral choice made not because of a simple sense of sympathy, but because "we are responsive to what Adam Smith called 'reason, principle, conscience,

21. Appiah, *Cosmopolitanism*, p. 156.

22. Adam Smith, *The Theory of Moral Sentiments*, ed. Knud Haakonssen (Cambridge: Cambridge University Press, 2002), p. 157.

23. Appiah, *Cosmopolitanism*, p. 157.

the inhabitant of the breast.' "[24] Cosmopolitanism, therefore, is not something natural or intuitive, but it requires a lot of sound thinking and reasonable comparison, a choice consciously made after careful deliberations.

In a learned essay on the theme of killing a Chinese mandarin, Carlo Ginzburg traces the idea of the moral implications of distance to Aristotle and then mainly to the works of Diderot and Chateaubriand, thus establishing a French lineage for Rastignac's question in *Le Père Goriot.* In speaking of pity as an emotional response to something terrible that happens to people, Aristotle used the expression "ten thousand years" as an extremely large figure "to suggest a time, either past or future, so remote that it prevents us from identifying, either in a positive or in a negative way, with the emotions of other human beings."[25] Distance diminishes the intensity of our emotional response, and this is further developed in Diderot's discussion of a man illicitly taking a sum of money away, far from home. "We agreed," says Diderot, "that perhaps distance in space or time weakened all feelings and all sorts of guilty conscience, even of crime. The assassin, removed to the shores of China, can no longer see the corpse which he left bleeding on the banks of the Seine. Remorse springs perhaps less from horror of oneself than from fear of others; less from shame at what one has done than from the blame and punishment it would bring if it were found out." As Ginzburg remarks, Diderot here seems to echo Aristotle's idea, but "it is Aristotle pushed to an extreme."[26] It is interesting that both Adam Smith and Diderot used China to suggest huge distance. In the eighteenth century, because of the Jesuit missionaries' letters and reports, China was very much on the minds of European thinkers, though for the average person, it was still a faraway place, probably on the margins of some imaginary *mappa mundi,* and thus suitable as a symbol of the greatest distance possible.

Ginzburg points out that the assassin who left Paris for China in Diderot's work reemerged in François-René de Chateaubriand's popular work, *The Genius of Christianity,* where the author writes, "I put to myself this question: 'If thou couldst by a mere wish kill a fellow-creature in China, and inherit his fortune in Europe, with the supernatural conviction that the fact would never be known, wouldst thou consent to form such a wish?' "[27] The question obviously responds to Diderot's hypothetical situation and is almost identical

24. Ibid., p. 174.

25. Carlo Ginzburg, "Killing a Chinese Mandarin: The Moral Implications of Distance," *Critical Inquiry* 21: 1 (Autumn 1994): 48.

26. Denis Diderot, "Conversation of a Father with his Children," in *This Is Not a Story and Other Stories,* trans. P. N. Furbank (Oxford: Oxford University Press, 1993), p. 143.

27. Viscount de Chateaubriand, *The Genius of Christianity; or the Spirit and Beauty of the Christian Religion,* trans. Charles I. White (Baltimore: John Murphy and Co., 1856), p. 188.

to Rastignac's in Balzac's novel. Chateaubriand, as Ginzburg notes, "created a new story: the victim is a Chinese; the murderer, a European; a reason for the murder—financial gain."[28] Chateaubriand, however, used that hypothetical murder of a Chinese to prove the ubiquitous presence of conscience, particularly from a Christian point of view. However he tried to rationalize the distant killing of a Chinese, eventually, says Chateaubriand, "in spite of all my useless subterfuges, I hear a voice in the recesses of my soul, protesting so loudly against the mere idea of such a supposition, that I cannot for one moment doubt the reality of conscience."[29] In Balzac's novel, Rastignac's friend likewise eventually rejects the temptation and chooses to extend his moral responsibility to a stranger despite the enormous distance. In fact, *tuer le mandarin* was a rather popular theme in the nineteenth century with a philosophical point, and we find variations on this theme in works as different as the Portuguese writer Eça de Queiróz's *The Mandarin*, in which the wealth suddenly acquired by the magic killing creates a huge problem, and Arnold Bennett's *The Grim Smile of the Five Towns*, in which Vera, a fashionable lady, was contemplating killing a mandarin by mere imagining in order to buy herself a brooch for her gown.[30] All these stories make an ethical point about comparison as a moral choice.

In *The Hypothetical Mandarin*, Eric Hayot considers "killing a Chinese mandarin" to be "a generic philosopheme for the question of how best to be, or to become, a modern, sympathetic human being."[31] In the "civilizing" process of European life and sentiments during the eighteenth and the nineteenth centuries, China was both on the margin as a sign of the distant "Other" *and* an "empire of cruelties," a barbaric foil to contrast with civilized Europe, "a horizon of horizons."[32] In an article on the same subject, Iddo Landau discusses killing a mandarin as a thought experiment, a philosophical hypothesis that reveals the deep-seated self-deception of all human beings, that people are often worse than they think they are, that most people "are ready to, or have significant difficulty in refusing to, murder a human being, if it is clear that we would never be caught," thus highlighting "the importance, or centrality, of society's supervision over us."[33] From a European or American point of view,

28. Ginzburg, "Killing a Chinese Mandarin," p. 54.

29. Chateaubriand, *The Genius of Christianity*, p. 188.

30. See Eça de Queiróz, *The Mandarin and Other Stories*, trans. Margaret Jull Costa (Sawtry, UK: Dedalus, 2009), and Enoch Arnold Bennett, *The Grim Smile of the Five Towns* (London: Penguin, 1946).

31. Eric Hayot, *The Hypothetical Mandarin: Sympathy, Modernity, and Chinese Pain* (Oxford: Oxford University Press, 2009), p. 8.

32. Ibid., p. 10.

33. Iddo Landau, "To Kill a Mandarin," *Philosophy and Literature* 29 (April 2005): 94.

a Chinese mandarin signifies an unknown person from a distant place, but the philosophical import of this thought experiment need not be limited to just European or American. In fact, the fantasy of killing a person at great distance without the risk of dire consequences is not at all an alien idea in Chinese imagination. In a satirical essay on "Chinese Fantasies," the influential modern writer Lu Xun observes: "There is another small fantasy. That is, with a gentle hum a man can send out a ray of white light from his nostrils and kill his hated enemy or opponent, no matter how far away it is. The white light will return and no one will know who's done the killing. How nice and carefree it is to be able to kill someone and have no troubles for it!"[34] The similarity between this Chinese fantasy of magic killing and the European idea of distant killing is rather striking. In his study of classical Chinese fiction, Lu Xun notes that such fantasies, stories of "riding on clouds and flying daggers," were quite old and already had become popular in the literature of the Song dynasty from the twelfth to the mid-thirteenth centuries.[35] Such fantasies of distant killing seem to anticipate the Western fantasy of killing a Chinese mandarin, but the significant difference is that the Chinese fantasy does not have a Frenchman or Englishman as the target. This lack of particularity reveals something specific about modern and European coloniality that we cannot relate to those classical stories of Chinese fantasies.

Hayot refers to a version of killing a Chinese mandarin in Gertrude Stein's *Everybody's Autobiography*, in which she remarks that "many people had thought it was funny when, in her opera *Four Saints in Three Acts*, 'they asked Saint Therese what would she do if by touching a button she could kill three thousand Chinamen and the chorus said Saint Therese not interested.' "[36] Saint Therese here shows her saintly quality and moral conscience, but thanks to the progress of science and technology, particularly in the manufacturing of increasingly more sophisticated and powerful modern weaponry, the distant killing of thousands of people by pushing a button in a bomber or a missile base is no longer an abstract philosophical hypothesis or literary fantasy, but a real choice available for the politicians and military commanders to make (and have made) in the world today. On the one hand, the development of

34. Lu Xun, "Zhongguo de qixiang" [Chinese Fantasies], *Lu Xun quanji* [*Lu Xun's Complete Works*], 16 vols. [Beijing: Renmin wenxue, 1981], 5:239.

35. See Lu Xun, *Zhongguo xiaoshuo shi lue* [*A Concise History of Chinese Fiction*], *Lu Xun quanji* [*Lu Xun's Complete Works*], 9:100.

36. Gertrude Stein, *Everybody's Autobiography* (New York: 1971), pp. 89–90; quoted in Hayot, *The Hypothetical Mandarin*, p. 205.

science has made it possible to kill from a distance, but on the other, because the fantasy of distant killing has become a real and lethal possibility and, more importantly, a possibility no longer exclusively European and American, killing a Chinese mandarin has lost its guarantee of safety in its original imaginary form. In comparison with the time of Diderot and Balzac, then, science and moral sensibility in our time have almost eliminated the distance—physical and psychological—between China and the West, and has given the metaphor of killing a Chinese mandarin a definite feel of datedness, an unsavory flavor of Western racism and imperialism, which the original metaphor purports to question and challenge in the works of Adam Smith, Diderot, Chateaubriand, Balzac, and others.

When Adam Smith imagined an earthquake that destroyed "the great empire of China," he probably had in mind the real, devastating earthquake that had destroyed the city of Lisbon in 1755, which inspired Voltaire to write his *Poème sur le désastre de Lisbonne* and *Candide*, in which he satirized Leibniz's optimistic idea of "the best of all possible worlds." That famous earthquake had a profound influence on the Enlightenment philosophers and helped change European thinking and society in many ways. If the Lisbon earthquake was indeed the background for Smith's imaginary earthquake in China, for at the time China seemed so far away from Europe that such natural disasters could only be imagined by the Europeans, then we may compare Smith's imaginary earthquake with the real and hugely destructive Sichuan earthquake that shook China in May 2008, or the horrible earthquake, tsunami, and dangerous radioactive leaks at the Fukushima nuclear power plant in Japan in March 2011. Both of these earthquakes in Asia were immediately reported the world over through satellite TV and extensive international news coverage that made them a compelling reality felt far beyond China or Japan, at least in people's consciousness, such that it became rather difficult for an average European or American with any degree of decency to brush it aside as if nothing had happened. Intercontinental travel, Internet, e-mail, Facebook, Twitter, television, and world news reports—all these common features of the digital age—have made the world seem much smaller. What was distant one hundred years ago now seems close to home in the so-called global village.

If distance diminishes the intensity of emotional responses, then, compared with the time of Adam Smith or Balzac, have modern science and technology diminished the distance between different parts of the world, say, between China and Europe? That killing a Chinese mandarin has gone out of currency in the usage of our time may suggest a positive answer. And yet, whether one is to extend one's moral responsibilities to distant strangers as compared to one's relatives and close neighbors is still a choice to be made, still a matter of comparison each time we face a real issue. We find ourselves still facing a crossroads that calls for careful comparisons and reasonable decisions.

A Critique of Untranslatability

Translation is all about comparison, about finding comparable or equivalent expressions in one language for those in another, and in recent theoretical reflections, translation is often taken to be a model for comparative literature. "Global translation is another name for comparative literature," as Emily Apter puts it.[37] So far, I have argued for the necessity of comparison, so translation as inherently comparative is also, I would argue, always necessary and possible. Much of recent Western theorizing, however, has focused on the notion of untranslatability, the idea that translation is impossible. Apter's "Twenty Theses on Translation" begins with "nothing is translatable," though paradoxically or dialectically, it ends at just the opposite position: "everything is translatable."[38] Untranslatability in Apter's argument, however, does not really mean incomparability and therefore does not mean the impossibility of translation. Untranslatability is a misnomer.

There is always this dream of untranslatability, what John Sallis calls "the dream of nontranslation": "What would it mean not to translate?" asks Sallis. "What would it mean to begin thinking beyond all translation?"[39] If thinking is speaking to oneself, as Plato and Kant have argued, it is already thinking in language and therefore, Sallis asserts, "it will never have outstripped such translation. . . . In other words, for thinking to begin beyond such translation would mean its collapse into a muteness that could mean nothing at all; incapable of signification, it would have ceased—if thinking is speaking to oneself—even to be thinking. It would have risked a captivation that falls short even of silence, if indeed silence is possible only for one who can speak."[40] But mystics and philosophical mysticism have always dreamed of that silence, and despite his effort to refute it, Sallis has to admit that "attestations to

37. Emily Apter, *The Translation Zone: A New Comparative Literature* (Princeton, NJ: Princeton University Press, 2006), p. xi.

38. Ibid., pp. xi, xii.

39. John Sallis, *On Translation* (Bloomington: Indiana University Press, 2002), p. 1.

40. Ibid., p.2.

untranslatability abound."[41] They abound particularly in recent theorizing in translation studies, in which the idea of untranslatability denies languages their basic comparability.

In her introduction to a volume of essays on translation, Sandra Bermann reminds us that the semantic "overlap" of words in different languages, on which translation is based, can only be partial, that words seemingly synonymous are in fact untranslatable, "as is attested by Benjamin's famous example of '*Brot*' versus 'pain' or Saussure's equally well-known discussion of '*mouton*' versus the English 'mutton' *and* 'sheep.' "[42] That no two languages or linguistic expressions totally overlap is a basic fact that calls for comparison and translation in the first place, but when Benjamin claims that "the word *Brot* means something different to a German than the word *pain* to a Frenchman, that these words are not interchangeable for them, that, in fact, they strive to exclude each other," he is making a clear distinction, "distinguishing the intended object from the mode of intention." As though to forestall misunderstanding, Benjamin immediately goes on to add: "As to the intended object, however, the two words mean the very same thing."[43] For Benjamin, the mode of intention or the way in which the intended object manifests itself is always couched in a particular language and makes sense only in that language. *Brot* makes sense in German and differs from *pain* in French, but using the concepts in German phenomenology, he also argues that different languages with their different modes of intention can intend "the very same thing," or relate to the same referential intentionality. Benjamin does not, in other words, endorse the idea of untranslatability. On the contrary, he emphatically states that "the translatability of linguistic creations ought to be considered even if men should prove unable to translate them."[44] Benjamin argues that beyond their different idioms and modes of intention, all languages want to express a deep intention realized in a "pure language."[45] It is this pure language that one tries to translate, and it is in this pure language that translation finds its ultimate legitimacy.

Benjamin's idea of the task of the translator, as Antoine Berman comments, "would consist of a search, beyond the buzz of empirical languages, for

41. Ibid., p. 112.

42. Sandra Bermann, "Introduction," in Sandra Bermann and Michael Wood (eds.), *Nation, Language, and the Ethics of Translation* (Princeton, NJ: Princeton University Press, 2005), p. 5.

43. Walter Benjamin, "The Task of the Translator," in *Illuminations*, trans. Harry Zohn (Glasgow: Fontana, 1973), p. 74.

44. Ibid., p. 70.

45. Ibid., p. 74.

the 'pure language' which each language carries within itself as its messianic echo. Such an aim, which has nothing to do with the ethical aim, is rigorously metaphysical in the sense that it platonically searches a 'truth' beyond natural languages."[46] For Benjamin, translatability is rooted in the very nature of languages and their comparable intentionality, it is confirmation of the possibility of translation on a conceptual level, even though on a technical level, some words or expressions may prove to be untranslatable. "The very aim of translation—to open up in writing a certain relation with the Other, to fertilize what is one's Own through the mediation of what is Foreign," says Berman, "is diametrically opposed to the ethnocentric structure of every culture, that species of narcissism by which every society wants to be a pure and unadulterated Whole."[47] The idea of untranslatability is wrong because it is based, wittingly or unwittingly, on that narcissistic desire of cultural and linguistic purity, the ethnocentric illusion that one's own language and culture are unique, superior to, and incomparable with, any other. Or, in a different way, it is wrong because it keeps the Other as absolutely Other, as totally different from one's self, with no possibility of comparison, understanding, and communication. Translation as comparison of the Other with what is one's Own is thus deeply ethical as the act of communication and the establishment of a human relationship.

In a discussion of the ethics of translation, however, Robert Eaglestone deliberately goes against the widely accepted view "that translation is central to the ethical philosophy of Emmanuel Levinas," and puts forward his own counterargument that challenges such a consensus. "Levinas's work," says Eaglestone, "offers an understanding of ethics that suggests the impossibility of translation."[48] According to Eaglestone, "Levinas's thought is about translation—but that movement is heading out from the community to the other, precisely where translation is impossible. Levinas argues for an unending (and so infinite) ethical responsibility incumbent on each of us. The counterintuitive conclusion is that we are each responsible for those we do not, cannot, and could not understand."[49] But with such total alienation and lack of understanding, how can one establish an ethical relationship with the Other in an

46. Antoine Berman, *The Experience of the Foreign: Culture and Translation in Romantic Germany*, trans. S. Heyvaert (Albany: State University of New York Press, 1992), p. 7.

47. Ibid., p. 4.

48. Robert Eaglestone, "Levinas, Translation, and Ethics," in Bermann and Wood (eds.), *Nation, Language, and the Ethics of Translation*, p. 127.

49. Ibid., p. 137.

intense engagement, what Levinas calls "the face-to-face with the Other"?[50] What Levinas calls "face" denotes the presence and alterity of the Other, but he speaks of human relationships, not of automatons. "Face to face with the other man that a man can indeed approach as presence," the thinking subject is exposed, says Levinas, "to the defenseless nakedness of the face, the lot or misery of the human," ". . . to the loneliness of the face and hence to the categorical imperative of assuming responsibility for that misery." For Levinas, it is the "Word of God" that commits us to such a moral responsibility, hence "a responsibility impossible to gainsay."[51] With such an absolute moral command, ethics is injected into hermeneutics, and the dialogic relationship with the Other in understanding is recast as the real and practical questions of human relationships and responsibilities: questions of comparison and moral choice. Denying understanding is thus to deny recognition of the "face" of the Other, its suffering and misery, its basic humanity; it is to put the Other at the fantastic end of exoticism as pure difference, or at the endlessly remote distance where untranslatability turns into total indifference. The ethical implication of translation as communication is the comparison of the Other with one's self, the extension of moral responsibilities to the Other in comparison with one's own relatives and one's own community.

When Emily Apter draws on Alain Badiou to "rethink translation studies from the standpoint of the presumption that 'nothing is translatable,'" she acknowledges that her notion of "the translation zone is established on the basis of the philological relation."[52] To limit comparison to philological relations with common etymons in languages and shared sociohistorical conditions, however, is a very limited view, almost of the old-fashioned *littérature comparée* with its positivistic emphasis on *rapports de fait*. What Badiou does is to discard all those philological and cultural relations in the comfort zone and to compare a classical Arabic poet Labîd ben Rabi'a with the French poet Mallarmé across huge chasms and gulfs in culture and language. Badiou does not have much faith in the old-fashioned comparative literature, nor does he consider much translation of great poets adequate, but he is not at all inimical to comparison. On the contrary, he believes "in the universality of great poems, even when they are represented in the almost invariably disastrous approximation that translation

50. Emmanuel Levinas, *Time and the Other [and Additional Essays]*, trans. Richard A. Cohen (Pittsburgh, PA: Duquesne University Press, 1987), p. 79.

51. Emmanuel Levinas, *Outside the Subject*, trans. Michael B. Smith (Stanford, CA: Stanford University Press, 1994), p. 158.

52. Apter, *The Translation Zone*, p. 85.

represents." "Comparison," says Badiou, "can serve as a sort of experimental verification of this universality."[53] Translation may be miserably inadequate as "disastrous approximation," but it is surely not impossible. Here we may recall Benjamin's remark that "the translatability of linguistic creations ought to be considered even if men should prove unable to translate them." For Badiou, it is comparison that makes understanding possible despite disastrous translations. In his comparative work, as Apter well describes it, "for all the obstacles posed by translation, 'great poems' surmount the difficulty of being worlds apart and manage to achieve universal significance. This poetic singularity against all odds challenges the laws of linguistic territorialization that quarantine language groups in communities 'of their own kind' (as in Romance or East Asian languages) or enforce a condition in which monolingualisms coexist without relation."[54] That is exactly what comparative literature for our time should be—comparison not just within but beyond and across philologically linked language groups, across Romance and East Asian languages. "Badiou's literary universalism, built on affinities of the Idea ("une proximité dans la pensée") rather than on philological connections or shared sociohistorical trajectories," says Apter, "defines a kind of *comparatisme quand même* that complements the militant credo of his political philosophy."[55] For Badiou, the very act of comparison bears witness and serves as "experimental verification" of the universality of radically different literary works brought into comparison. That, in my view, holds out an exciting and promising prospect for comparative literature more effectively than the translatability of everything into everything else by, into, or through digital codes in an age of advanced computer technologies.

Concluding Remarks: The Inevitability of Comparison

The Self and the Other are invariably correlated as identity and difference, or more precisely, as identity through comparison and differentiation. This can find another formulation in Spinoza's famous motto *omni determinatio est negatio*—"determination is negation."[56] To determine or ascertain one's Self

53. Alain Badiou, *Handbook of Inaesthetics*, trans. Alberto Toscano (Stanford, CA: Stanford University Press, 2005), p. 46.

54. Apter, *The Translation Zone*, pp. 85–86.

55. Ibid., p. 86.

56. Benedict de Spinoza, *Correspondence, The Chief Works of Benedict de Spinoza*, trans. R. H. M. Elwes, 2 vols. (New York: Dover Publications, 1951), 2:370.

is necessarily to relate to the Other in an act of comparison and differentiation; thus Spinoza puts forth the following as an *ethical* proposition: "Every individual thing, or everything which is finite and has a conditioned existence, cannot exist or be conditioned to act, unless it be conditioned for existence and action by a cause other than itself."[57] Freud and Saussure made the same argument in psychoanalysis and linguistics, which all confirm that comparison or differentiation is ontologically and epistemologically necessary, inevitable, and always already functioning. That is also the core of my argument in this chapter.

Parallelism and antithesis are obviously predicated on comparison, while the conceptual metaphors of a crossroads and distant killing help bring out the necessity as well as the challenge of comparison as a risky business with moral and political implications. Cosmopolitanism as a moral choice is seen as deeply comparative in the sense that it measures the distance of the Other against one's loyalty to one's relatives and local community, and argues for extension of one's responsibilities to distant strangers and outsiders. Finally, translation is inherently comparative as it involves the Self and the Other, what is one's Own and what is Foreign, the close and the distant, the local and the global. It is essential not only because it engages different languages and their comparability, but because understanding and communication are, in a broad sense, necessary for forming any human relationships. Translation, in that sense, is then a fundamental form of communication like dialogue, and thus a form as essential to Mikhail Bakhtin as it is to Levinas. Bakhtin puts it very well: "To be means to communicate dialogically. When dialogue ends, everything ends. Thus dialogue, by its very essence, cannot and must not come to an end."[58] We may say in the same vein that comparison, by its very essence, cannot and will not come to an end. Bakhtin's insistence on dialogue thus becomes as much a moral imperative as Benjamin's insistence on translatability or Badiou's insistence on *comparatisme quand même*. Comparison, we realize, is what we must always do to exist and to act, and therefore what and how we compare—and what follow as consequences of our comparison—truly deserve our critical attention.

57. Spinoza, *The Ethics,* Ibid., 2:67.

58. Mikhail Bakhtin, *Problems of Dostoevsky's Poetics,* ed. and trans. Caryl Emerson (Minneapolis: University of Minnesota Press, 1984), p. 252. Katerina Clark and Michael Holquist first made the connection between Bakhtin and Levinas. They emphasize Bakhtin's skeptic attitude toward systematizing and put him in a tradition of thinkers "from Heraclitus to Emmanuel Lenivas, who have preferred the powers that inhere in the centrifugal forces." See Clark and Holquist, *Mikhail Bakhtin* (Cambridge, MA: Harvard University Press, 1984), p. 8.

2

The Complexity of Difference

Individual, Cultural, and Cross-Cultural

Difference is a basic fact in life and in our understanding of life. As individual human beings, we are all different from one another in genetic makeup as well as in physiognomic traits. Take a walk in the bustling streets of a city like Hong Kong, where I now live; you have human diversity thrust upon you as you find yourself in a motley crowd of Cantonese-speaking locals, Mandarin-speaking mainlanders, European or American expatriates, Filipinos, Thais, Indians and other south or southeast Asians, visitors or tourists from all corners of the earth, uttering a polyphonic heteroglossia or a spate of English of diverse accents. Such variety and marked differences make each of us identifiable as a person with distinctly personal characteristics as unique as our DNA sequences or our fingerprints. As I have argued in the last chapter, individual identity is possible only in comparison with and differentiation from others. And yet, as social groups, communities, and nations, individual identities coalesce and people display certain in-group features that are common and shared by members of the same group while differentiating them from those of other groups. Language and ethnicity are examples of such socially constituted features, which become markers of collective identities; and as the study of collective identities often has more weight than that of individuals (for even the study of an individual, say, biography as a genre, must examine the individual in a collective or social context), group features, or differences on the collective level, are most likely to become the center of activities in academic research, particularly in social sciences and the humanities. In other words, critical attention in scholarly discourse tends to focus on cultural differences, culture being the term for a community's collective ways of living, the form of life in a particular society. As a result, cultural differences stand out prominently, while individual differences are often obscured, even though they may be just as important in our lives.

Ethnography, which aims at the study of cultures, usually cultures of other groups than the ethnographer's own, is predicated on the understanding and interpretation of cultural differences. According to George Marcus, ethnographers traditionally believe that cultural difference "can be fully *consumed*, that is, assimilated to theory and description by cracking codes of structure, through better translation, and so forth." In this postmodern age of ours, however, the idea of "radical or surplus difference" comes to dominate the field "with the premise that difference can never be fully consumed, conquered, experienced." The prominence of difference is now the distinct mark of postmodern ethnography. "In any attempt to interpret or explain another cultural subject," says Marcus, "a surplus of difference always remains."[1] The emphasis on cultural difference thus assumes a paradigmatic role in ethnography or cultural anthropology, and that is indicative of what happens in many other fields and disciplines as well.

In this connection, we may understand why Thomas Kuhn's idea of incompatible paradigms has exerted such a huge influence far beyond the study of the history of science, and why his concept of radical incommensurability has so often been borrowed in discussing cultural differences. Indeed, Kuhn himself draws an analogy between scientific revolution and political revolution. "Like the choice between competing political institutions," he remarks, "that between competing paradigms proves to be a choice between incompatible modes of community life."[2] Different paradigms, he further argues, are "not only incompatible but often actually incommensurable."[3] Scientists working under different paradigms not only have different standards and definitions, ask different questions, give different interpretations, but they "practice their trades in different worlds," which Kuhn considers to be the "most fundamental aspect of the incommensurability of competing paradigms."[4] If scientists working under different paradigms live in different worlds of mutual incomprehension, such an idea of incommensurability easily offers a model for social sciences and the humanities to look at different cultures as radically incommensurable worlds.

As Kuhn's ideas circulate in general discourse in the study of cultures, incommensurability quickly becomes a theoretical notion that serves not only

1. George E. Marcus, *Ethnography through Thick and Thin* (Princeton, NJ: Princeton University Press, 1998), p. 186.

2. Thomas S. Kuhn, *The Structure of Scientific Revolution*, 2nd enlarged ed. (Chicago: University of Chicago Press, 1970), p. 94.

3. Ibid., p. 103.

4. Ibid., p. 150.

to emphasize difference, but also, and unfortunately, to legitimize the segregation of social groups and communities. The concept may mirror social reality already in place; it may also exert certain influence on how people perceive reality and thus help create such a reality. In any case, as an influential concept, incommensurability has its consequences. It becomes a paradigmatic idea in what Lindsay Waters dubbed the "Age of Incommensurability." It functions, as Waters complains, as "justification for a resurgent tribalism." In its worst form, it even fosters "a blinkered, absolutist, nonpluralist relativism."[5] Incommensurability thus gives theoretical endorsement to a radical relativism, the dubious idea of mutually incomprehensible cultures and societies. Particularly in the humanities and social sciences, such a conceptual relativism predominates in much of academic discourses, especially in understanding different cultures and alien societies.

Influential as they are, Kuhn's ideas have nevertheless given rise to controversies and met with a good deal of criticism. Hilary Putnam argues, for example, that Kuhn's concept of incommensurability "seems to signify nothing more than intertheoretic meaning change, as opposed to uninterpretability"; and he questions whether scientists under different paradigms really have no common language or common measurement to gauge the change of meaning. The Copernican heliocentric and the Ptolemaic geocentric astronomers certainly shared the same language in which they debated with one another on the nature of the universe and presented their different views. "When two theories conflict, then, although the common theoretical terms generally have different meanings," says Putnam, "that does *not* mean that there is no 'common language' in which one can say what the theoretical terms of both theories refer to."[6] Donald Davidson points out an inherent difficulty of the relativist paradigm. "The dominant metaphor of conceptual relativism, that of differing points of view, seems to betray an underlying paradox," says Davidson. "Different points of view make sense, but only if there is a common co-ordinate system on which to plot them; yet the existence of a common system belies the claim of dramatic incomparability."[7] It is ironic that cultural relativists, who maintain that language, cognition, and knowledge are all generated within the system of one culture and do not obtain across cultures, nonetheless claim

5. Lindsay Waters, "The Age of Incommensurability," *Boundary 2* 28:2 (Summer 2001): 144, 145.

6. Hilary Putnam, *Realism with a Human Face*, ed. James Conant (Cambridge, MA: Harvard University Press, 1990), p. 127.

7. Donald Davidson, *Inquiries into Truth and Interpretation*, 2nd ed. (Oxford: Clarendon Press, 2001), p. 184.

to have cross-cultural knowledge about fundamentally different and incommensurable cultures.

In response to his critics, Kuhn tried in his later years to modify his earlier claim and redefined incommensurability as "a sort of untranslatability, localized to one or another area in which two lexical taxonomies differ." Such a localized linguistic incommensurability does not, he insists, "bar intercommunity understanding. Members of one community can acquire the taxonomy employed by members of another, as the historian does in learning to understand old texts."[8] But if that is the case, then, to equate incommensurability with untranslatability would hardly make sense. Historians certainly can find ways to understand and translate texts of the past. "Instead of living in different worlds," as Davidson comments dryly, "Kuhn's scientists may, like those who need Webster's dictionary, be only words apart."[9] In other words, we may question whether Kuhn's redefined notion may still hold on to the concept of incommensurability. The real problem is, however, that Kuhn's redefined notion, though meant to modify his earlier and more radical claims, comes a bit too late to curb the circulation of the concept of incommensurability or its relativist interpretations in the discourse of social sciences and the humanities. As a result, Kuhn's notion helps create a blinkered, dichotomous relativist paradigm in the study of cultures.

The idea that different social groups or communities have nothing in common and cannot be brought into comparison for mutual illumination proves to be especially entrenched when it comes to the understanding of non-Western cultures. Of course, the opposition of West and East, Europe and Asia, or Greece and China, long predates Kuhn's work and the popularization of the idea of incommensurability, as the emphasis on difference has a long history in Western discourse on the non-European Other with different motivations and consequences. Much of that history illustrates the difficulty of cross-cultural understanding and shows the tenacity of what I have called the "myth of the Other."[10] Sometimes, as with the French poet and Sinophile Victor Segalen in

8. Thomas S. Kuhn, *The Road since Structure: Philosophical Essays, 1970–1993, with an Autobiographical Interview*, ed. James Conant and John Haugeland (Chicago: University of Chicago Press, 2000), p. 93.

9. Davidson, *Inquiries into Truth and Interpretation*, p. 189.

10. Since the time of Marco Polo (c. 1254–1324) and particularly Matteo Ricci (1552–1610), China has been understood differently in the West and the image of China has played different roles in European imagination and self-understanding. What becomes important for our time, I argue, is the demythologizing of China for real cross-cultural understanding. See Zhang Longxi, *Mighty Opposites: From Dichotomies to Differences in the Comparative Study of China* (Stanford, CA: Stanford University Press, 1998), pp. 19–54.

the early twentieth century, a culturally exotic China with all its peculiarities and differences is indispensable for the possibility of poetry and the appreciation of exotic beauty. "Exoticism," says Segalen, "is nothing other than the notion of the different; the perception of diversity; the knowledge that something is not oneself."[11] In contemporary theories, however, the emphasis on cultural difference is more a matter of conceptual or epistemological contrast than aesthetic sensibilities.

Perhaps nothing is more exotic than Michel Foucault's mind-boggling "*heterotopia*," an unthinkable space generated by an incomprehensible "Chinese encyclopaedia" and its illogical way of classifying animals. In the preface to *The Order of Things*, Foucault quotes from Borges's essay on John Wilkins a most curious passage of animal classification, which defies any logic, but that strange passage does not come from any real "Chinese encyclopaedia"; it is a fictional piece created by Borges himself, who does not, however, mean to use it to symbolize an incomprehensible exotic system of thought. And yet, Foucault takes it to be genuinely Chinese and representative of the way the Chinese mind operates, which threatens to "collapse our age-old distinction between the Same and the Other," casting a spell, an "exotic charm of another system of thought," while showing "the limitation of our own, the stark impossibility of thinking *that*."[12] In Foucault's description of such a bizarre "Chinese way of thinking," a totally different system is constructed to set off the normality of European thinking, the *epistemes* or cultural codes of a familiar system. That strange classification is so illogical and so impossible to conceive that it can only inhabit, according to Foucault, the unthinkable "*heterotopia*," a conceptual place fundamentally different from the Western fantasy of a Utopia.

Another significant example of China as a symbol of fundamental difference is Jacques Derrida's use of Chinese writing as the opposite of Western phonetic writing, which embodies "logocentrism" or the "metaphysical hierarchy" of thinking, speech, and writing. "Logocentrism," the debasement of writing and the elevation of the voice in speech, the loss of which the alphabetic form of writing tries to recuperate, says Derrida, "is also a phonocentrism: absolute proximity of voice and being, of voice and the meaning of being, of voice and the ideality of meaning."[13] In Western thinking about language, therefore, there is an entrenched tradition of the debasement of writing, the prejudice

11. Victor Segalen, *Essai sur l'exotisme: une esthétique du divers* (Paris: Fata Morgana, 1978), p. 23.

12. Michel Foucault, *The Order of Things: An Archaeology of the Human Sciences* (New York: Vintage, 1973), p. xv.

13. Jacques Derrida, *Of Grammatology*, trans. Gayatri Chakravorty Spivak (Baltimore, MD: Johns Hopkins University Press, 1976), pp. 11–12.

against the inadequacy of language, particularly in the form of writing. Derrida insists that logocentrism in its "original and non-'relativist' sense" is "an ethnocentric metaphysics. It is related to the history of the West."[14] Based on Ernest Fenollosa and Ezra Pound, he understood Chinese written characters as forming a totally different system of writing unrelated to the speaking voice. The "largely nonphonetic scripts like Chinese or Japanese," he declares, can stand as "the testimony of a powerful movement of civilization developing outside of all logocentrism."[15]

Now neither Foucault nor Derrida is a Sinologist, nor are they concerned with the understanding of China as such when they made those claims about the Chinese language and thinking. And yet, they all use China or Chinese writing to contrast with the West, and to highlight cultural differences as some sort of an impossible place as "*heterotopia*" or the ultimate "*différance*." Given their tremendous influence in social sciences and the humanities, the East-West dichotomies they set up offer a model in thinking about China as the opposite of Europe. Indeed, in Sinology and Asian studies in general, as in ethnography discussed earlier, the relativist emphasis on cultural difference assumes a paradigmatic role. More than twenty years ago, David Buck as editor of the American *Journal of Asian Studies* already stated in his introduction to a forum on universalism and relativism that "relativist interpretations are advanced with much more frequency among Asianists, and indeed in the *JAS*'s pages, than universalist ideas."[16] Having looked at various forms, Buck comes to the conclusion that relativism is basically a skeptic view on "the issue of

14. Ibid., p. 79.

15. Ibid., p. 90. Insofar as the Chinese written characters are concerned, however, Fenollosa and Pound are unreliable and patently misleading. In the Chinese philosophical tradition, the inadequacy of language, and in particular the debasement of writing, has a long genealogy and many articulations. The Greek word *logos* contains the duality or tension between speaking and that which is spoken, and that hierarchic relationship forms the basis of Derrida's naming of the Western tradition as "logocentrism." By an interesting and perhaps revealing coincidence, the word *tao* in Chinese also signifies both speaking and that which is spoken, and the "logocentric" idea of language incapable of fully expressing what it is supposed to mean is clearly expressed in such classic works as the *Tao te ching*, which begins with the statement that "the *tao* (often translated as Way) that can be spoken of (which in the original is also *tao*) is not the constant *tao*." In other words, *tao*, the "Way," or whatever is considered the highest in philosophical or religious thinking, is ineffable and beyond language. The "metaphysical hierarchy" of thinking, speech, and writing thus exists in China as it does in the West. That is the main thesis in my critique of Derrida for setting up an absolute East-West dichotomy. See Zhang Longxi, *The Tao and the Logos: Literary Hermeneutics, East and West* (Durham, NC: Duke University Press, 1992).

16. David D. Buck, "Forum on Universalism and Relativism in Asian Studies: Editor's Introduction," *The Journal of Asian Studies* 50:1 (Feb. 1991): 32.

whether any conceptual tools exist to understand and interpret human behavior and meaning in ways that are intersubjectively valid."[17] In other words, most Asianists are skeptic about the availability of conceptual tools that can be useful "across the boundaries of language, geography, culture, and time."[18]

More recently, Richard Nisbett has given the relativist paradigm yet another strong affirmation when he focuses on "Asians" and "Westerners" and their fundamental differences. Despite the consensus of cognitive scientists about some general commonality among all human beings, Western scholars in the humanities and social sciences, according to Nisbett, have found differences between peoples and cultures more important and crucial. "Human cognition is not everywhere the same," says Nisbett. "First, that members of different cultures differ in their 'metaphysics,' or fundamental beliefs about the nature of the world. Second, that the characteristic thought processes of different groups differ greatly. Third, that the thought processes are of a piece with beliefs about the nature of the world: People use the cognitive tools that seem to make sense—given the sense they make of the world."[19] According to Nisbett, people differ as social groups, for these groups hold different belief systems and their "thought processes" differ collectively. Here, incredibly large groups (all Asians and all Westerners) are said to think and behave in collective and fundamentally different ways, thereby cultural differences are highlighted in a clear-cut East-West dichotomy with no room for individual variations.

It is in the context of such an intellectual climate—the predominance of a relativist paradigm that puts an overemphasis on cultural differences—that we may come to fully appreciate the significance of Geoffrey Lloyd's work that tries to bring some sense and balance to the current situation of scholarship. As it often happens in theoretical discourse, a valid point tends to develop until it turns into its opposite by going to the invalid and unhelpful extreme. Against the false universalism of the colonialist or imperialist times, when European concepts and standards were used as universal measurements to judge non-European cultures and found them lacking, the emphasis in our times on cultural difference and the internal validity of value systems makes a lot of sense morally, politically, and philosophically. To deny the possibility of cross-cultural understanding and to insist on the incommensurability of the East and the West, however, only lead to the other extreme of the isolation of cultures and

17. Ibid., p. 30.

18. Ibid., p. 29.

19. Richard Nisbett, *The Geography of Thought: How Asians and Westerners Think Differently . . . and Why* (New York: The Free Press, 2003), pp. xvi–xvii.

the danger of clash of civilizations. In emphasizing the fundamental differences between Asians and Westerners, Nisbett clearly sees that possible danger, but he accepts it as something unavoidable. "If people really do differ profoundly in their systems of thought," says Nisbett in a sober-minded vein, "then efforts to improve international understanding may be less likely to pay off than one might hope."[20] Given the conflict we find in much of our world today, however, the important question is: Do we need to try to improve international or cross-cultural understanding despite all the difficulties? To acknowledge the difficulty is one thing, but to give up the effort is quite another.

To reduce the tendency toward such extremisms, the first thing in order should be an effort to avoid simplistic collective categorization in the study of cultures and societies. In this regard, we may appreciate the methodological value of Lloyd's critique of Lévy-Bruhl's concept of collective mentalities. In attributing a shared mentality to a social group, even an entire nation, such a crude differentiation of peoples into rigid mental phalanxes "always risks ignoring or playing down individual variations. Collectivities do not think, only individuals do," says Lloyd, "but it is not that *any* group, *any* society consists of individuals with entirely uniform mental characteristics."[21] To pay attention to the "individual variations" within a supposedly homogeneous mentality is crucial for recognizing the richness and diversity of a cultural tradition. The problem with cultural relativism is that it overemphasizes cultural or cross-cultural differences while ignoring individual ones; that it minimizes differences within cultures so that differences between cultures can be pushed to the foreground.

This is precisely the problem with Nisbett's ignoring the distinction between one individual's personal opinion and that of an entire community or even all "Asians." He started his book with an anecdotal account of what "a brilliant student from China" told him: "You know, the difference between you and me is that I think the world is a circle, and you think it's a line." That student went on to explain and said: "The Chinese believe in constant change, but with things always moving back to some prior state. They pay attention to a wide range of events; they search for relationships between things; and they think you can't understand the part without understanding the whole. Westerners live in a simpler, more deterministic world; they focus on salient objects or people instead of the larger picture; and they think they can control events because they know the rules that govern the behavior of objects."[22]

20. Ibid., pp. xvii–xviii.

21. G. E. R. Lloyd, *Demystifying Mentalities* (Cambridge: Cambridge University Press, 1990), p. 5.

22. Nisbett, *The Geography of Thought*, p. xiv.

Apparently, that student from China is not that "brilliant" after all, for he has no idea that circle, reversal, and return are often discussed in the West. "The eye is the first circle; the horizon which it forms is the second," says Ralph Waldo Emerson in a well-known essay entitled "Circles." For Emerson, circle or circular movement is "the primary figure," "the highest emblem in the cipher of the world."[23] Circle is the symbol not only of the world, but of the life of man as well. "The life of man," Emerson continues to argue, "is a self-evolving circle, which, from a ring imperceptibly small, rushes on all sides outwards to new and larger circles, and that without end."[24] Again, that student has no idea that "you can't understand the part without understanding the whole" is by no means uniquely Chinese, because it is what the "hermeneutic circle" in the German tradition is all about. And yet, for Nisbett, this one person's ill-informed view not only represents the views of all Chinese, but of all Asians. As there are millions and millions of Chinese and Asians, it is obviously misguided to take one individual's opinion as collectively valid. We cannot ignore individual differences and subsume them under group or cultural differences.

Nisbett has, however, made some more specific claims. The ancient Greeks, he says, "more than any other ancient peoples, and in fact more than most people on the planet today, had a remarkable sense of personal *agency*—the sense that they were in charge of their own lives and free to act as they chose. One definition of happiness for the Greeks was that it consisted of being able to exercise their powers in pursuit of excellence in a life free from constraints."[25] I am sure we can cite some Greek sources to prove the correctness of this claim, but we can just as easily cite many other instances—and important classical ones at that—to disprove the validity of such a claim. It is a critical commonplace that ancient Greek tragedies are often tragedies of destiny, of which Sophocles' *Oedipus the King* can serve as a classic example, in which the striking ancient Greek idea is precisely a remarkable sense of the *lack* of personal agency, the recognition that individual human beings are pathetically limited in their knowledge and wisdom, and that they are *not* "in charge of their own lives and free to act as they chose." At the end of *Oedipus the King*, the Chorus sums up that sense of destiny in their song that expresses a notion of happiness very different from what Nisbett describes:

23. Ralph Waldo Emerson, *Essays and Letters*, ed. Joel Porte (New York: Library of America, 1983), p. 403.

24. Ibid., p. 404.

25. Nisbett, *The Geography of Thought*, pp. 2–3.

> Before that final day when one can say
> his life has reached its end with no distress or grief,
> no man should be called happy.[26]

What we have here is a deep sense of tragic pathos, a sense of the helplessness of man trapped in an unpredictable and indeed unknowable destiny. Who is to say that what Sophocles expressed so effectively here is not typically Greek? "Oedipus confronts the mystery of being alive in a world that does not correspond to a pattern of order or justice satisfactory to the human mind," as Charles Segal argues. "He places us in a tragic universe where we have to ask whether the horrible suffering we witness is all due to design or to chance, whether our lives are random or entirely determined. If everything is by accident—a view to which the modern reader is probably more inclined than the ancient one—then life seems absurd. If it is all by design, then the gods seem cruel or unjust, and life is hell."[27] The play may indeed have different interpretations, but there is certainly a tremendous sense of "a mysterious doom or destiny, will of the gods."[28] If Nisbett's sweeping generalization about the Greek sense of happiness and personal agency does not convince us of its validity, how can we trust him to come up with a general truth about all Asians, who are so numerous and have among them such complex and significant differences in terms of language and culture, race and ethnicity, historical experience and social structures? The point is that differences exist within cultures as much as between cultures, and sweeping generalizations about Greeks and Asians as opposites are hardly sustainable as a serious argument. What comes out of such sweeping generalizations is often a simplistic caricature that presents a distorted picture of a culture rather than an approximation of its reality. If we are serious about paying attention to differences, we should pay as much attention to individual differences as we do to group and collective ones.

Another significant aspect of Lloyd's work is his effort to bring the cultural tradition of ancient China into comparison with that of ancient Greece. Given the overemphasis on cultural difference, China and Greece are mostly kept apart in much of modern scholarship, and if they are brought together

26. Sophocles, *Theban Plays: Oedipus the King, Oedipus at Colonus, Antigone*, trans. Ruth Fainlight and Robert J. Littman (Baltimore, MD: Johns Hopkins University Press, 2009), p. 63.

27. Charles Segal, "The Greatness of Oedipus the King," in Harold Bloom (ed.), *Sophocles' Oedipus Plays: Oedipus the King, Oedipus at Colonus, & Antigone* (Broomall, PA: Chelsea House Publishers, 1999), p. 74.

28. Ibid., p. 75.

at all, they are often put in a sharp contrast to highlight the differences these two traditions are supposed to exemplify. François Jullien, for instance, repetitively uses China as a negative mirror to look for what Europe is not, and his method is always to put China and Greece in a mutually exclusive opposition. "Indeed, if one wants to 'go beyond the Greek framework,' and if one searches for appropriate support and perspective," says Jullien, "then I don't see any voyage possible other than 'China-bound,' as one used to say. This is, in effect, the only civilization that is recorded in substantial texts and whose linguistic and historical genealogy is radically non-European." Using Foucault's "*heterotopia*" as a conceptual frame and the idea of Far East as non-Europe, Jullien declares that "strictly speaking, *non-Europe* is China, and it cannot be anything else."[29] Jullien often draws up two columns of contrastive categories, one Greek and the other Chinese. Those columns of opposites, however, have more to do with Jullien's contrastive methodology than with Greek or Chinese thought and culture as such, for it is his dichotomous argument that turns his image of China into the reverse of Greece, so much so that whatever he finds in China is very predictably the opposite of Greece, thus always an unfailing confirmation of fundamental cultural differences.

Against such crude contrastive outcomes, we find Lloyd's views much more nuanced and balanced. Lloyd sees both Greece and China as richly diverse in their respective development of thought and culture. These two traditions are certainly different in important ways, but they also have significant similarities that make it impossible to reduce everything to an absolute dichotomy. It is "not just hazardous but often downright misleading," says Lloyd, "to generalise about Greek thought, culture and politics, ignoring the immense diversity within the philosophies proposed, the scientific work undertaken, the political systems developed in theory and in practice, at different periods." And it is just as misleading and "clearly impossible," he continues, "to advance generalisations valid for the whole of Chinese history or for the totality of the many diverse traditions of thought exemplified in Chinese culture."[30] At the same time, Lloyd does not play down cultural differences, but he acknowledges them where appropriate. Greek mathematics as exemplified by Euclid, for example, proceeds by deductive operations "from a single set of indemonstrable but self-evident axioms," but such axiomatic-deductive demonstration was "quite foreign to Chinese mathematics right down to modern times, that is until after the

29. François Jullien with Thierry Marchaissse, *Penser d'un Dehors (la Chine): Entretiens d'Extrême-Occident* (Paris: Éditions du Seuil, 2000), p. 39.

30. Lloyd, *Demystifying Mentalities*, p. 106.

translation of Euclid undertaken by the Jesuits and their followers."[31] Likewise in the study of medicine, important differences are not to be overlooked: "where the Greeks generally focused on the study of structures and organisms, in China the emphasis was more often on processes, on interaction, on resonances."[32] Even today, these are still conspicuous differences, for Western medicine and the biomedical and pathological theories underlying medical treatment are quite different from the Chinese practice of acupuncture, herbal medicine, and their theoretical justifications. These important differences between China and Greece would put any simplistic universal claim into question.

Differences are a matter of degree, however, not of kind, and more or less understanding and communication have always worked across linguistic and cultural gaps. "Empirically," as Lloyd puts it, "there is no human society with which communication has proved to be totally impossible, however hard mutual understanding—always imperfect, to be sure—may sometimes be to attain. Logically, if indeed we are confronted with a conceptual scheme that is incomprehensible in our terms, then we cannot, by definition, make any sense of it."[33] That is to say, if things are really incommensurate, then, no one can even make the claim that they are incommensurate, because to make such a claim presupposes that one knows both sides of the dichotomy and knows them to be truly incommensurate, and yet, such cross-cultural knowledge is precisely what the incommensurability argument precludes and denies. By pointing out this logical difficulty, we can effectively dislodge the incommensurability argument.

Cognitive Variations, a more recent of Lloyd's books, is impressive in dealing with a wide range of topics from color perception, spatial cognition, animal and plant classifications, to such less determinable issues as emotions, sense of health and well-being, self and agency, the nature-culture dichotomy, and the question of rationality. Lloyd gives each of these subjects a detailed discussion, based on readings of a large amount of scholarship from social anthropology, linguistics, history, philosophy, developmental psychology, evolutionary psychology, neurophysiology, and several areas of cognitive science. The central issue is again the question of whether in all these different disciplines we can detect cross-cultural universals or the predominance of cultural relativities, and in his discussion of all these issues, Lloyd not only examines

31. G. E. R. Lloyd, *Ancient Worlds, Modern Reflections: Philosophical Perspectives on Greek and Chinese Science and Culture* (Oxford: Clarendon Press, 2004), p. 29.

32. Ibid., p. 30.

33. Ibid., p. 40.

contemporary scientific studies for the insights they offer as well as their limitations, but he also draws on historical arguments in ancient Greece and ancient China to throw light on modern debates. In all these different areas of human cognition, there is what Lloyd calls the "multidimensionality" of data or phenomena, of positions, perspectives, methodologies, styles of enquiries, etc., so much so that in each and every case, we realize that neither the universalist nor the relativist has the monopoly of truth. The problem with both universalist and relativist claims is that they only recognize collective identities without proper consideration of individual variations, that they either see no difference between cultures, or see nothing but cultural differences. The truth is that the complexity of difference, i.e., the presence of difference on various levels, makes any simple generalization invalid. Difference exists not just collectively between cultures and groups, but also individually among people within the same culture or the same group.

The multidimensionality of things or the complexity of difference can help us detect the limitations of both the universalist and the relativist positions. Individual differences obviously make universal claims difficult to sustain as each member of the same group or cultural tradition differs from the other members. Individual and group differences also make cultural relativist claims untenable as differences are not just between one culture and another, but between groups within the same culture. For example, S. C. Levinson shows that in locating objects in space, there are basically three distinct frames of reference—the intrinsic, the relative, and the absolute. That is reasonable enough, but what becomes problematic is the claim that "the acquisition of one or other frame of reference is strongly influenced by culture in general and by language in particular."[34] The use of linguistic determinism of the Sapir and Whorf kind, or what Levinson calls a neo-Whorfian approach, creates a problem because difference in spatial orientation does not fall neatly along linguistic lines, and people sharing the same language and culture may use different frames of reference in locating objects or orienting themselves.

As Lloyd observes, "there was no uniformity among the ancient Greeks on several problems concerning space, place, and the void, and on the relations between them, including on the question of whether it makes sense to talk of up and down, right and left, with regard to the cosmos as a whole. This already suggests that on those questions, at least, the Greek language, used by all the participants in those debates, certainly did not dictate determinate

34. G. E. R. Lloyd, *Cognitive Variations: Reflections on the Unity and Diversity of the Human Mind* (Oxford: Clarendon Press, 2007), p. 24.

solutions to the problems."[35] Likewise in China, there is no uniformity on the issue of spatial cognition, because people in the north mostly use an absolute frame of reference in locating objects in space, while most southerners use a relative frame of reference; yet both northerners and southerners largely share the same language and culture. The difference between the north and the south often plays a significant role in China. As early a text as the ancient *Book of Rites* already states that "what is considered strong in the south is tolerance, not taking vengeance for wrongs," but "what is considered strong in the north is being equipped with weapons and leather armours and not shrinking from death."[36] In Chan Buddhism as in traditional Chinese painting, the northern and the southern schools are clearly differentiated. "To relate geographical areas like the 'south' and the 'north' with two distinct modes of thinking or styles of learning," says Qian Zhongshu, arguably the most erudite scholar in modern China, "can be found as early as in the Six Dynasties (420–589), and the division of Chan Buddhism in the Tang dynasty (618–907) into the southern and the northern schools matched or closely followed the old ideas in the Six Dynasties."[37] This north-south differentiation is certainly true of spatial cognition as well. When asking a northerner for direction in China, you will be told to go north, south, east, or west, and an absolute frame of reference is used, but in the south, a relative frame is used to direct you to go straight or turn left or right, using some landmark as a point of reference. The same language is used in all these cases, and frames of reference are not mutually exclusive, either, as some combination is possible by either northerners or southerners. The Sapir and Whorf thesis of linguistic determinism is erroneous because, as Lloyd remarks, "we often find divergent views expressed in the same language by different members of the same society."[38] Here again, individual variations are always possible, and generalizations on collective basis tend to mislead. "China is not a mass of self-enclosed atomic facts but vast regions and networks of human experience," as Benjamin Schwartz reminds us. "The universalistic claims of externally imposed paradigms must be constantly and mercilessly exposed to the complexity of concrete experience, which may challenge the

35. Ibid., p. 29.

36. *Liji zhengyi* [*The Correct Meaning of the Book of Rites*], in Ruan Yuan (ed.), *Shisan jing zhushu* [*The Thirteen Classics with Annotations*], 2 vols. (Beijing: Zhonghua, 1980), 2:1626b.

37. Qian Zhongshu, "Chinese Poetry and Chinese Painting," *Qi zhui ji* [*Collection of Seven Essays*] (Shanghai: Shanghai guji, 1985), p. 9.

38. Lloyd, *Cognitive Variations*, p. 174.

paradigms themselves."[39] The concrete experience of individuals is always variable, though we must also realize that individual flexibility is confined within limits of the range of possibilities available in a particular group or society.

Let me conclude by returning to ethnography and the understanding of different cultures. A joke about ethnography has it that the ethnographer, coming back from field work in a remote land, reports that the language of the exotic tribe he has visited has only one word. It turns out that the word means "finger," for every time he pointed at something with his finger and asked what it was, the native informant answered, correctly, "finger." As good ethnographers know, jokes are often revealing, and given the presumption that the exotic people must be fundamentally different from us, the joke's point is precisely to demystify ethnography's presumption of a "surplus of difference." It is unthinkable that *our* language has only one word, but it becomes conceivable to describe the language of the Other as having just one word, as the ethnographer expects that language to be fundamentally different from *our* own, unthinkable in *our* terms. As Renato Rosaldo maintains, to judge the adequacy of an ethnographical report, a plausible criterion could be "a thought experiment: how valid would we find ethnographic discourse if it were applied to ourselves?"[40] Here the underlying assumption is of course the shared humanity among different peoples with different cultural values and belief systems. "Despite the indeterminacy of translation and the real problems of 'culture-boundedness,'" again as Schwartz argues, "it is possible to grasp the concerns which lie behind the discourse of other cultures. Difference is ever present but it is not ultimately inaccessible."[41] Differences make all of us distinct as individuals, as groups, communities, and nations, but despite and beyond all the differences, we share the same globe as human beings and as neighbors. The universalist's denial of individual and cultural differences obviously gives us a false picture of the world, and the relativist's insistence on all difference without similarity equally distorts the true condition of our world, the possibility of cross-cultural understanding and cooperation. The reality is always more complex than such either/or dichotomy would lead us to believe, and we may do well to choose to know the complexity of reality than to believe in the false picture of either all unity or total difference.

---

39. Benjamin Schwartz, *China and Other Matters* (Cambridge, MA: Harvard University Press, 1996), p. 5.

40. Rosaldo, Renato, "Where Objectivity Lies: The Rhetoric of Anthropology," in John S. Nelson, Allan Megill, & Donald N. McCloskey (eds.), *The Rhetoric of the Human Sciences: Language and Argument in Scholarship and Public Affairs* (Madison: University of Wisconsin Press, 1987), p. 90.

41. Schwartz, *China and Other Matters*, p. 7.

3

Difference or Affinity?

A Methodological Issue in Comparative Studies

In comparative studies, should one put emphasis on difference or on affinity between the things we bring into comparison? This is a question that not only often gets asked by students in practice, but also has real methodological and theoretical implications. Things are of course *either* different *or* similar, and very often they are *both* different with distinctive features *and* comparable in certain aspects. The question of difference or affinity is a general one and has been discussed by both Chinese and Western thinkers and scholars past and present. In ancient China, Mencius (c. 385 BCE–c. 304 BCE), for example, believed in the commonality of human nature and the universality of taste—taste in the gastronomic sense and, metaphorically, in an aesthetic or moral sense. He claims that "all palates have the same predilection in taste; all ears tend to the same preference in sound; all eyes have the same appreciation in beauty. Thus how can hearts alone have nothing in common? What are common to all hearts? Reason and rightness . . . So reason and rightness please my heart in the same way as meat pleases my palate."[1] With the increasing importance of Mencius since the Tang dynasty (618–907), his emphasis on commonality has a major influence in the Chinese tradition.

In some other ancient Chinese texts, however, we find a different understanding of taste that puts emphasis on diversity rather than commonality, arguing that it is by blending different ingredients that we get what we appreciate as good taste. A subtle distinction is made between sameness and harmony. For example, in a famous passage from *Zuo zhuan* or *Zuo's Commentaries on the Spring and Autumn Annals* (in "the twentieth year of Duke Zhao"), Duke

1. Jiao Xun (1763–1820), *Mengzi zhengyi* [*The Correct Meaning of the Works of Mencius*], xi.7, in *Zhuzi jicheng* [*Collection of Master Writings*], 1: 451.

Jing of the State of Qi asked his chief advisor: "Are harmony and sameness different?" "They are indeed different!" replied his advisor by making analogies to food and music: "Harmony is like making a soup: water and fire, vinegar, meat paste, salt, plums are all put together to cook with fish and meat; the cook puts logs on the fire and mixes up the ingredients, adding to what is insufficient and reducing what is excessive." Thus the tasty soup is not just one thing, but the combination of many elements. The same is true of music; it is by combining sounds of different pitch, tempo, and rhythm in harmony that a fine piece of music is produced. "But if one only adds water to water, who would eat that? If lute and zither all produce the same one sound, who would listen to it? So sameness will not do."[2] In another text, *Discourses of the States*, we find articulation of a similar idea: "Harmony indeed produces a variety of things, but sameness generates no progeny . . . Therefore we blend five flavors to suit our palate, strengthen the four limbs to protect our body, combine six tunes to please our ears . . . Sounds made one produce no music; things made one display no pattern; flavors made one offer no delicacy; and things made one provide no choice."[3] Here we find a slightly different emphasis from Mencius, but the two arguments are not contradictory to one another; rather, they highlight different aspect of things—either the diversity within unity or unity with diversity.

Among Greek philosophers, Heraclitus has expressed ideas very close to what we have seen above in ancient China, for in fragment 45 he says: "Things taken together are whole and not whole, <something which is> being brought together and brought apart, in tune and out of tune; out of all things there comes a unity, and out of a unity all things."[4] Again in fragment 49 we read: "What is opposed brings together; the finest harmony (*harmonia*) is composed of things at variance, and everything comes to be in accordance with strife."[5] The idea of a dialectic relationship between unity and diversity becomes an important principle in Western thinking, and it is also prominent in traditional Chinese philosophy. From this we should come to the conclusion

2. *Chunqiu Zuo zhuan zhengyi* [*The Correct Meaning of Zuo's Commentaries on the Spring and Autumn Annals*], in Ruan Yuan (ed.), *Shisan jing zhushu* [*The Thirteen Classics with Annotations*], 2:2093–94.

3. Fu Gengsheng (ed.), *Guo yu xuan* [*Selections from Discourses of the States*] (Beijing: Renmin wenxue, 1959), pp. 212–13.

4. Heraclitus, fragment 45, in *A Presocratics Reader: Selected Fragments and Testimonia*, ed. Patricia Curd, trans. Richard D. McKirahan, Jr. (Indianapolis, IN: Hackett, 1996), p. 34.

5. Ibid., fragment 49, p. 35.

that difference and affinity—the specific and the general, the diverse and the universal—are all complementary to one another with emphasis put on one side or the other; so we should not overstress one at the expense of the other. Difference or affinity has no value in and of itself; therefore it is pointless to ask, without a specific context, whether we should lay emphasis on difference or affinity in comparative studies. If we think of scholarship in terms of a hermeneutic dialogue, any study or argument can then be conceptualized as a presentation in answer to a specific question, and it is in that dialogic context, in answering a specific question, that we may decide whether difference or affinity should be the focus.

In arts and literature, we normally desire a rich variety rather than sameness or uniformity. The Chinese are justly proud of the rich ideas and lively debates in pre-Qin philosophy at the early stage of their history, which they usually describe as "a hundred flowers match in full bloom, and a hundred schools contend to raise their voices." Those different schools of thought indeed constitute a rich source of ideas influential in the Chinese tradition, and it is futile to force them into a unified orthodoxy. The First Emperor of Qin in the third century BCE tried to burn books and to bury scholars alive in his draconian effort to control people's minds, but he only succeeded in locking himself in the pillory of shame in history, winning the notoriety of a prototypical tyrant despised by all later generations. So we indeed appreciate diversity and difference in arts and literature, and in those studies where the purpose is to define or distinguish an object from other objects, emphasis on difference or the specific distinctiveness becomes the legitimate concern. "Determination is negation," as Spinoza puts it.[6] On the level of textual details, we may say that every work of literature is unique—each poem, each novel or play is different from any other. And yet, uniqueness is only relative and not absolute, for no work of literature is so different as to deny itself the possibility of comparison with other works. After all, the literary language itself is not different from our normal, daily language, and it is only the writer's skillful use of the language that makes all the difference. As Oscar Wilde puts it, "the morality of art consists in the perfect use of an imperfect medium."[7] A truly unique, private language would become unintelligible and thus defeats the very purpose of literary expression and communication. Poems, novels, and plays can be seen to constitute a certain form and tradition with common features

6. Benedict de Spinoza, *Correspondence*, in *The Chief Works of Benedict de Spinoza*, 2:370.

7. Oscar Wilde, Preface to *The Picture of Dorian Gray*, in *The Portable Oscar Wilde*, rev. ed., eds. Richard Aldington and Stanley Weintraub (Harmondsworth, UK: Penguin, 1981), p. 138.

when we look at them from the point of view of literary genres, treat them as parts of literature as a whole, and study them as exemplary works in literary history. It is precisely the commonality of shared features of different literary works that lays the very foundation of comparative literature as a discipline.

The ground for comparison, however, is more specifically concerned with the commonality or comparability of different literary traditions and is often debatable. It becomes an even more challenging problem when comparative literature develops beyond the European or Euro-American boundaries. In China and the West, we often encounter an argument that insists on the fundamental difference between Chinese and Western literatures and cultures. In the late seventeenth and the eighteenth centuries, the so-called Chinese rites controversy flared up in the Vatican to condemn the Jesuit "accommodation approach," which, according to the doctrinaire purists, gave too much concession to the Chinese and their pagan culture and language. The use of *tianzu* or *shangdi* as Chinese equivalents to the Christian God or Lord was officially condemned by popes from Clement XI in 1704 to Benedict XIV in 1742, and transliteration of the Latin *Deus* was allowed to be used as the only adequate word for conveying the idea of God. Insofar as the Vatican was concerned, God spoke Latin, even though the Bible was originally in Hebrew and Greek. The Catholic Church reassured the spiritual uniqueness and the fundamental difference between Christianity and the pagan Chinese culture, and the idea of untranslatability became not just a linguistic, but a conceptual issue that has cast a long shadow on later discussions of East-West cross-cultural understanding.

Now differences are obvious between China and the West in many ways—in language, culture, history, social customs, political institutions, and so on. No one can overlook those differences and claim an unproblematic universality between the East and the West. Those who insist on fundamental differences, however, are not concerned with such obvious and concrete differences, but they argue for difference on a more conceptual or philosophical level, the radical incommensurability of the modes of thinking, and therefore the impossibility of East-West comparative literature or cross-cultural studies. Some have argued, for example, that Chinese-Western comparative literature is "essentially a *utopian* project," that is, a sort of pure fantasy, an imaginary endeavor "inscribed" in an "impossible disciplinary space."[8] Some of the most commonly held dichotomous views include such clear-cut oppositions: a Chinese synthetic mode of thinking versus a Western analytic mode of thinking,

8. David Palumbo-Liu, "The Utopias of Discourse: On the Impossibility of Chinese Comparative Literature," *Chinese Literature: Essays, Articles, Reviews* 14 (December 1992): 165.

Chinese emphasis on collectivity versus Western predilection for individualism, Chinese harmonious relationship with nature versus Western conquest of nature and its dire consequences of pollution and the destruction of the world's ecological system, etc.

Not only some Westerners hold such views, but some Chinese and Asian scholars as well, for whom such simplistic dichotomies may serve to strengthen the stereotypes they have of the West and blame the West for all the environmental disasters and other problems we face in the world today. In his discussion of East-West dichotomies, Raghaven Iyer finds a "glass curtain" between Asia and Europe. We cannot ignore such a "glass curtain," he says, but we must also try our best to overcome the obstacle. In cross-cultural studies, he argues, "the real difficulty is that the smug denial of any serious obstacle to mutual understanding is met by the repeated insistence that there is nothing less than an 'eternal antithesis,' an 'obstinate schism' between Asia and Europe."[9] He not only enumerates many European prejudices against Asia, including some racist and colonialist views, but he also points out some equally simplistic Asian prejudices. Prejudices are often exaggerated opinions not totally baseless, but they distort and overemphasize, and they create big problems for cross-cultural understanding. Iyer says:

> Modern Asian writers have also been more or less complacent (or defensive) in their own sweeping contrasts between Asia and Europe, between Eastern and Western thought and culture. We have, for example, Liang Ch'i-ch'ao's contrast between Eastern wisdom and Western learning, Kitaro Nishida's distinction between the rule of the intellect in European culture and the stress on feeling in Eastern culture, Kitayama's opposition of 'space' and 'time' cultures, and Nagayo's emphasis on the difference between 'soul training' and 'mental culture.' Okakura held that Christian Europe never ascended above a human godhead to the Eastern vision of the universal in its 'eternal search for unity in variety.'[10]

Iyer made his argument in the mid-1960s, but it is surprising to see that the situation has not changed as much as one might have hoped. In the West, Jonathan Spence once remarked that to set up "mutually reinforcing

9. Raghavan Iyer, "The Glass Curtain between Asia and Europe," in Iyer (ed.), *The Glass Curtain between Asia and Europe* (London: Oxford University Press, 1965), p. 5.

10. Ibid., pp. 20–21.

images and perceptions" of an exotic China "seems to have been a particularly French genius."[11] Spence's description of the "French exotic" is of course by no means applicable just to the French, though it is true that quite a few French Sinophiles and Sinologues seem to have a particular predilection for a kind of Chinese exoticism. Victor Segalen is probably the first to theorize the charm of an exotic China in a series of notes for a pamphlet in the early twentieth century, but as I said earlier, he was more interested in the poetic possibilities of cultural difference, the aesthetic appeal of the exotic or what he called *"l'esthétique du divers*."[12] Some French scholars in our time, however, are more determined to conceptualize China as the opposite of Europe and thereby to set up a more absolute dichotomy between the East and the West.

For example, in his study of the Chinese rites controversy, Jacques Gernet imputed the failure of the Christian mission in China to the fundamental difference "not only of different intellectual traditions but also of different mental categories and modes of thought."[13] The fundamental difference between a Chinese mentality and its European counterpart is often illustrated by the contrast between Greek abstract thinking and the lack thereof in China, and it is often the conclusion of such contrastive studies to present China as the opposite to Greece. Thus, Gernet claims that the Chinese language has no grammatical categories that European languages possess. "There was no word to denote existence in Chinese, nothing to convey the concept of being or essence, which in Greek is so conveniently expressed by the noun *ousia* or the neuter *to on*. Consequently, the notion of being, in the sense of an eternal and constant reality, above and beyond that which is phenomenal, was perhaps more difficult to conceive, for a Chinese."[14] This is a general claim not only of the untranslatability of particular Western words or terms into Chinese, but one that evaluates the nature and quality of the entire Chinese language, and also of the capabilities of the Chinese "mode of thinking." When the Christian missionaries went to China in the late seventeenth century, what they came in contact with, according to Gernet, was a civilization that "differed fundamentally, not on particular points but as a whole, from all that had become familiar to them by virtue of their own long traditions." The world those mis-

11. Jonathan D. Spence, *The Chan's Great Continent: China in Western Minds* (New York: W. W. Norton, 1998), p. 145.

12. See Segalen, *Essai sur l'exotisme*.

13. Jacques Gernet, *China and the Christian Impact: A Conflict of Cultures*, trans. Janet Lloyd (Cambridge: Cambridge University Press, 1985), p. 3.

14. Ibid., p. 241.

sionaries faced was so very different that they, says Gernet, "found themselves in the presence of a different kind of humanity."[15] The emphasis on cultural and ethnic difference and incommensurability can hardly be expressed more emphatically than what we see here, but Gernet is not the only one to put such emphasis on the absolute alteriry of China.

Again, as I discussed earlier, another prolific French scholar writing today, François Jullien, goes even further in setting up the dichotomies between ancient China and ancient Greece. In his many books and articles, Jullien has reiterated the same point repeatedly and repetitively, namely that China, among all ancient civilizations, is the only one that had no contact with Greece and therefore could provide a negative mirror for the West to look at the self for what it is not. In his effort to create a Greek-Chinese polarity, Jullien brings a series of contrastive categories into play. For example, he makes a systematic contrast between Greek philosophy and its search for truth on the one hand, and Chinese wisdom and its alleged unconcern with truth on the other. Reminiscent of Gernet's remarks on the Greek notion of being, Jullien argues that the Greek concept of truth is linked with that of being, but because the Chinese "did not conceive of the existential sense of being (the verb *to be*, in that sense, does not even exist in classical Chinese), it had no concept of truth."[16] The idea of way in the West, he continues, leads to truth or a transcendental origin, but in China, "the way recommended by wisdom leads to nothing. No truth—revealed or discovered—constitutes its destination."[17] In ancient Greece, however, there are more than one concept of truth or the accessibility to truth, and it is impossible to single out one as *the* representative Greek concept of truth. Geoffrey Lloyd argues that we can broadly distinguish three main families of positions about truth in ancient Greece: "These are the objectivist, the relativist, and the sceptical."[18] Parmenides, Plato, and Aristotle, their differences notwithstanding, all hold the objectivist view of truth as objective reality distinct from mere appearance and human perception. Then Protagoras may be seen as representing the relativist position in seeing man as the measurement of all things, and therefore what is true or false is also measured from a human being's subjective point of view. The most interesting is perhaps the skeptic Gorgias, who maintains "first that nothing

15. Ibid., p. 247.

16. François Jullien, "Did Philosophers Have to Become Fixated on Truth?" trans. Janet Lloyd, *Critical Inquiry* 28:4 (Summer 2002): 810.

17. Ibid., p. 820.

18. G. E. R. Lloyd, *Ancient Worlds, Modern Reflections*, p. 53.

exists, secondly that if it did, it cannot be known, and thirdly that if it did and were known, it cannot be communicated to anyone else." For all practical purposes, then, truth does not exist and cannot be known or articulated. "I recall them here first to emphasize that there is no one Greek concept of truth," says Lloyd. "It is not just that the Greeks disagreed on the answers to the questions: they disagreed on the questions themselves."[19] Likewise, there are different positions about truth in ancient China. Confucius famously set forth the project of "rectification of names," which aims to have names or linguistic terms correspond to reality.[20] Laozi made a distinction between truth and beauty in his remark that "true words are not beautiful, and beautiful words are not true."[21] Another Taoist philosopher Zhuangzi (Zhuang Zhou) expressed a radically skeptical view of truth and reality by questioning whether his dream of being a butterfly is real or the reality is just a dream, when he woke up from that dream and wondered "whether it was Zhou who dreamed of being a butterfly or it was the butterfly who had dreamed of being Zhou."[22] So, just as in ancient Greece, evidently there are different positions in ancient China concerning the question of truth; therefore Jullien's absolute contrast of Greece as having the concept of truth while China as lacking the notion of truth does not stand up to scrutiny.

The West may achieve self-understanding by looking at China as the opposite—that is the point Jullien repeatedly makes in one argument after another. Of course, it is perfectly all right for a Western scholar to use China as an aid for self-understanding and for thinking from the outside, but the problem with Jullien's argument is that it becomes utterly predictable as his study is always already predetermined to find differences between China and Greece, and he always finds them one way or another. In one of his earlier works, *La valeur allusive*, Jullien criticized the Chinese scholar Qian Zhongshu for making China and Europe "more or less alike."[23] But that is a gross simplification, because Qian Zhongshu never simply proclaims that something Chinese is similar or equivalent to something European, but his argument

19. Ibid., p. 55.

20. Liu Baonan (1791–1855), *Lunyu zhengyi* [*The Correct Meaning of the Analects*], xiii.3, in *Zhuzi jicheng* [*Collection of Masters Writings*], 1:80.

21. Wang Bi, *Laozi zhu* [*Laozi with Annotations*], ibid., 3:47.

22. Guo Qingfan (184–1895), *Zhuangzi jishi* [*The Variorum Edition of the Zhuangzi*], ibid., 3:53–54.

23. François Jullien, *La valeur allusive: Des catégories originales de l'interprétation poétique dans la tradition chinoise (Contribution à une réflexion sur l'altérité interculturelle)* (Paris: École française d'Extrême-Orient, 1985), p. 126, no. 1.

always starts with a particular textual detail, typically a quotation from an ancient Chinese classic, and proceeds with quotations from various other sources, supplemented with his own commentaries to bring all the textual evidences together for an insight, an elucidation, or a major critical point. Qian's text is characteristically a dense web of quotations from texts in Chinese, English, French, German, Italian, Spanish, or Latin, in which brilliant ideas are always well-connected with one another to demonstrate the affinities, or sometimes crucial differences, of cultures and traditions East and West. The intertextual correspondences and mutual illuminations in Qian's work always present an argument based on detailed comparisons and logical connections, and its persuasive power is supported not by mere claims, but always by a wealth of textual evidence. Without the same kind of textual structure, convincing evidences, and persuasive argument, it is hardly possible to take Jullien's contrastive claims seriously, because simply to declare that all things East and West are "more or less different" can hardly be regarded as serious scholarship. It is no ground-breaking news that China is in Asia and Greece is in Europe, that the Chinese speak a language different from Greek, that ancient Chinese thinkers talked about language, society, truth, or beauty in ways very different from that of Greek philosophers. What else can we expect with regard to the differences between China and Greece? But does that preclude any possibility of comparison, translation, and cross-cultural understanding?

In an intriguing analysis of the European image of the non-European, Henri Baudet traced the dichotomous thinking to ancient times and followed its development throughout the centuries. He found that there are two very different relations that the Europeans have often established with the non-European: one is "in the realm of political life in its broadest sense," i.e., real contact with concrete non-European countries and peoples, and the other is an imaginary relation "of all sorts of images of non-Western people and worlds which have flourished in our culture—images derived not from observation, experience, and perceptible reality but from a psychological urge," says Baudet. "That urge creates its own realities which are totally different from the political realities of the first category. But they are in no way subordinate in either strength or clarity since they have always possessed that absolute reality value so characteristic of the rule of the myth."[24] That is to say, the urge to see the non-European Other as the opposite of the European self can be so strong that it creates a myth of the Other despite the reality and lived experience of the

24. Henri Baudet, *Paradise on Earth: Some Thoughts on European Images of Non-European Man*, trans. Elizabeth Wenthold (Middletown, CT: Wesleyan University Press, 1988), p. 6.

non-European people. That may explain the persistence of the dichotomous view that seems so attractive to many European scholars when it comes to conceptualize the non-Europe. But should such a dichotomy still dominate our view of the world today? Is it time that we went beyond such a dichotomy and made efforts at cross-cultural understanding based not on self-generated myth, but on reality, on the real concerns about real people outside our own group or community?

Cultural differences certainly exist, but there is also affinity beyond whatever differences we may have as human beings. Moreover, differences exist not just between cultures, but also in the same culture. Let me return to the initial question of difference or affinity and reiterate my argument: it is pointless to ask whether we should put emphasis on difference or on affinity in comparative studies without considering the context within which we conduct our study. The meaning and value of difference or affinity emerge only in a particular context or situation, in answering specific questions with concrete argument and textual evidences. Affinity does not mean sameness without diversity, and difference does not mean incommensurability that denies the very possibility of comparison. And that, I would argue, should be the basis of comparative studies of literature and culture as a field of study and a worthy subject in the discipline of the humanities.

4

Heaven and Man

From a Cross-Cultural Perspective

Before a sudden and debilitating financial crisis struck Asia in 1997–98, a discourse on "Asian values" was actively presented as a cultural explanation for the extraordinary economic growth and prosperity in East and Southeast Asia—Japan, and particularly South Korea, Singapore, Taiwan, and Hong Kong, the so-called "four little dragons of East Asia." At the same time, the discourse on "Asian values" was also presented as an argument for offering an alternative social and political model distinct from "hegemonic Western norms," particularly democracy and human rights. Highly visible advocates of "Asian values" included politicians, notably the Singaporean Prime Minister Lee Kuan Yew and the Malaysian Prime Minister Mahathir Mohamad, both strong leaders with authoritarian political outlooks. Lee Kuan Yew in particular, according to Michael Barr, "is the undisputed architect of the 'Asian values' argument."[1] The discourse on "Asian values" also appeals, however, to many Asian (and non-Asian) intellectuals for various reasons, including such eminent scholars as William Theodore de Bary and Tu Wei-Ming. In order to distinguish Asian from European or Western values, many who argue for Asian values tend to construct a systematic contrast between Eastern and Western "ways of thinking," often understood as an opposition between a "holistic" and an "analytic," or an "individualistic" and a "communitarian" approach in thinking and action. For example, a group of scholars claim that the Western "Cartesian way of thinking" always tends "to look at a part, or an aspect of the reality separated

1. Michael D. Barr, *Cultural Politics and Asian Values: The Tepid War* (London: Routledge, 2002), p. 3. In a chapter on Singapore and Malaysia, Barr maintains that one can precisely trace "the origins and development of the 'Asian values' reaction, because in each country the 'Asian values' agenda was written by a particular person: Lee Kuan Yew in Singapore and Mahathir Mohamad in Malaysia" (p. 30).

from the whole assuming that it is the whole and the reality," whereas the Eastern "holistic approach or mind," they maintain, "would never look at an aspect, or part, separate from the whole. It sees everything as interconnected, overlapping, inseparable, every part as held together by every other part or aspect. They are one."[2]

This reminds us of what Nisbett said "a brilliant student from China" had told him, for that student also claimed that the holistic view of seeing the correlation of parts and the whole was uniquely Chinese or Eastern, without knowing at all that the correlation of the parts and the whole constitutes a traditional German concept of the hermeneutic circle. As H. G. Gadamer observes, "Schleiermacher follows Friedrich Ast and the whole hermeneutical and rhetorical tradition when he regards it as a fundamental principle of understanding that the meaning of the part can be discovered only from the context—i.e., ultimately from the whole."[3] This suggests that ignorance often lies behind the courage to make sweeping generalizations about the East and the West, and it is often the case that the less one knows, the more willingly one makes a claim about the East-West dichotomy without hesitation. Such dichotomous views seem rather popular with a number of academics and, according to the same group of scholars, the differences between Asian and Western "ways of thinking" are not just epistemological, but also ethical and political. They continue to build up a rigid dichotomy when they argue:

> In the Western mind, good is good, bad is bad. It is an 'either or.' You must make your choice. The good must win over the bad. In fact, it is an absolutist position. In the Chinese mind, there is a dynamic balance between good and bad. Although they are conflictual, each is relatively good and relatively bad. There is no such thing as a victory of good over bad for otherwise there would not be a dynamic interplay of opposites. In political terms, capitalism is neither absolutely good, nor absolutely bad. Similarly, communism is neither absolutely good, nor absolutely bad. The Cold War propaganda of bad communism and good capitalism is contrary to *yin* and *yang*, and reflects the Cartesian mind.[4]

2. Josiane Cauquelin, Paul Lim and Birgit Mayer-König, "Understanding Asian Values," in Cauquelin, Lim and Mayer-König (eds.), *Asian Values: An Encounter with Diversity* (Surrey, UK: Curzon, 1998), p. 15.

3. Hans-Georg Gadamer, *Truth and Method*, 2nd rev. ed., translation revised by Joel Weinsheimer and Donald G. Marshall (New York: Crossroad, 1991), p. 190.

4. Cauquelin et al., "Understanding Asian Values," p. 17.

As a Chinese myself, I find this statement rather amusing. The clear-cut contrast between a rigid, Western "absolutist position" and an ambiguous, equivocal "Chinese mind" sounds like a "either/or" opposition straight from a "Cartesian mind" these scholars themselves described. Obviously these scholars do not live in China, nor are they writing under the political condition of contemporary Chinese society, for if they were, I wonder what might happen to them and their statement that capitalism or communism "is neither absolutely good, nor absolutely bad." In Mao's China from the 1950s to the 1970s, such a statement might land them in jail or some other forms of trouble, to say the least; even today, it may still be difficult for them to get that statement loudly announced and published in China. The discrepancy between the claim made by this group of academics outside China and the sociopolitical reality in China as I have experienced it leads me to conclude that either their statement about the "Chinese way of thinking" is completely erroneous or contemporary China has been so Westernized that it has lost its traditional "way of thinking" as they described. The latter argument is of course heard from time to time, particularly in the West, but that argument has the fundamental flaw of a certain type of Western anthropological discourse, what Johannes Fabian called the "denial of coevalness," i.e., "*a persistent and systematic tendency to place the referent(s) of anthropology in a Time other than the present of the producer of anthropological discourse.*"[5] That is to say, in this Western anthropological discourse, China with its "pure" tradition, as the Western anthropologist envisions it in his imagination, is frozen in time and sealed off from the history of change and transformation, whereas history, particularly modern history with the crucial concepts of evolution and progress, is something only the West has gone through and possesses. Hegel's Eurocentric view of history is typical of such a discourse. For Hegel, as Haun Saussy observes, China is not contemporary but permanently ancient. "Essential China is historical China, just as the essential Greece is the Greece of Pericles and the essential England is the England of the worldwide mercantile empire. And what essential China brought to the world is something that lies deep in the past of historical Prussia, and of all humanity."[6] The problem with such a Hegelian view is that China names a continuous cultural heritage, a living tradition that reaches from antiquity to the present; and that China as it exists today is as vibrantly

5. Johannes Fabian, *Time and the Other: How Anthropology Makes Its Object* (New York: Columbia University Press, 1983), p. 31.

6. Haun Saussy, *Great Walls of Discourse and Other Adventures in Cultural China* (Cambridge, MA: Harvard University Asia Center, 2001), p. 95.

modern and continually changing as the modern West. To see China as the reverse mirror image of the West, the exemplary Derridean *différance* or a Faucaultian *heterotopia*, as the opposite of the West, only exposes a spot of blindness in the Western theoretical perspective.

The incredibly fast development and the emergence of China as an economic and political world power in the last few decades should have broken many of the old stereotypes and misconceptions about a frozen, permanently ancient, and timeless Oriental stasis. A visit to Beijing, Shanghai, and many other cities in China today should permanently cure a Western visitor of those nineteenth-century romantic images of an exotic, static China immune to change and temporal events. China as a living culture is a contemporary presence, not an archaeological specimen of a frozen past. "Students of modern China," as Saussy remarks, "have no problem in recognizing that all of us inhabit 'the same time.' "[7] And yet, old ideas and stereotypes persist; not surprisingly, we are witnessing a comeback of the discourse on "Asian values," which subsided for a while in the wake of the Asian financial crisis, but never completely disappeared despite economic difficulties and even the SARS epidemic in 2003.

Here I would like to examine a certain type or a particular variation of the "Asian values" discourse, namely the argument about a perfectly harmonious relationship between "heaven and man" in traditional Chinese cosmology and philosophical thinking as opposed to an allegedly antagonistic attitude toward nature in the West. Quite often, such an argument is easily combined with a strong sentiment of nationalism and patriotism, and thus becomes a sort of proclamation, a profession of one's faith in the superiority of Eastern culture, a proclamation with emotional appeal rather than a careful examination of facts and cool reasoning. For example, Professor Ji Xianlin, a well-respected senior scholar in China, became quite famous in the last few decades for making such arguments. As a champion for the values of Eastern culture, he always set up an absolute East-West dichotomy and maintained that the fundamental differences between the East and the West "ultimately come from the differences in the modes of thinking," because "the Eastern mode of thinking is synthetic, while the Western mode of thinking is analytic."[8] For him, analysis somehow equals aggression and violence in dealing with nature, for "the guiding principle in Western thinking is to conquer nature; while the guiding

7. Ibid., p. 96.

8. Ji Xianlin, "New Interpretation of the Unity of Heaven and Man," in Ji Xianlin and Zhang Guanglin (eds.), *Dong Xi wenhua yilun ji* [*Essays on Eastern and Western Cultures*], 2 vols. (Beijing: Economics Daily Press, 1997), 1: 82.

principle in Eastern thinking, with its basis in a synthetic mode, advocates the merging with nature and all things. The West attacks nature vehemently and takes all natural resources by force and with violence"; while Eastern culture, operating under the principle of "the unity of heaven and man," treats nature with love and caring tenderness.[9] According to him, the aggressive Western analytic mode of thinking is responsible for all the ills of the world today. With Western culture prevailing in the modern times, he says:

> The world's ecological balance is destroyed, acid rain causes havoc everywhere, fresh water resources are drastically reduced, air is polluted, the ozone layer is damaged, rivers, seas, and oceans suffer from pollution, some species become extinct, new diseases emerge, and all these put the future development, and even the very existence, of mankind in jeopardy. If these disasters and threats are not overcome, humanity will not be able to survive in less than a hundred years.[10]

That was written in the late 1990s, but the situation, particularly air and water pollution and environmental problems, seems to describe China today. In any case, while issuing such an apocalyptic warning of the imminent end of humanity, Professor Ji offers Eastern culture as the necessary remedy. "Is there any way of salvation?" he asks. The answer is, of course, yes: the world will be fine so long as we "bring the synthetic mode of thinking in Eastern culture to rescue the collapse of the Western analytic mode of thinking. People must first follow the philosophical thinking of the Chinese or the Easterners, of which the most important is the idea of 'the unity of heaven and man'; they must make friends with nature and mend their ways completely from evil to good. Only with such changes," he concludes, prophet-like, "can humanity continue to exist in happiness."[11] One can hardly find a more absolute dichotomy between the Eastern and Western "modes of thinking," nor can one find a more forceful articulation of the spirit of Chinese nationalism, the belief in the superiority of Chinese or Eastern culture over the West. But what exactly is this "unity of heaven and man"? Is such an idea uniquely Chinese and diametrically opposed to the "Western way of thinking"? What happens if we go beyond the dichotomy and look at that idea historically, try to find some

9. Ibid., p. 83.

10. Ibid., p. 84.

11. Ibid.

textual evidence, some exemplary quotations, and examine that idea from the perspective of cross-cultural studies?

Tian ren he yi, literally "heaven and man merging into one," is indeed an old idea in Chinese thinking that can be traced back to concepts and notions first manifested in several ancient books and their commentaries. The idea of *tian* or heaven as the supreme authority that keeps all things in order and legitimates the kingly rule on earth already existed in such old classics as the *Book of Changes*, the *Book of Poetry*, the Confucian *Analects*, the *Spring and Autumn Annals*, etc. It is an idea held by philosophers of different schools, not just the Confucians. In the chapter on the "Will of Heaven (*tian zhi*)" of the book of *Mozi*, for example, we find a clear expression of this idea: "When the son of heaven does something good, heaven can reward him. When the son of heaven does evil, heaven can punish him."[12] The son of heaven refers to the ruler, a king or an emperor, and Mozi here articulates the ancient idea that heaven has the power to reward or punish the ruler for what he does, and to accord a political regime its legitimacy. In Mozi's conceptualization, as a modern commentator observes, heaven becomes an anthropomorphic deity with will and power, "a religious force that all must obey and do as its will dictates."[13] This idea is assimilated into Confucian political philosophy, and the assimilation is very important for the development of Confucianism. It is not just Mozi, however, but also other schools of ancient Chinese thinking that understand heaven as a supreme power over and beyond the human world. This can be seen, for instance, in the chapter on the "Revolution of Heaven (*tian yun*)" in the Taoist book *Zhuangzi*: "Heaven has six dimensions and five constant elements. Following heaven, the king will rule in good order, but going against heaven, the king will bring about disasters."[14] The relationship between heaven and the ruler is clearly established in a framework of correspondence and unity, in which to follow the will of heaven is crucial for a good and successful government. The Gongyang school of commentaries on the *Spring and Autumn Annals* in particular adumbrated the idea of the unity of heaven and man, which was then further developed during the Western Han dynasty (206 BCE–25 CE).

12. Sun Yirang (1848–1908), *Mozi jiangu* [*Annotations on the Mozi*], in *Zhuzi jicheng* [*Collection of Masters Writings*], 4:123.

13. Huang Pumin, *Tian ren he yi: Dong Zhongshu yu Handai ruxue sichao* [*Unity of Heaven and Man: Dong Zhongshu and Confucian Thoughts in the Han Dynasty*] (Changsha: Yuelu shushe, 1999), p. 64.

14. Guo Qingfan, *Zhuangzi jishi* [*Variorum Edition of the Zhuangzi*], in *Zhuzi jicheng* [*Collection of Masters Writings*], 3:219–20.

The famous scholar and statesman Dong Zhongshu (179–104 BCE) is a key figure in the history of Confucianism. As an erudite scholar who played an important role in assimilating much of the knowledge available in his time—the theories of *yin* and *yang*, of the five elements that constitute the world, of stars and the other heavenly bodies and their influences, of the medical understanding of the human body as corresponding to the body of nature, of the unity of the cosmos as a model for political unity on earth, and so on and so forth—Dong Zhongshu was mainly responsible for turning Confucianism into a state-sanctioned orthodoxy. As a modern commentator observes, theorizing about the "unity of heaven and man" is "the most basic feature and the main pillar of Dong Zhongshu's Confucian teaching."[15] The core of Dong's cosmology, says another scholar, "is the correspondence between heaven and man, and its goal is essentially political."[16] Indeed, in his major work—*Chun qiu fan lu* or *Exuberant Dews of the Spring and Autumn*—and other writings, Dong Zhongshu put forward a cosmological as well as a political theory, or a systematic theory of government based on the correlations between heaven and man, formulated as a strict and orderly hierarchy of social status and political power. This cosmological and political theory has such a profound influence on Chinese history and culture that no discussion of the idea of the "unity of heaven and man" can ignore its argument.

In Dong's argument, heaven is the highest authority, the ultimate source of social and political power, the authority that provides the political power on earth with a kind of divine legitimacy. The way power operates is strictly hierarchical, and the hierarchy, as typical of Confucian teachings, has a moral basis in family relationships. Dong Zhongshu writes:

> The son of heaven takes orders from heaven; the nobles take orders from the son of heaven; the son takes orders from the father; male

15. Huang Pumin, *Tian ren he yi: Dong Zhongshu yu Handai ruxue sichao* [*Unity of Heaven and Man: Dong Zhongshu and Confucian Thoughts in the Han Dynasty*], p. 76. For a study in English of Dong's contribution to the institutionalization of Confucianism during the Han dynasty, see Sarah A. Queen, *From Chronicle to Canon: The Hermeneutics of the Spring and Autumn, according to Tung Chung-shu* (Cambridge: Cambridge University Press, 1996).

16. Zhou Guidian, *Dong xue tan wei* [*Exploring the Intricacies of Dong Zhongshu's Doctrine*] (Beijing: Beijing Normal University Press, 1989), p. 61. Huang Pumin makes an effort to differentiate Dong's theory of the "unity of heaven and man" from an earlier idea of the "correspondence between heaven and man," but that difference comes down to little more than the fact that Dong's theory is more systematic and more developed than earlier ones. See Huang, *Tian ren he yi* [*Unity of Heaven and Man*], pp. 83–86. In this essay, I shall not focus on such a minute difference and treat the two as similar and closely related ideas.

> and female subordinates take orders from their master; the wife takes orders from her husband. All who take orders revere their superior as heaven; so it can be said that all take orders from heaven.[17]

From this citation we can see clearly that Dong Zhongshu's theory of "heaven and man merging into one" is first and foremost a theory aimed to establish moral authority and political unification in a hierarchical social order and to legitimize that order. In this theoretical frame, the ruler is endowed with the mandate of heaven or the divine right to rule, and the hierarchical relationship between the ruler and his subjects is duplicated in the family and in society at large. In addition, Dong builds up an elaborate analogy between heaven and man to argue for their correlation and correspondence, and presents nature and man as similarly constituted. "Heaven uses the numbers of a whole year in making the human body," he says, "so there are three hundred and sixty-six small joints to correspond to the number of days, and twelve big joints to correspond to the number of months. Inside the human body, there are five organs to correspond to the number of five elements. On the outside, there are four limbs to correspond to the number of four seasons." The opening and closing of eyes correspond to day and night; breathing in and out correspond to the blowing of air and winds; sorrow, joy, and the other kinds of mood correspond to the changing condition of the seasons. In all these correspondences, man and heaven are seen as similar to one another; if heaven assumes the shape of an anthropomorphic god, man is also turned into a miniature universe. "The human body," as Dong puts it, "is like that of heaven."[18] Because of such perfect correspondences, one can understand the abstract and the general by looking at the concrete and the particular. As Dong argues, "one can display the visible to reveal the invisible, and take the countable to reveal the uncountable. That is to say, the way to understand should be looking at the correspondence of categories, just like looking at what is visible, and examining the matching of numbers."[19]

That may explain the importance of observing the movement of heavenly bodies, recording natural calamities and any unusual things or events as signs and omens sent by heaven. That may also highlight the necessity of interpreting what one has observed, the close relationships of hermeneutics with politics

17. Dong Zhongshu, *Chun qiu fan lu* [*Exuberant Dews of the Spring and Autumn*], annotated by Ling Shu (Shanghai: The Commercial Press, 1937), chap. 70, p. 241.

18. Ibid., chap. 56, p. 205.

19. Ibid., pp. 205–06.

and ethics, the necessity of understanding the will of heaven through proper reading of natural signs. "All calamities have their roots," says Dong, "in the defects of a state." Natural calamities serve as heaven's warnings sent to man; therefore, those who rule "must endeavor to see the will of heaven through calamities."[20] That is the political significance of the idea of "heaven and man merging into one," a political concept that has little to do with the love of nature or the idea of pure harmony.

Whatever happens in heaven is correlated with and has influence on the human world—that is indeed an old idea in China, but that idea, or what we would now call astrology, is by no means uniquely Chinese. Observing stars or heavenly bodies as a way to understand the will of heaven is a common practice in almost all ancient civilizations. "God invented and gave us sight to the end that we might behold the courses of intelligence in the heaven, and apply them to the courses of our own intelligence which are akin to them"; this may sound like Dong Zhongshu, but actually here Plato is speaking.[21] In ancient times, observation of heavenly bodies and recording of their movements often served a divinatory purpose. Geoffrey Lloyd has discussed the investigation of heavenly bodies in ancient Mesopotamia, China, and Greece, and noticed that in all three civilizations there was the belief that "the heavens sent messages that bore on human destinies, not determining their fate, but rather sent as warnings that the wise should take into account."[22] That is exactly what Dong Zhongshu says about natural calamities. "When the defects of the state first start," says Dong, "heaven would send calamities as warnings. If such warnings do not make the state to change its ways, strange things would appear to strike fear in men's hearts, but if men are not frightened and do not know fear, catastrophes would come as punishment."[23] The striking similarities here in understanding calamities as warnings sent by heaven, which we find in Greece as well as in China, lead us to the realization that the correlation of heavenly bodies with the human body, of natural phenomena with the human world, or the "unity of heaven and man," is not a uniquely Chinese idea, but can also be found in the West from antiquity, the medieval time, up to and even beyond the eighteenth century.

20. Ibid., chap. 30, p. 144.

21. Plato, *Timaeus* 47bc, trans. Benjamin Jowett, in Edith Hamilton and Huntington Cairns (eds.), *The Collected Dialogues of Plato, including the Letters* (Princeton: Princeton University Press, 1961), p. 1175.

22. G. E. R. Lloyd, *Ancient Worlds, Modern Reflections*, p. 20.

23. Dong Zhongshu, *Chun qiu fan lu* [*Exuberant Dews of the Spring and Autumn*], chap. 30, p. 144.

Such a "holistic" view of the natural and the human world as a world of order, hierarchy, and correspondences has been famously discussed in such classic works as Arthur Lovejoy's *The Great Chain of Being* and E. M. W. Tillyard's *The Elizabethan World Picture*. "One is tempted to call the medieval habit of life mathematical," says Tillyard, "or to compare it with a gigantic game where everything is included and every act is conducted under the most complicated system of rules."[24] Perhaps the Western concept of the Great Chain of Being may be more systematically religious, but evidently in both Chinese and Western cultures the various correspondences between heaven and man, or macrocosm and microcosm, connect everything in the universe with everything else, thus offering the rich opportunity for cross-cultural comparative studies.

We have seen Dong Zhongshu describing the human body as corresponding numerically to the four seasons, the twelve months, the three hundred sixty-six days in a year, and so forth; in a way this is also how the Western concept of correspondences link man and the universe together in a perfect match, for "man's very anatomy corresponded with the physical ordering of the universe," says Tillyard in quoting many textual evidences to prove that in traditional Western understanding, there was this "physical correspondence between microcosm and macrocosm."[25] The Western idea of man as a microcosm or a little world modeled on macrocosm or the world of nature, the metaphor of the body politic, and the idea of man as somehow special and distinct from all other animals and creatures—all these have parallel expressions in Dong Zhongshu's works. It is often said that the Chinese concept of *qi* is untranslatable, because it is a kind of air or vapor that fills the universe and man and carries with it a vital energy, for which one does not easily find an equivalent expression in any of the Western languages. According to Dong, "the *qi* of *yin* and *yang* always exists between heaven and earth, in which man is submerged, just like the way fish is submerged in water. The only difference from water is that it is invisible while water is visible."[26] It is this *qi* that connects man with the movement of the entire universe, and indeed it is difficult to translate this term precisely into a European language. But let us look at how Tillyard describes the traditional European theory of the humors: "The four humours created in the liver are the life-giving moisture of the body. They generate a more active life-principle, vital heat, which corresponds to the fires in the centre of the earth, themselves agents in the slow formation of the metals. . . . The

24. E. M. W. Tillyard, *The Elizabethan World Picture* (New York: Vintage, 1959), pp. 6–7.

25. Ibid., p. 68.

26. Dong Zhongshu, *Chun qiu fan lu* [*Exuberant Dews of the Spring and Autumn*], chap. 81, p. 278.

natural spirits are a vapour formed in the liver and carried with the humours along the veins."[27] The similarities here with the Chinese idea of *qi* as an "active life-principle, vital heat," and "a vapour," are quite remarkable. The two are surely not identical, but they seem to have similar functions.

Likewise, the Western concept of the body politic, a conceptual metaphor that can be traced back to Plato and clearly articulated by John of Salisbury (c. 1120–1180) in the twelfth century, also has a similar expression in Chinese political thinking. According to John of Salisbury, the king is "the head in the republic," the senate its heart, "judges and governors of provinces" perform "duties of the ears, eyes and mouth," officials and soldiers are the hands, while those who assist the king are "comparable to the flanks."[28] Li Gang (1083–1140), a Chinese statesman of the Song dynasty slightly earlier than John of Salisbury, also described the state or "all under heaven" as "just one human body. The royal house inside is the heart, offices outside reaching in four directions are the four limbs, and laws, rules, and penal codes are the veins and arteries."[29] This of course reminds us of Dong Zhongshu's description of the human body as similarly constituted as that of heaven or the universe in an essentially social and political theory. Formulated so strikingly similarly in ancient Chinese political thinking and in Western political philosophy, the body politic and the correspondence between the human body and the natural world can really serve as powerful testimonies to the affinities of the human minds across linguistic and cultural differences.

It is true that man as God's favorite creation is clearly acknowledged in the Bible to be a special being above all other creatures in his environment, for he would "have dominion over the fish of the sea, and over the fowl of the air, and over every living thing that moveth upon the earth" (Gen. 1:28). This biblical elevation of man above all others, together with the idea that "God created man in his own image" (Gen. 1:27), proves to be vitally important for the rise of humanism during the Renaissance, but it may also have caused some "Asian values" advocates to blame the West for a human-centered ideology that pits man against nature, and for an aggressive "Western way of thinking" bent

27. Tillyard, *The Elizabethan World Picture*, p. 69.

28. John of Salisbury, *Policraticus: Of the Frivolities of Courtiers and the Footprints of Philosophers*, 5:2, in Cary J. Nederman and Kate Langdon Forhan (eds.), *Medieval Political Theory—A Reader: The Quest for the Body Politic, 1100–1400* (London: Routledge, 1993), p. 38. See also Plato, *Republic* V.464b, *The Collected Dialogues*, p. 703.

29. Li Gang, "On Curing the State," *Liangxi ji* [*Li Gang's Collected Writings*], *juan* 157, in *Siku quanshu* [*Complete Collection of the Four Treasuries*] (Shanghai: Shanghai guji, 1987 reprint), vol. 1126, pp. 683b–684a.

on conquering nature and destroying man's harmonious relationship with it. As we have seen earlier in this essay, those critics seem to argue that man in Chinese or Eastern culture is completely at peace with nature and not above any other creature, and that the "unity of heaven and man" puts man on an equal footing with everything else in the universe. When we check such a claim against Dong Zhongshu's works, however, we find it completely wrong and false. "Man is above and beyond all ten thousand things," Dong Zhongshu declares in no ambiguous terms, "and is thus the noblest of all under heaven."[30] "When we look at the human body," he wonders, "how much higher above everything else it is, and how much closer to heaven!" He goes on to argue that because other creatures take less of the essence of heaven and earth, when compared with human beings, they are all shaped in such a way as to bend down or prostrate when they move, while "man alone stands erect and is truly worthy."[31] To relate the upright human shape with man's worth and dignity may remind us of John Milton's great encomium of Adam and Eve, the first two human beings created in God's image in the Garden of Eden. In Book 4 of his great epic *Paradise Lost*, Milton thus describes the first couple:

> Two of far nobler shape erect and tall,
> Godlike erect, with native Honor clad
> In naked Majesty seem'd Lords of all,
> And worthie seem'd, for in thir looks Divine
> The image of thir glorious Maker shone.
> (*Paradise Lost*, iv.288–92)

The appreciation of man as the noblest and superior creature on earth is indeed shared by both the humanistic tradition in the West and the Confucian tradition in China. Dong Zhongshu definitely put man on top of all other creatures under heaven. In fact, Confucian teachings are clearly human-centered. As we read in the *Analects*, when Confucius came back home one day and found the stable in his house burned down in a fire, he immediately asked: " 'Is anybody hurt?' But he did not ask about the horses." For him, the supreme virtue of *ren* or benevolence meant nothing but to "love human beings."[32] To

30. Dong Zhongshu, *Chun qiu fan lu* [*Exuberant Dews of the Spring and Autumn*], chap. 81, p. 277.

31. Ibid., chap. 56, p. 204.

32. Liu Baonan, *Lunyu zhengyi* [*The Correct Meaning of the Analects*], x.17, xii.22, in *Zhuzi jicheng* [*Collection of Masters Writings*], 1:228, 278.

put human beings above other creatures, however, does not necessarily mean to destroy the balance between man and nature, and it is misleading to insist that either you have to conquer and destroy nature or you must give up all human interests and desires to preserve nature. Such an "either/or" opposition, as I have argued at the very beginning, is false and unhelpful, serving only to intensify the cultural differences and confrontations arbitrarily set up between the East and the West. What we need in our world today is an open-minded acceptance of different perspectives and views that bring to us the best of all cultures. In fact, in the world's great cultures and traditions, we can find ideas, insights, and visions that are fundamentally commensurate and mutually enriching, and it is the task for a scholar and an intellectual to recognize the values of humanity's common ideas, insights, and visions, and promote the mutual understanding, rather than the confrontation, of Asia and Europe, the East and the West. It is not so much Asian values as human values that we must learn to appreciate, and in this effort, cross-cultural understanding offers the hope of true knowledge, the hope of humanity's future.

5

The True Face of Mount Lu

On the Significance of Perspectives and Paradigms

Viewed horizontally a range; a cliff from the side,
It differs as we move high or low, or far or nearby.
We do not know the true face of Mount Lu,
Because we are all ourselves inside.

—Su Shi, "Written on the Wall of the Temple of West Woods"

We understand differently, *if we understand at all.*

—H.-G. Gadamer, *Truth and Method*

The short poem on Mount Lu by one of the greatest Chinese poets, Su Shi (1037–1101), which reads like a Chan Buddhist *gāthā,* is well-known for articulating philosophical insights into the interaction between recognition and perspective, and it has often been understood as a reflection on the limitation and blindness of an insider's point of view, or the difficulty of knowing something up close. "Because we are all ourselves inside," says the poet in the famous last two lines, the very interiority of the location makes it impossible for us to know "the true face of Mount Lu." The implication seems to be that one must get out of the mountain to command a full view of it, and therefore an outsider may see it more clearly than someone inside the mountain. Such a reading would privilege an outsider's view, which of course has particularly positive implications for Sinology or China studies in the West that tries to understand China not from within, but from the outside. By virtue of being an outsider, a Sinologist or China specialist may occupy a better position than a native Chinese to understand China at some critical or reflective distance. That is indeed the view held by many China specialists in the West, justifiable to some extent, and apparently supported by a great Chinese poet's philosophical insight into the nature of horizons and perspectives, the limitation and blindness of someone inside the object of study.

Horizon or perspective happens to be an important concept in philosophical hermeneutics. Friedrich Nietzsche and Edmund Husserl made use of the concept, which was further developed by Hans-Georg Gadamer into a crucial term for understanding the very nature of understanding. "The horizon is the range of vision that includes everything that can be seen from a particular vantage point," says Gadamer. "Applying this to the thinking mind, we speak of narrowness of horizon, of the possible expansion of horizon, of the opening up of new horizons, and so forth. Since Nietzsche and Husserl, the word has been used in philosophy to characterize the way in which thought is tied to its finite determinacy, and the way one's range of vision is gradually expanded."[1] We all have our particular horizons or vantage points from which we see and understand things, and what we see must be within the range of our vision, tied to our "finite determinacy." Thus horizon constitutes the precondition of understanding or what Heidegger called the fore-structure of understanding. Before we understand anything, we already have some idea about that which we are to understand, that is, our anticipations or prejudgments, and the process of understanding appears to move in a "hermeneutic circle."

It is therefore inevitable that a Western China scholar would understand China from the horizon and perspective of a Westerner. The point of the hermeneutic circle, however, is not to confirm the necessity of circular movement, and certainly not to legitimize the circularity of understanding or the subjectivity of one's own horizon. Although he lays much emphasis on the fore-structure of understanding, "the point of Heidegger's hermeneutical reflection is not so much to prove that there is a circle as to show that this circle possesses an ontologically positive significance," says Gadamer. "All correct interpretation must be on guard against arbitrary fancies and the limitations imposed by imperceptible habits of thought, and it must direct its gaze 'on the things themselves.'"[2] When we examine Sinology or China studies in the light of such a philosophical insight, then, we realize that to privilege an outsider's view is not really justifiable because it tends to overemphasize the significance of one's own horizon and perspective at the expense of what the other, and internal, perspective might have to offer.

1. Gadamer, *Truth and Method,* p. 302.

2. Ibid., pp. 266–67.

That is precisely the major point Paul Cohen made almost thirty years ago in *Discovering History in China*, in which he consciously proposed a new paradigm in China studies, different from older ones in which Western scholars looked at China only from the outside, with an outsider's horizon. In his review of the development of American Sinology, Cohen found that most American China scholars in the 1950s were unable to break away from the theoretical framework of "Western impact and Chinese response" in their interpretation of recent Chinese history from the Opium Wars and the Boxer Uprising to the founding of the Chinese Republic. They all maintained that China would have remained stagnant and immobile if there were no impact from the West. The impact-and-response framework constituted the basic horizon for their understanding of Chinese history from the nineteenth to the early twentieth century.

Closely related to this was the theoretical framework of "modernization," which regarded modern Chinese history as a history of modernization and "equated *modern* with *Western* and *Western* with *important*."[3] As a result, the West and Western ideas became essential elements in the study of modern Chinese history, whereas Chinese elements unrelated to modernization were considered less important in such a framework. During the late 1960s, however, as the Civil Rights movement and the popular protest against the war in Vietnam raged all over America, a strong tendency of self-critique arose in the intellectual climate in the United States and in the West at large. In China studies a new framework emerged, which Cohen calls the framework of "imperialism." It is in fact a framework of anti-imperialism, a radically self-critical theoretical perspective that maintained that the study of modern Chinese history should be focused on the issue of how Western imperialism had stifled and impeded China's social development. Sharply critical of the West, this framework nevertheless understood modern Chinese history as basically a history of Western impact, even though it condemned the consequences of such an impact rather than viewing it in a positive light.

According to Cohen, these three paradigms—the frameworks of "impact and response," "modernization," and "imperialism"—all look at China from an outsider's perspective with little or no attention paid to the internal development of Chinese history, and "all three, in one way or another, introduce Western-centric distortions into our understanding of nineteenth- and twentieth-century China."[4] Against such West-centric distortions, Cohen advocates a "China-

3. Paul A. Cohen, *Discovering History in China: American Historical Writing on the Recent Chinese Past* (New York: Columbia University Press, 1984), p. 2.

4. Ibid., p. 3.

centered" approach to the study of Chinese history, an approach that lays emphasis on Chinese language materials and Chinese points of view. Cohen characterizes this approach in the following manner:

> The main identifying feature of the new approach is that it begins with Chinese problems set in a Chinese context. These problems may be influenced, even generated, by the West. Or they may have no Western connection at all. But either way they are *Chinese* problems, in the double sense that they are experienced in China by Chinese and that the measure of their historical importance is a Chinese, rather than a Western, measure.[5]

Of course, it is impossible to demand that Western China scholars all turn themselves into native Chinese. "The great challenge for Western historians is not the impossible one of eliminating all ethnocentric distortion," Cohen admits; "it is the possible one of reducing such distortion to a minimum and in the process freeing ourselves to see Chinese history in new, less Western-centered ways."[6] The main point of Cohen's "China-centered history" is the recognition that modern Chinese history evolves along a path of its own, with its own structure, rather than being a passive receptacle of decisive outside influences from the West. To emphasize the history "experienced in China by Chinese" is obviously meant to emulate an insider's perspective, the horizon of those participants in the historical events. The use of the term "China-centered," says Cohen, "is intended to delineate an approach to recent Chinese history that strives to understand what is happening in that history in terms that are as free as possible of imported criteria of significance."[7] By putting emphasis on using Chinese language materials and identifying internal factors in Chinese history that played decisive roles in its development, Cohen tries to transcend the limitations of an outsider who lacks the sense of tangible reality and only has a blurred view of what is going on in China, to emulate an insider's perspective, horizon, and experience, and to set up a "China-centered" paradigm beyond the biased view skewed toward the West.

In a more recent book, Cohen clearly states that his "abiding concern" throughout his career as a historian has been his "determination to get inside China, to reconstruct Chinese history as far as possible as the Chinese them-

5. Ibid., p. 154.

6. Ibid., p. 1.

7. Ibid., p. 196.

selves experienced it rather than in terms of what people in the West thought was important, natural, or normal . . . in short, to move beyond approaches to the Chinese past that bore a heavy burden of Eurocentric or Western-centric preconceptions."[8] The key feature of his "China-centered" paradigm, Cohen later reiterates, is "to reconstruct the Chinese past as the Chinese themselves experienced it rather than in terms of an imported sense of historical problem."[9] For an American scholar, such a conscious effort to overcome the limitations of an outsider's perspective, to break away from the bias of West-centrism, and to understand Chinese history from the inside, following the route of its internal development, readily exemplifies the effort to reach a "correct interpretation" as Gadamer describes, namely, always to "be on guard against arbitrary fancies and the limitations imposed by imperceptible habits of thought," with one's gaze always directed "on the things themselves." Such an approach is certainly a respectable and responsible one in the study of history.

And yet, there is no guarantee of a full grasp of historical reality when the historian gets inside and tries to "reconstruct the Chinese past as the Chinese themselves experienced it." In terms of the theory of history, Cohen's paradigm seems to resemble what Giambattista Vico had advocated, or what Wilhelm Dilthey in particular had argued for in the nineteenth century in his *Lebensphilosophie*. Dilthey once claimed that "the first condition of possibility of a science of history is that I myself am a historical being, that the person studying history is the person making history."[10] This certainly reminds us of Vico, who, in reaction against Cartesian skepticism with only the certainty of mathematical knowledge of nature to stand against it, asserted the convertibility of the true and the made (*verum ipsum factum*), and thus the authenticity of historical knowledge. Nature was created by God and therefore only God could know it, but "the world of nations, or civil world," says Vico, "since men had made it, men could come to know."[11] In the eighteenth and the nineteenth centuries, Vico's argument elevated history as the most reliable human knowledge above the study of nature.

Gadamer is not quite satisfied with that argument, however, because Vico's thesis has not solved the problem of historical understanding. Gadamer

8. Paul A. Cohen, *China Unbound: Evolving Perspectives on the Chinese Past* (London: Routledge-Curzon, 2003), p. 1.

9. Ibid., p. 186.

10. Wilhelm Dilthey, *Gesammelte Schriften*, VII, p. 278, quoted in Gadamer, *Truth and Method*, p. 222.

11. Giambattista Vico, *The New Science of Giambattista Vico*, trans. Thomas Goddard Bergin and Max Harold Fisch (Ithaca, NY: Cornell University Press, 1968), section 331, p. 96.

argues that "positing homogeneity as its condition conceals the real epistemological problem of history. The question is how the individual's experience and the knowledge of it come to be historical experience." As each individual human being is limited in his or her horizon, experience, and knowledge, "the important question remains how such infinite understanding is possible for finite human nature."[12] Vico and Dilthey never really gave a satisfactory answer to such questions. In reconstructing past history, historians must of course try to experience the social condition or event empathetically as best as they can by imagining what people in the past might have experienced, but "empathy" does not replace the historian's horizon, nor does it endow historical knowledge as such with "objectivity." But isn't that the point made clear in Su Shi's poem? "We do not know the true face of Mount Lu, / Because we are all ourselves inside." Thus, by emulating an insider's perspective through the act of empathetic understanding, the historian has acquired only a particular insider's point of view still limited by its own finite determinacy.

While advocating an empathetic reconstruction of Chinese history from the perspective of an insider and participant in the historical process, Cohen also tries to cope with the incomprehensibility of the totality of history by disaggregating China "horizontally" into different regions, provinces, prefectures, counties, and cities, and "vertically" into different levels and social strata, thereby promoting the study of regional and local history on the one hand, and popular and non-popular lower-level history on the other. The huge and multifaceted China is thus cut up and divided into smaller, manageable pieces. In so doing, as Cohen acknowledges himself, he proposed an approach that "is not *China*-centered at all, but region-centered, or province-centered or locality-centered."[13] In his survey of China studies in America since the 1970s, he mentioned with approval quite a few works accomplished by applying anthropology, systems theory, and other social-science theories and methodologies to the study of Chinese history. Cohen's "China-centered" paradigm thus acquires yet another distinct feature, namely that "it welcomes with enthusiasm the theories, methodologies, and techniques developed in disciplines other than history (mostly, but not exclusively, the social sciences) and strives to integrate these into historical analysis."[14] As these social-science theories, methodologies, and techniques are all fruits of Western scholarship, however, their applications to the study of Chinese history often clash, almost necessarily, with the "China-

12. Gadamer, *Truth and Method*, pp. 222, 232.

13. Cohen, *Discovering History in China*, p. 162.

14. Ibid., pp. 186–87.

centered" paradigm. They may even surreptitiously sabotage that paradigm when such Western theoretical models generate a sense of superiority and the arrogance of "theoretical sophistication" on the part of those who apply them to Chinese materials. Indeed, the actual condition of China studies in America since the 1970s does not have much to show for the success of the "China-centered" paradigm, and when we look at scholarship in the West as a whole, the influence of such a paradigm is even less noticeable.

The French scholar François Jullien in his many publications, as I have mentioned earlier, always starts from the position of a Western scholar and sees China as the exemplary "Other." He clearly announces that the purpose of studying China is to "return to the self," that "China presents a case study through which to contemplate Western thought from the outside."[15] Indeed, one of his more recent books is significantly titled *Penser d'un dehors (la Chine)* or *Thinking from the Outside (China)*, which treats China as the foil to the West. Following Foucault, Jullien declares that "strictly speaking, *non-Europe* is China, and it cannot be anything else."[16] Though it is perfectly fine for a Western scholar to insist on using China as a mirror to reflect on the Western self, the problem with Jullien's contrastive approach is its very predictable contrastiveness: since it has set the goal of finding contrasts between Chinese and Western concepts, ideas, and values, whatever Jullien finds in his argument is always already predetermined at the outset. This argument thus becomes rather repetitive and predictably contrastive, and eventually turns out to be little more than a reaffirmation of his own anticipations and prejudgments rather than an observation and recognition of what "things themselves" may look like without the distortion of a contrastive perspective.

In his examination of the cultural conflict manifested in the so-called "Chinese rites controversy" during the seventeenth and the eighteenth centuries, Jacques Gernet, another French scholar, also reduced all the differences between Christianity and Chinese culture to the most fundamental level of language and thinking, arguing that these are "not only of different intellectual traditions but also of different mental categories and modes of thought."[17] Gernet maintains that the Chinese are not capable of abstract thinking, that the Chinese language has no grammar, and, pushing the idea to the area of philosophy, he remarks that as a result, "the notion of being, in the sense of

15. François Jullien, *Detour and Access: Strategies of Meaning in China and Greece*, trans. Sophie Hawkes (New York: Zone Books, 2000), p. 9.

16. Jullien with Thierry Marchaisse, *Penser d'un dehors (la Chine)*, p. 39.

17. Gernet, *China and the Christian Impact*, p. 3.

an eternal and constant reality, above and beyond that which is phenomenal, was perhaps more difficult to conceive, for a Chinese."[18] In the area of Chinese literary studies, Stephen Owen holds somewhat similar views. He maintains that the Chinese language, unlike the alphabetic Western languages with their artificial and arbitrary sign systems, "is itself natural," and that Chinese poetry, unlike Western literature as imaginative fiction in the imitation of nature, is a kind of natural manifestation.[19] Whereas the Western poet creates, in imitation of God the first Maker, a fictional world *ex nihilo*, the Chinese poet only "participates in the nature that is." Whereas Western poetry is a literary creation, a Chinese poem presents an "uncreated world," and the Chinese poet, following the example of Confucius, only "transmits but does not create."[20] Consequently, Chinese poetry is said to be "nonfictional" and its statement "strictly true," to be literally understood, without the possibility of metaphor, allegory, and imaginative fictionality.[21]

These are only a few examples from Sinological studies that set up an either/or opposition between the East and the West, and all such oppositional arguments share the same problem of predetermination, namely, that they all set up a Western self against which the various aspects of Chinese culture are brought up as its contrast or as a reverse mirror image. These are self-consciously outsiders' points of view, and in their discussions of Chinese language, literature, thought, and culture, these scholars almost totally ignore the insiders, that is, Chinese scholars and their works written in Chinese. This certainly runs counter to the spirit of the "China-centered" paradigm, which tries "to get inside China, to reconstruct Chinese history as far as possible as the Chinese themselves experienced it." For a long time in the twentieth century, there might have been a legitimate reason or a reasonable excuse to ignore native Chinese scholarship because much of that scholarship was under the heavy influence, even the tight ideological control, of official Marxism or Maoism, and hardly any native Chinese scholar was free from the dogmatic ideas of a Marxist or Maoist orthodoxy, particularly in history and the other fields in the humanities and social sciences. But if that was largely, though by no means completely, true of the condition of Chinese scholarship in much of the twentieth century, it is no longer true in China today. The condition of

18. Ibid., p. 241.

19. Stephen Owen, *Traditional Chinese Poetry and Poetics: Omen of the World* (Madison: University of Wisconsin Press, 1985), p. 20.

20. Ibid., 84; quoting Confucius, *The Analects*, vii.1.

21. Ibid., p. 34.

scholarly work in China, along with other aspects of Chinese social life, has changed dramatically in the last twenty to thirty years, and Chinese intellectuals themselves have mostly abandoned the ideological orthodoxy of the past. In fact, things have changed so much that it becomes no longer wise or practical for Western China scholars to ignore native Chinese scholarship.

For example, the very concept of "China" and its meaning in history have become debatable issues in recent scholarship, for which it is quite necessary to hear what Chinese scholars themselves have to say. Western discussions of nation-states are naturally predicated on European history and thus have come to the consensus that the formation of nation-states is a concomitant process as the medieval world came to an end and evolved into early modernity. Immanuel Wallerstein, for example, discusses the nation-state from the perspective of world-systems analysis and declares: "The modern state is a sovereign state. Sovereignty is a concept that was invented in the modern world-system."[22] Wallerstein's analysis of the nation-state is based completely on European history since the Renaissance and the sixteenth century, but Chinese history, that is, the history of China as a cultural and political entity with a clear distinction between *hua* and *yi* or *civilized* and *barbarian*, goes back to a much earlier period than the Renaissance in Europe. With earliest mention already found in oracle bones and bronze vessels, the word *Zhongguo* or "China" appears in nearly thirty pre-Qin texts. As a concept, the word in ancient classics may have different meanings. "Geographically, it identifies China as the geographical center of the ancient world, while whatever lies outside China in the four directions were considered border areas," says Huang Chun-chieh in discussing the concept of *Zhongguo* in ancient times. "Politically, China was the area of kingly rule . . . while outside was where the ferocious barbarians dwelled. Culturally, China was the center of the civilized world, and outside it were uncivilized areas, called pejoratively *man, yi, rong*, and *di*."[23] At least as early as the Song Dynasty (960–1279) and partly because of the invasion by neighboring nomadic people to the north, the concept of China as a nation-state with well-defined borders and a clear sense of sovereignty was thrust upon the Chinese, mainly the ethnic Han nationals. The sense of being a nation or state among others, the consciousness of being "Chinese" as different from others,

22. Immanuel Wallerstein, *World-Systems Analysis: An Introduction* (Durham, NC: Duke University Press, 2004), p. 42.

23. Huang Chun-chieh, "The Idea of *Zhongguo* and Its Transformation in Early Modern Japan and Contemporary Taiwan," *Taiwan Dong Ya wenmin yanjiu xuekan* [*Taiwan Journal of East Asian Studies*] 3: 2 (Dec. 2006): 93.

as Ge Zhaoguang argues, not only helped legitimize "China" and its "civilization (mainly that of the Han nationality)" in ancient times, but also "became a distant source of the ideology of Chinese nationalism in more recent history."[24] It is of course a gross anachronism to believe that China has always been like what it is today, because both borderlines and the various ethnic components of what we call China have undergone many changes throughout the centuries in history. China today is surely different from China in the past, but it is also a gross mistake to tailor the history and reality of China in order to fit the yardstick of postmodern and postcolonial theories and to think of China as a mere ideological construct, a purely "imagined community."

The way Prasenjit Duara discusses modern Chinese history in *Rescuing History from the Nation* may offer an example of the kind of paradigmatic difficulties one encounters in applying concepts and theoretical approaches formulated in the context of European historical studies to the study of Chinese history. It is certainly admirable for Duara to "rescue history" from the fictitious constructs of the nation-state and to put into question and interrogate the subject of "Enlightenment history" and the teleological model of a "linear history." Against that model, Duara proposed what he calls a "bifurcated" conception of history, though that conception has been questioned by some Chinese scholars.[25] On the one hand, Duara criticizes the grand narratives of national unity constructed from the perspective of nationalism, arguing that "national history secures for the contested and contingent nation the false unity of a self-same, national subject evolving through time."[26] On the other hand, however, he has no alternative but to acknowledge that "it is—as yet—impossible to radically displace the nation as the locus of history."[27] The nation is not, after all, a completely fictitious construct. As a scholar originally from India, Duara is almost intuitively suspicious of the discourse of the nation-state modeled on European examples, and thus he cannot come to a complete agreement with the idea that the nation-state is a modern product. In discussing some

24. Ge Zhaoguang, "The Rise of the Consciousness of China in the Song Dynasty—A Distant Source of the Ideology of Nationalism in More Recent History," in *Gudai Zhongguo de lishi, sixiang yu zongjiao* [*History, Ideas, and Religion in Ancient China*] (Beijing: Beijing Normal University Press, 2006), p. 151.

25. See Li Meng, "Whose History to Rescue?" *Ershi yi shiji* [*Twenty-First Century*], no. 49 (October 1998): 128–33.

26. Prasenjit Duara, *Rescuing History from the Nation: Questioning Narratives of Modern China* (Chicago: University of Chicago Press, 1995), p. 4.

27. Ibid., p. 6.

Western scholars' concept of the nation-state in terms of a particular identity, he remarks, quite insightfully:

> In privileging modern society as the only social form capable of generating political self-awareness, [Ernest] Gellner and [Benedict] Anderson regard national identity as a distinctly modern mode of consciousness: the nation as a whole imagining itself to be the cohesive subject of history. The empirical record does not furnish the basis for such a strong statement about the polarity between the modern and the premodern. Individuals and groups in both modern and agrarian societies identify simultaneously with several communities, all of which are imagined; these identifications are historically changeable and often conflicted internally with each other. Whether in India or China, people historically identified with different representations of communities, and when these identifications became politicized, they came to resemble what is called modern "national identities."[28]

This shows that quite appropriately Duara has a sense of alertness, a kind of postcolonial sensibility, toward theoretical models based on European history. He realizes that the Chinese in the past already had a strong sense of identity and that "the representation of the ethnic nation is most evident in the Song."[29] And yet, his discussion of India and China is very far from the kind of "China-centered" approach Cohen espoused. In fact, he has raised a number of questions about Cohen's approach. "Do Chinese historical materials," asks Duara, "prefigure a certain narrative of their own which Western and Chinese historians have to listen closely to and then reproduce as best they can? Or are the historical materials simply 'noise,' heterophony, the meaning of which is disclosed by the narratives through which the historian 'symbolizes' them?"[30] In discussing recent Chinese history, Duara borrows heavily from contemporary Western theories, concepts, and terms in the humanities and social sciences, and his writing has all the typical discursive features of a Western scholarly argument. At the same time, Cohen has his own reservations about the kind of "postmodern scholarship" in the works of Duara and James

28. Ibid., p. 54.

29. Ibid., p. 59.

30. Ibid., p. 26.

Hevia, finding in them "a deplorable tendency, through the unchecked use of abstract conceptual formulations and neologisms, to build intellectual walls around themselves and what they are up to."[31] As Cohen sees it, these works, burdened by neologisms and novel ideas borrowed from Western theories, are still a far cry from the "China-centered" historiography he has advocated, and they are, to a large extent, West-centered works very different from what a Chinese participant in Chinese history would have experienced.

By now it should be clear that I do not see any particular epistemological advantage in either Cohen's "China-centered" approach or a Western Sinological perspective; or to put it differently, neither insiders nor outsiders have privileged access to knowledge in understanding China, its history, society, culture, and tradition. At best, insiders and outsiders are all limited in their respective horizons and finite determinacy, and at worst, the insider's blind spots are matched only by the outsider's ignorance and lack of sensitivity. In an insightful 1972 essay, the famous sociologist Robert Merton had already exposed the limitations of both insiders and outsiders who claim to have a *monopolistic* or *privileged* access to certain kinds of knowledge. "In structural terms," says Merton, "we are all, of course, both Insiders and Outsiders, members of some groups and, sometimes derivatively, not of others; occupants of certain statuses which thereby exclude us from occupying other cognate statuses." This is obvious in any individual or social group, but more important is "the crucial fact of social structure that individuals have not a single status but a status set: a complement of variously interrelated statuses which interact to affect both their behavior and perspectives."[32] More recently, Amartya Sen puts emphasis on the same crucial fact when he argues that it is the illusion of singular and exclusive identities that breeds conflict and war in our world. "Violence is fomented," says Sen, "by the imposition of singular and belligerent identities on gullible people, championed by proficient artisans of terror."[33] In making sense of identities, he goes on to argue, we must realize that we always have plural affiliations and multiple identities: "We are all individually involved in identities of various kinds in disparate contexts, in our own respective lives, arising from our background, or associations, or social activities."[34] As I have

31. Cohen, *China Unbound*, p. 193.

32. Robert K. Merton, "The Perspectives of Insiders and Outsiders," in *The Sociology of Science: Theoretical and Empirical Investigations*, ed. Norman W. Storer (Chicago: University of Chicago Press, 1973), p. 113.

33. Amartya Sen, *Identity and Violence: The Illusion of Destiny* (New York: W. W. Norton, 2006), p. 2.

34. Ibid., p. 23.

argued earlier, particularly in the second chapter, there are different levels of identities or differences, from individual to collective, from cultural to cross-cultural, and we need to pay attention to all the levels and must not fixate on one particular identity at the expense of our other identities.

With such insights into our plural and interrelated "statuses" or multiple "identities," we can now come to the conclusion that it is foolish to believe that only Chinese can understand China or, equally absurdly, that only a Sinologist can give us true and objective knowledge about China. The point is that no particular horizon or perspective can guarantee better knowledge, but that knowledge or scholarship as such should be assessed with a set of intellectual criteria that transcends the simple opposition between native scholarship and Sinological lore, or an insider's historical experience and an outsider's critical reflection. Understanding China and Chinese history requires integration of different views from different perspectives, but such integration is not a simple juxtaposition of insiders' and outsiders' views; it is more of an act of interaction and mutual illumination than adding up native Chinese scholarship and Western Sinology. "We no longer ask whether it is the Insider or the Outsider who has monopolistic or privileged access to social knowledge," to quote Merton's apposite words again, "instead, we begin to consider their distinctive and interactive roles in the process of seeking truth."[35] In the pursuit of knowledge, being an insider or an outsider is often functionally irrelevant, and we must negotiate among our plural affiliations and multiple identities as well as those of others in order to reach a better understanding.

Let us now return to the poem by Su Shi quoted at the beginning of this essay and to the whole issue of horizons and perspectives, insiders and outsiders. The last two lines of this poem are the most famous, and they definitely speak of the limitation and blindness of an insider's perspective. In a sense the entire poem falls victim to the success of its last two lines, because a careful reading will reveal that Su Shi's poem actually does not privilege any particular point of view; that the "true face of Mount Lu" is presented not as one single face, but many faces, changing as the viewer moves to different locations and takes different positions, "high or low, or far or nearby." Mount Lu can be seen as a range, but it may also appear as a cliff, and neither is the only "true face." What we get from this little poem is the limitation of human knowledge because of our finite horizons and perspectives. Such limitations, the fact that understanding is always tied to one's "finite determinacy," are part of the human condition of our existence; therefore neither insiders nor

35. Merton, *The Sociology of Science*, p. 129.

outsiders have privileged access to true knowledge. To read Su Shi's poem as privileging the outsider's view is only to misread it. Either inside or outside, we do not know the true face of Mount Lu; or, either from the inside or the outside, far away or up close, we always see the mountain from a particular angle, with a particular point of view.

The mountain metaphor for understanding history is quite appropriate, and this metaphor is not only used by Su Shi in his poem on Mount Lu, but by the English historian E. H. Carr, who argues that, though we should discard the positivistic notion of "objectivity," the finite determinacy of our own horizon cannot erase the existence of "the things themselves." Carr remarks, as though in conversation with Su Shi:

> It does not follow that, because a mountain appears to take on different shapes from different angles of vision, it has objectively either no shape at all or an infinity of shapes. It does not follow that, because interpretation plays a necessary part in establishing the facts of history, and because no existing interpretation is wholly objective, one interpretation is as good as another, and the facts of history are in principle not amenable to objective interpretation.[36]

The mountain metaphor works to the extent that historical events always happen at particular locations and geographical territories, in concrete circumstances and with materiality of their own. Nation, sovereignty, people and their cultures all have spatial connotations. History as such, however, means more than just the concrete, material, and territorial, and therefore its richness and complexity cannot be captured entirely by the mountain metaphor. Historiography not only as record but also as interpretation involves more than what the concrete mountain metaphor may suggest, as it must have the historian's engagement and participation, thus the limitations of horizons and perspectives. In that sense, Su Shi's poem on Mount Lu is more instructive than a simple description of a mountain, for it speaks more of the difficulty of understanding than the presence of "things themselves," though the existence of the mountain is tacitly acknowledged. This difficulty, the limitation of our horizons and our finite determinacy, the difficulty of knowing something far away or up close, constitutes the challenge of China studies as it does all other humanistic disciplines. But it also encourages us to open up to different perspectives and other views, to look from various angles, to judge all with a set

36. E. H. Carr, *What is History?* (Harmondsworth: Penguin Books, 1964), pp. 26–27.

of intellectual criteria that transcends group allegiances and local identities, and to reach what might be a closer approximation of Mount Lu, or whatever it is that we set out to study.

6

History and Fictionality

Insights and Limitations of a Literary Perspective

The fact that the written record of history or historiography is a narrative account of past events has received much scholarly attention in humanistic studies, particularly as a result of the expansion of the domain of literary theory to other disciplines and fields. To understand the phenomenon in a broad perspective of twentieth-century development in the humanities, this may be seen as an inevitable step for scholars to move away from nineteenth-century biases of scientism and positivism, and from a rigid concept of objective truth as discovery of the impersonal laws of nature and society unadulterated by human subjectivity and imagination. History as what happened in the past and as a story about what happened—and here one thinks of the French word *histoire* that designates both history and story—seems to contain the tension or a double-bind from the very beginning between truth and imagination, objective account and subjective projection, reality and fiction. Indeed, in the early stages of the Western tradition, we already find two different models of historical writing in the works of Herodotus and Thucydides. The latter was obviously distancing himself from his predecessor when he set up a clear contrast between his austere but realistic history of past events and Herodotus's interesting and lively account which does not, as David Grene observes, make an effective distinction "between the reality of verifiable truth and imaginative reality."[1] And that, in Thucydides' eyes, is more of a rhetorical exercise than a reliable historical record. "My narrative," says Thucydides, "will seem less pleasing to some listeners because it lacks an element of fiction." But pleasing fiction is not what he set out to write, as he goes on to say: "My work was composed not as a prizewinning exercise in elocution, to be heard and then

1. Herodotus, *The History*, trans. David Grene (Chicago: University of Chicago Press, 1987), p. 6.

forgotten, but as a work of permanent value."[2] Thucydides seems to contrast his own history as written records with his predecessor's as oral history, a contrast of writing that preserves the past in permanent signs with speech that is as fleeting as sounds, heard for a moment, but gone and forgotten immediately after.

What is of permanent value in Greek thinking, however, may not favor the kind of history Thucydides claimed to write. In effect, it is not the record of historical actuality that matters, but what goes beyond the actual and the transitory to reveal something of a permanent and universal nature. Such a Greek emphasis on the eternal objects of knowledge constitutes what R. G. Collingwood called "a rigorously anti-historical metaphysics."[3] It was philosophy against history, and in ancient Greece, philosophy won. The idea also comes out clearly in Aristotle's famous remark about the distinction between history and poetry that "the former relates things that have happened, the latter things that may happen. For this reason poetry is a more philosophical and more serious thing than history; poetry tends to speak of universals, history of particulars."[4] Aristotle's philosophical defense of poetry offers an answer to Plato's attack on poetry as imitation not of reality but of the appearance of reality and therefore as "concerned with the third remove from truth."[5] In the long apologetic tradition of literary criticism, Aristotle's remark has often been cited as a powerful plea for the superior value of poetry over history, but the *Poetics* was not widely known in Europe in antiquity or medieval times, and it did not become the great classic in Western criticism until the latter half of the sixteenth century. "The three books of *On Poets*, and the six or more books of *Homeric Problems* (presumably not in dialogue form)," as Stephen Halliwell observes, "were in fact the two chief works in which Aristotle's ideas on poetry were disseminated in the ancient critical tradition; while the *Poetics*, originally produced for use within the philosophical school, never became at all readily available or widely known."[6]

In any case, the distinction Aristotle made between poetry and history cannot be rigidly understood, because history also aims to recuperate what is

2. Thucydides, *The Peloponnesian War*, trans. Walter Blanco (New York: W. W. Norton, 1998), p. 11.

3. R. G. Collingwood, *The Idea of History*, ed. Jan van der Dussen (Oxford: Clarendon Press, 1993), p. 20.

4. Aristotle, *Poetics*, 51b, trans. Richard Janko (Indianapolis. IN: Hackett Publishing Co., 1987), p. 12.

5. Plato, *Republic*, x.602c, trans. Paul Shorey, in *The Collected Dialogues*, p. 827.

6. Stephen Halliwell, "Aristotle's Poetics," in George A. Kennedy (ed.), *The Cambridge History of Literary Criticism*, vol. 1, *Classical Criticism* (Cambridge: Cambridge University Press, 1989), p. 149.

generally applicable as a lesson or an insight from specific past events, to rescue historical knowledge as *epistēmē* from whatever transitory *doxa* or opinions that came to pass at the time. If Thucydides meant to compose a work of permanent value, Herodotus's aim in writing his *History* was no less an attempt at permanency by saving what is valuable from the passing moments so that "time may not draw the color from what man has brought into being, nor those great and wonderful deeds, manifested by both Greek and barbarians, fail of their report."[7]

This idea of writing against time is remarkably similar to what Sima Qian, the great Chinese historian, considered as the purpose of historical writing. For a historian, Sima Qian says, "no offense is greater than failing the sagely monarchs by neglecting to put their virtues and accomplishments in record, erasing the names of great heroes, illustrious families, and good officials by passing over their achievements in the narration, and letting the words of our ancestors fall into oblivion."[8] Thus writing in this sense becomes the best means to resist death and oblivion in view of the mortality of human life; history, like poetry, as W. B. Yeats put it so elegantly in "Sailing to Byzantium," gathers all men and their past into "the artifice of eternity," telling endless stories "Of what is past, or passing, or to come."

In the actual writing of history, both Herodotus and Thucydides used narrative techniques to represent what had fallen into the irretrievable abyss of the bygone past by preserving what happened and what was said in written records, which could always offer a contemporaneous experience in reading. Here I am referring to the concept of contemporaneity (*Gleichzeitigkeit*) as Gadamer discussed in *Truth and Method* with reference to Kierkegaard's religious understanding of the idea. As a religious concept, contemporaneity designates the task of a believer "to bring together two moments that are not concurrent, namely one's own present and the redeeming act of Christ, and yet so totally to mediate them that the latter is experienced and taken seriously as present (and not as something in a distant past)."[9] Gadamer develops this into an important hermeneutic concept of historical understanding, that is, understanding of a past event as "being present." For Gadamer, contemporaneity specifically "belongs to the being of the work of art," as he explains that the concept "means that in its presentation this particular thing that presents itself to us achieves full presence, however remote its origin may be."[10] In that

7. Herodotus, *The History*, p. 33.

8. Sima Qian, *Shi ji* [*Record of History*] (Beijing: Zhonghua, 1959), p. 3266.

9. Gadamer, *Truth and Method*, pp. 127–28.

10. Ibid., p. 127.

sense, the reading of history can be just as contemporaneous an experience as the experience of contemplating a work of art, because a good historical narrative may indeed present past events as though they were present, and in the "contemporaneous" experience of that presentation, we do appreciate the aesthetic appeal of historical writing. In the West and in China, whether it is Herodotus or Thucydides, Sima Qian or Sima Guang, Gibbon or Trevelyan, great histories always appeal to us for their literary quality as well as their value as enduring records of the past, and their literary value has always been appreciated by generations of readers. History as literature is thus by no means a new discovery in contemporary theory, though the distinction between history and literature has always been maintained and never put in question in such a fundamental way till the recent development of postmodern theories.

Prior to the French Revolution, as Hayden White observes, "historiography was conventionally regarded as a literary art. More specifically, it was regarded as a branch of rhetoric and its 'fictive' nature generally recognized." In the nineteenth century, however, historians came "to identify truth with fact and to regard fiction as the opposite of truth, hence as a hindrance to the understanding of reality rather than as a way of apprehending it." Historians in the nineteenth century seemed to have accepted the Aristotelian distinction between history and poetry in a reverse order: "History came to be set over against fiction, and especially the novel, as the representation of the 'actual' to the representation of the 'possible' or only 'imaginable.'"[11] But of course the historian uses the same kind of narrative techniques in writing history as the novelist does in fiction, and this simple fact undermines the clear-cut distinction between history and fiction. It is true, however, as Hayden White emphasized, that radical tendencies in contemporary critical theory have made it possible to reject the post-Romantic belief "that fiction is the antithesis of fact (in the way that superstition or magic is the antithesis of science) or that we can relate facts to one another without the aid of some enabling and generically fictional matrix."[12] But as early as 1742, the German scholar Johann Martin Chladenius already argued that our perceptions and conceptions of things are all determined by a particular "viewpoint," and that when histories are "related to us by someone who perceives them from another viewpoint, we do not believe that they actually took place and they appear therefore to be a fiction to us."[13] That

11. Hayden White, *Tropics of Discourse: Essays in Cultural Criticism* (Baltimore, MD: Johns Hopkins University Press 1978), p. 123.

12. Ibid., p. 126.

13. Johann Martin Chladenius, "On the Interpretation of Historical Books and Accounts," in Kurt Mueller-Vollmer (ed.), *The Hermeneutics Reader: Texts of the German Tradition from the Enlightenment to the Present* (New York: Continuum, 1990), p. 68.

is to say, if a historical narrative appears to be fantastically incredible, it may well be that the historical event has been conceived differently and interpreted from a different point of view. The actuality of the event itself, however, is not in doubt. Chladenius maintains that "the event is one and the same, but the concept of it different and manifold. There is nothing contradictory in an event; the contradictions arise from the different conceptions of the same thing."[14]

In an address to the Berlin Academy of Sciences in 1821, Wilhelm von Humboldt went much further. He argued that a historical event or "what has taken place" is "only partially visible in the world of the senses," so the historian must make up for the invisible part, for "the remainder must be added through feeling, deduction, and conjecture."[15] The bare facts of what has happened, says Humboldt, offer only "the skeleton of the event," nothing more than "the necessary foundation for history, its material, but not history itself." It is the task of the historian to find out "the essential inner truth founded in the causal relationships," and in so doing, the historian, like the poet, "must take the scattered pieces he has gathered into himself and work them into a whole."[16] Humboldt gives full credit to the role of imagination in historical writing and finds history and poetry comparable. "Historical depiction, like artistic depiction," says Humboldt, "is an imitation of nature. The basis of each is the recognition of true shape, the discovery of the necessary, and the separation of the accidental."[17] Thus we realize that even in the nineteenth century, the literary quality of historical writing was fully recognized.

In our time, when positivism has lost its grip on our understanding of reality and the different ways we approach it, the rigid opposition between history and fiction collapses, and we become more appreciative of the power of representation in narrative fiction. In a way reminiscent of Humboldt's idea of history as the establishment of invisible causal links on the basis of "the skeleton of the event," Daniel Aaron argues that since "the historian writing from hindsight can never fill in the lost connections," it is necessary and important to make connections through creative imagination, which is what a novelist does best. Therefore, even though Gore Vidal's literary portrait of Lincoln may not satisfy a historian's strict definition of a reliable account, his Lincoln is more convincing as a historical figure in *Lincoln: A Novel* (1984) than the lifeless image recorded in old archives. "Hence truth is what is best

14. Ibid., p. 69.

15. Wilhelm von Humboldt, "On the Task of the Historian," ibid., p. 105.

16. Ibid., p. 106.

17. Ibid., p. 109.

imagined," says Aaron, "and the novelist is obviously better qualified than the historian to locate and reattach invisible historical links."[18] The positivist "custodians of history" may lay claim to historical actuality in their tedious "clinical monographs," but novelists may actually give us a better sense of past history in their imaginative and fictional reconstructions.[19]

Reflecting on the difficulties involved in gathering information for writing a historical account of the literary left during the 1920s and 30s, Aaron speaks of the "treachery of recollection," the deliberate or unintended distortion of what actually happened in the "recollections of people who have conscious or unconscious motives for selective remembering or forgetting, who are themselves parties to the events described, whose view of the past is blurred by ignorance, hostility, or sentimentality."[20] If recent history is so difficult to grasp, it would only be a self-deception to believe that accounts of past history are all that reliable. So Aaron asks: "how much history, whether written by contemporaries or by historians centuries later, has been the work of misinformed people relying upon incomplete data?"[21] Nevertheless, the distinction between history and fiction is maintained, and Aaron concludes by reaffirming the usefulness of the historian's work for offering "a reasonably accurate facsimile," in which history and fiction are not set apart as mutually exclusive, and the historian learns to participate in "Henry James's delight in what he called 'a palpable imaginable *visitable* past.' "[22] In contemporary scholarship in the West, many historians would not insist on the simple distinction between history as factual account and literature as fiction, but would see historical narrative as representation of reality in language and thus lending itself to the kind of literary analysis applicable to narrative fiction.

When we turn to a different tradition and look at the historical writings in China, we find that chronicles and biographies are combined from early on in the transmission of historical knowledge, in which accounts of actual events and fictional narration are closely intertwined. An early historical work is *Zuo zhuan* or *Zuo's Commentary on the Spring and Autumn Annals* (c. mid-4th century BCE), which is one of three ancient commentaries on a yet earlier work, but the most literary of the three. The way speech is reported in *Zuo zhuan* is

18. Daniel Aaron, "What Can You Learn from a Historical Novel?" *American Heritage* 43:6 (Oct. 1992): 56.

19. Ibid., p. 62.

20. Daniel Aaron, *American Notes: Selected Essays* (Boston: Northeastern University Press, 1994), p. 12.

21. Ibid., p. 16.

22. Ibid., p. 17.

a particularly noteworthy literary technique. For example, an episode in that work tells the story of a man by the name of Jie Zhitui, who followed Duke Wen of the state of Jin for many years in exile. When the Duke returned to rule over Jin and rewarded his followers, Jie Zhitui thought none of them worthy of the reward and decided to retire to a mountain and live the life of a recluse. He had a conversation with his mother to discuss the decision. She first urged him to claim his reward as everybody else did, but Jie Zhitui replied: "I would err even more if I follow those whom I've blamed for their errors. Moreover, I have complained against them and refused to take any emoluments." His mother said: "Why not tell them and let them know then?" But he answered: "Words are like the body's decorations. When the body is going to hide, why bother to decorate it? That would be too much like a show." His mother then said: "If you can do this, I am going with you in seclusion."[23] So they went into hiding and finally died in the mountains. Another episode tells the story of Chu Ni, a warrior sent by Duke Ling of Jin to assassinate Zhao Dun, an honorable official who had offended the Duke by speaking straightforwardly and repeatedly giving advice too hard for the willful Duke to accept. This is what happened according to the narrative in *Zuo zhuan*:

> Chu Ni went very early in the morning and found the door to the bedchamber open and Zhao Dun already dressed in his official robe for presentation at the court. As it was too early to go, Zhao was sitting there, dozing off. Chu Ni stepped back and said with a deep sigh: "He never forgets to respect his duties and office, and is indeed the lord of the people. To murder the lord of the people is disloyalty, but to give up my sovereign's orders is a breach of trust. I would rather die than doing either of these." So he dashed his head into an ash tree and died.[24]

Now these may make very interesting readings with dramatic details, but the veracity of such reported speech has not gone unquestioned. The eminent modern scholar Qian Zhongshu cites several remarks made by past readers who have expressed doubts about the possibility of anyone eavesdropping on Jie Zhitui's conversation with his mother or overhearing Chu Ni's soliloquy

23. *Chunqiu Zuo zhuan zhengyi* [*The Correct Meaning of Zuo's Commentaries on the Spring and Autumn Annals*], in Ruan Yuan (ed.), *Shisan jing zhushu* [*The Thirteen Classics with Annotations*], 2:1817ab.

24. Ibid., 2:1867a.

before his suicide, but Qian considers such reported speech a legitimate construction in historical narratives and praises *Zuo zhuan* for its literary quality. "In writing about real people and real events in hindsight," he remarks, "the historian often needs to feel vicariously what the historical figures felt and imagine how past events happened; he must put himself in the situation and enter the minds of others with sympathetic understanding so that what he writes makes good sense and bears sufficient credibility." He points out that "the recorded speech in *Zuo zhuan* is in fact imagined speech or speech on behalf of historical figures, which becomes, it is not too farfetched to say, the antecedent of dialogues or asides in novels and plays of later times." This does not mean, however, that such imagined speech has no place in historical writing, and Qian quotes Quintilian and Hegel to support the view that literary and historical elements should not be taken as opposed to one another: "Quintilian in his *Institutio oratoria* praised Livy for making words in the speech always suit the person or the situation (*ita quae dicuntur omnia cum rebus tum personis accomodata sunt*), and Hegel in his *Philosophy of History* commended Thucydides for making speeches that were not alien to the historical speaker, even if those words were the historian's invention (*Wären nun solche Reden, wie z. B. die des Perikles . . . auch von Thukydides ausgearbeitet, so sind sie dem Perikles doch nicht fremd*)."[25]

Indeed, even Thucydides constructed speeches in imagination, and he was fully aware of their constructedness. For the speech in his work, he readily admits that "it has been difficult for me and for those who reported to me to remember exactly what was said. I have, therefore, written what I thought the speakers must have said given the situations they were in, while keeping as close as possible to the gist of what was actually said."[26] Some Sinologists have argued that Chinese poetry is grounded in actual and particular historical circumstances, but Qian Zhongshu points out that it would be naïve and untenable "to believe that poetry is all verifiable factual account while not to know the fictional embellishment in historical writing, or only to realize that poets use the same techniques as historians while not to understand the poetic quality of historiography."[27] Not only should we recognize the historical grounding of literary fiction, but we must also appreciate the literary value of good historical writing that can itself be read, to some extent and in some

25. Qian Zhongshu, *Guan zhui bian* [*Limited Views*], 2nd ed., 5 vols. (Beijing: Zhonghua, 1986), 1:166.

26. Thucydides, *The Peloponnesian War*, p. 11.

27. Qian Zhongshu, *Tan yi lu* [*Discourses on the Art of Literature*], expanded ed. (Beijing: Zhonghua, 1984), p. 363.

ways, as imaginative literature. To achieve vividness of narration, historiography sometimes has to resort to imagined conversation.

In addition to imaginative reported speech in history, there is also the matter of narrative structure of historical writing. When historians try to make sense of the seemingly random pile of data and discover some kind of "inner truth," or when they try to draw some moral lesson from it, they must make choices and put their materials in perspective so that an intelligible pattern will appear. Herodotus thus draws this moral lesson from the fall of Troy when he says that "as the Trojans perished in utter destruction, they might make this thing manifest to all the world: that for great wrongdoings, great also are the punishments from the gods."[28] In *Zuo zhuan*, the narrative clearly has a moral structure to supply historical lessons to the reader. As Ronald Egan observed long ago, the shape of the narrative is determined by its moralistic and didactic purpose. The actual battle between the states of Jin and Chu, for example, is very scantily described without giving the number of soldiers, their training, equipment or deployment, but more attention is given to preliminary matters that predetermine the outcome of the battle in moral terms. "The emphasis throughout the narrative is on establishing the right and wrong of the situation and on distinguishing the just from the selfish leader," says Egan. "Once this has been done, the outcome of the battle is predictable, and there is a noticeable lack of interest in depicting the main event."[29] In traditional parlance, this is known as *wei yan da yi* or "great meanings in few words," supposedly characteristic of the Confucian classic of the *Spring and Autumn Annals*. More recently, Anthony Yu also argues that traditional history in China always tries to provide a "moral cause" for the explanation of any turn of events or change of situation, and that historical narratives always put events "within the fold of an absolute moral order."[30] In *Zuo zhuan* in particular, says Yu, one can detect "an attempt to weave a moral pattern wherein not only are the good and bad clearly distinguished but they are also 'encouraged or censured (*cheng'e quanshan*)' accordingly."[31] In Chinese historiography as in many traditional Chinese novels, narratives clearly have a moral pattern and didactic interest, and the development of events seeks to reveal the causal links between men's words and deeds and their consequences. It is in this context that we may

28. Herodotus, *The History*, p. 181.

29. Ronald Egan, "Narratives in *Tso chuan*," *Harvard Journal of Asiatic Studies* 37: 2 (Dec. 1977): 335.

30. Anthony C. Yu, *Rereading the Stone: Desire and the Making of Fiction in Dream of the Red Chamber* (Princeton, NJ: Princeton University Press, 1997), p. 39.

31. Ibid., p. 40.

fully understand why Sima Guang's (1019–1086) monumental work of history is entitled *Zi zhi tongjian* or *The Comprehensive Mirror for Governance*. Insofar as it aims to offer an intelligible pattern and a moral lesson out of the random pile of information, history as narrative is structured like poetry or fiction, with a sense of poetic justice embedded in its movement from the beginning, through the middle, and toward a meaningful end.

In contemporary discussions, Hayden White is perhaps most influential in emphasizing the close parallel construction of historiography and the various literary forms, especially the novel. He calls it "a fiction of the historian that the various states of affairs which he constitutes as the beginning, the middle, and the end of a course of development are all 'actual' or 'real' and that he has merely recorded 'what happened' in the transition from the inaugural to the terminal phase," because the movement from the beginning to the end are all "inevitably poetic constructions, and as such, dependent upon the modality of the figurative language used to give them the aspect of coherence."[32] What should interest us, says White, is not the distinction of history as fact and poetry as fiction, but what he calls the "fictions of factual representation." Even if we acknowledge that novelists deal with imaginary events while historians with real ones, it is important to realize that "the process of fusing events, whether imaginary or real, into a comprehensible totality capable of serving as the *object* of a representation is a poetic process. Here the historians must utilize precisely the same tropological strategies, the same modalities of representing relationships in words, that the poet or novelist uses."[33] In effect, White argues for reading history as literature.

All this is reasonable enough as we understand that historical narrative is also a kind of narrative, and that the coherence of meaning, if we seek meaning in history at all, is constructed in the context of a poetic or imaginative structure. But as I have shown earlier, to recognize the literary quality of historiography is not really new; what is new and has become the specific impact of postmodern theory on the study of history is a radical reconceptualization of history as literature or as a form of textuality underpinned by a particular ideology. When Hayden White says: "What is at issue here is not, What are the facts? But rather, How are the facts to be described in order to sanction one mode of explaining them rather than another?" we seem to see the pendulum swinging toward the other extreme.[34] It is one thing to realize

32. White, *Tropics of Discourse*, p. 98.

33. Ibid., p. 125.

34. Ibid., p. 134.

that a historian uses imagination and literary techniques in writing history, but it is quite another to erase the distinction completely between history and fiction, which creates a host of other problems the literary theorist is either unwilling to investigate or incapable of solving.

In *Historical Representation,* F. R. Ankersmit draws an important distinction between literary theory and the philosophy of history. Without diminishing its contributions to the understanding of history, he discerns a serious problem in literary theory's hidden agenda to promote a kind of philosophy of language detached from social and historical reality. "Unfortunately, in literary theory's philosophy of language, reference and meaning are rarely more than a set of pathetic and ill-considered *obiter dicta,*" says Ankersmit. "This has no disastrous consequences for literary theory's aim to clarify literature, since truth and reference have no very prominent role to play there; but obviously this is not the case with historical writing, in which the weaknesses of literary theory as a philosophy of language may become a serious handicap, inviting historical theorists to cut through all the ties between historical narrative and what it is about."[35] For Ankersmit, "being about" is the crucial factor of historical representation, quite distinct from the simple description of reality as "reference."[36] The "aboutness" of representation guarantees certain ties or connections with reality as the represented or what representation is all about. In such a formulation, the insights of a literary perspective are fully acknowledged on the level of "speaking about speaking," in enquiring into the nature and complexity of historical representation, but the theorist does not lose sight of the question of "speaking," i.e., "the level where the historian describes the past in terms of individual statements about historical events, states of affairs, causal links, etc."[37] The question of truth or truth-claims is thus important in thinking about historical representation, that is, whether a set of criteria exists to enable us to discriminate between competing historical narratives and identify the one that is more reliable and credible than others as a representation true to historical reality. If there is no way to know what the facts are, or the question of facts becomes totally irrelevant, and if competing histories are nothing but different discursive constructions trying "to sanction one mode of explaining them rather than another," then how can we make a judgment of their relative values and credibility? Without ways of

35. F. R. Ankersmit, *Historical Representation* (Stanford, CA: Stanford University Press, 2001), p. 21.

36. Ibid., p. 41.

37. Ibid., pp. 41–42.

assessing the degree of truth or truth-claims, without serious concern about true representation of history, on what legitimate ground can we uphold truth and condemn its falsification, and strive for social justice against injustice and deception in past history as well as in our own time?

But what is truth? the relativist-skeptic might ask with a sneer, and the relativist-cynic might add: what else but power domination? Ironically, the relativist often takes the position of the absolutist: either the absolute All or the absolute Nothing. "First, an impossible demand is made, say, for unmediated presentness to reality as it is in itself or for an actual universal agreement about matters of value. Next, it is claimed that this demand cannot be met. Then, without any further ado," as Martha Nussbaum argues persuasively, the relativist concludes "that everything is up for grabs and there are no norms to give us guidance in matters of evaluation."[38] But human knowledge and what we recognize as truth is never absolute in that sense, and the fact that we can and often do improve our knowledge and make it more precise, that learning and self-cultivation, or the German idea of *Bildung*, is an endless process to move us one step closer to an approximation of truth, already locate our pursuit of knowledge somewhere in between the claim to absolute truth and the absolute denial of the possibility of truth. It is really a matter of basic human condition that our knowledge, like our very existence, is always *in medias res*. The relativist's demand for absolute truth is unreasonable, and the denial of the possibility of truth is even more obnoxious.

With regard to history, the denial of distinction between truth and fiction leads to the total collapse of certitude, which depends on the basic concept of language's referentiality and the availability of truth, and without which it becomes impossible to differentiate between what is reasonably true and what is patently false. This is of course part of a general postmodern tendency toward seeing everything as signifier or text, the so-called "linguistic turn" that holds language to be a closed system of signs, its meaning determined by and within that system rather than by any extra-linguistic reality. Ankersmit tries to differentiate the linguistic turn from literary theory and argues that "the linguistic turn does not question truth in any way but exclusively the standard empiricist account of the distinction between empirical and analytical truth."[39] But many other scholars understand the matter differently and find a total evaporation of reality in the linguistic turn, in which, as Roger Chartier

38. Martha Nussbaum, "Human Functioning and Social Justice: In Defense of Aristotelian Essentialism," *Political Theory* 20: 2 (May 1992): 209.

39. Ankersmit, *Historical Representation*, p. 36.

remarks, "reality is no longer to be thought of as an objective referent, exterior to discourse, because it is constituted by and within language."[40] Against this view, Chartier maintains that all historians "must take it into account that experience is not reducible to discourse, and all need to guard against unconstrained use of the category of the 'text'—a term too often inappropriately applied to practices (ordinary or ritualized) whose tactics and procedures bear no resemblance to discursive strategies." After all, discourse does not come out of nothing, but is itself socially determined. "Discursive construction thus necessarily refers back to the objective social positions and properties external to discourse that characterize the various groups, communities, and classes making up the social world."[41]

Chartier specifically raises several questions to Hayden White, taking him to task for championing "an absolute (and highly dangerous) relativism," and for depriving history of "all capacity to choose between the true and the false, to tell what happened, and to denounce falsifications and forgers."[42] After all, White has to admit that there *is* such a thing as historical fact when confronted with the real issue of "competing narratives" offered by the Nazi regime and the extermination of Jews and Gypsies. By reintroducing "a thoroughly traditional conception of the attested, certain, and identifiable historical event; for instance, the existence of the gas chamber," White only falls into self-contradiction because, says Chartier, such a traditional concept of the historical fact is totally incompatible with White's overall perspective and theoretical position. "How can one reconcile the evidence of the factual event with the quotation from Roland Barthes that White places in an epigraph to *The Content of the Form*: 'Le fait n'a jamais qu'une existence linguistique'? And on what basis, starting from what operations, using what techniques, can the historian establish that reality of the fact or verify whether a historical discourse is faithful to the 'factual record'?" By systematically ignoring the procedures proper to history, understood as a discipline of knowledge, says Chartier, "White leaves us powerless to answer such questions."[43]

Perhaps White himself never meant to dichotomize reality and historical narrative as absolutely as those who pick up his ideas and push them to the extreme, but the dichotomous tendency is definitely there to be reckoned with

40. Roger Chatier, *On the Edge of the Cliff: History, Language, and Practices*, trans. Lydia G. Cochrane (Baltimore, MD: Johns Hopkins University Press, 1997), p. 18.

41. Ibid., p. 20.

42. Ibid., p. 34.

43. Ibid., p. 37.

in rethinking about history and representation. Despite all the sophisticated theoretical argument about the textuality or linguistic nature of all discourses, including historical narratives, history as past event has a claim on us that is not at all linguistic in nature. Moreover, the denial of historical truth may have other than linguistic motivations, as the denial of the Holocaust shows. The denial of the Nanjing massacre by right-wing Japanese politicians and ideologues and the revision of Japanese textbooks of history may offer yet another example, which raises real questions about our present as inextricably linked with the past, and often flares up to create problems for Japan and its Asian neighbors, particularly Korea and China.

That leads us to another problem with the denial of the distinction between history and fiction, that is, the total neglect of the moral responsibility of historians to speak truth on behalf of those who cannot speak, to give voice to that which would otherwise remain forever silent. This is what Edith Wyschogrod calls the "ethics of remembering." Fully aware of the challenge by contemporary critical theories, Wyschogrod defines what she calls the "heterological historian" as one caught in between the promise to tell the truth on behalf of the dead and the philosophical aporias of the impossibility of representation, facing "the paradox that, on the one hand, there is no straightforward way to match our propositions about events with events themselves, yet, on the other hand, the historian is justified in claiming she can tell the truth."[44] She made a heroic effort to grapple with this paradox by negotiating a difficult position for her "heterological historian" in dialogue with a number of philosophers—Kant, Hegel, Nietzsche, Heidegger, Derrida,—attacking the issue from many different aspects, disciplines, and theoretical perspectives. For me, however, Lawrence Langer's words seem to speak more eloquently than theoretical abstractions about the issue of fact and fiction, narration, representation, and historical truth. Langer interviewed many Holocaust survivors and collected their narratives from memory as testimonies, and the questions of truth and reliability arise as real issues. "How credible can a reawakened memory be," asks Langer, "that tries to revive events so many decades after they occurred?" This may remind us of what Daniel Aaron calls the "treachery of recollection," discussed earlier in this chapter, but the problem here, Langer argues, is not with the testimonies as reconstructed narratives, but with the way the question is framed. Langer continues to say:

44. Edith Wyschogrod, *An Ethics of Remembering: History, Heterology, and the Nameless Others* (Chicago: University of Chicago Press, 1998), p. 3.

> I think the terminology itself is at fault here. There is no need to revive what has never died. Moreover, though slumbering memories may crave reawakening, nothing is clearer in these narratives than that Holocaust memory is an insomniac faculty, whose mental eyes have never slept. In addition, since testimonies are human documents rather than merely historical ones, the troubled interaction between past and present achieves a gravity that surpasses the concern with accuracy. Factual errors do occur from time to time, as do simple lapses; but they seem trivial in comparison to the complex layers of memory that give birth to the versions of the self that we shall be studying in this volume.[45]

This is, I would argue, how we should look at historical narratives. History is not merely a collection of historical documents, but a narrative with a human factor that raises certain questions and, to the extent possible, provides answers. As reconstructed narratives, history may be prone to errors and lapses, not to mention ideological biases and spots of blindness, but underneath all the layers of relations, descriptions, and imagined dialogues or motivations, there is a core of verifiable facts as the basis of all the narration. This core of facts together with non-linguistic artifacts, relics, and archaeological findings would form a firm ground for judging the veracity of historical narratives. Conceptual truth has a foundation in our perceptual beliefs, "the beliefs that are directly caused by what we see and hear and otherwise sense," as the philosopher Donald Davidson remarks. "These I hold to be in the main true because their content is, in effect, determined by what typically causes them." This is not just a simple or naive conviction because, as Davidson continues to argue: "Our concepts are ours, but that doesn't mean they don't truly, as well as usefully, describe an objective reality."[46]

In addition to the question of truth, there is also the important ethical concern in historiography. In ancient China, the virtue or ethical responsibility is an important quality to be appreciated in the historian, and a historical account of this can serve as an impressive example. In 546 BCE, Cui Shu usurped political power in the State of Qi, and, as we read in *Zuo zhuan*:

45. Lawrence L. Langer, *Holocaust Testimonies: The Ruins of Memory* (New Haven, CT: Yale University Press 1991), p. xv.

46. Donald Davidson, "Is Truth a goal of inquiry: Discussion with Rorty," in Urszula M. Żegleń (ed.), *Donald Davidson: Truth, Meaning and Knowledge* (London: Routledge, 1999), pp. 18–19.

> The grand historian of Qi put in written record that "Cui Shu committed regicide." Cui had the grand historian killed. His younger brother inherited the position and wrote the same; thus both were put to death. Their younger brother continued to write the same record, and at that point Cui gave up. The southern historian heard that all the historians in Qi were dead, so he had the record written on wooden slips and went to Qi. He returned when he heard that the correct written record was kept intact.[47]

The account of three brothers sacrificing their lives to bear the moral responsibility as historians and to uphold the truth of their historical record has always been held in high regard in the Chinese tradition as exemplary of the historian's virtue or moral strength, which cannot be vanquished by sheer political power. There is undoubtedly a moral intent built into this moving historical account itself, but its veracity is not to be questioned because of the moral exemplariness. When we admit that whatever truth recovered from the past in historical writing is not final and absolute, but forms an approximation of truth and also part of the history to be studied, we may find it possible both to accept the truth-claim of historiography and to subject that claim to further investigation. At the same time, we may also find it possible to appreciate the literary quality of historical writing, the aesthetic appeal of its narratives, just as we may learn about truth in narrative fiction, in great novels and great works of poetry. Perhaps in this context, we may begin to understand Keats's famous lines in his great "Ode on a Grecian Urn":

> "Beauty is truth, truth beauty,"—that is all
> Ye know on earth, and all ye need to know.

47. *Chunqiu Zuo zhuan zhengyi* [*The Correct Meaning of Zuo's Commentaries on the Spring and Autumn Annals*], in Ruan Yuan (ed.), *Shisan jing zhushu* [*The Thirteen Classics with Annotations*], 2:1984a.

7

In Search of a Land of Happiness

Utopia and Its Discontents

It is perhaps safe to say that the pursuit of happiness is a ubiquitous and universal desire since no one in any society would not wish to live in a better condition than what is available in reality, here and now. The desire for a better life in a better place, for a land of happiness, is perhaps one of the most basic human desires that has found many expressions in various forms—a paradise, a Golden Age, a Shangri-la, an ideal society or—generically speaking—a utopia. It is perhaps a desire that truly lasts through all times, *dall'antico al moderno*, and manifests itself in many literary traditions. Utopian fiction may be said to constitute an important genre in world literature. "The essential element in utopia is not hope, but desire—the desire for a better way of being," says Ruth Levitas in concluding her study of various definitions and forms of utopias.[1] Indeed, a simple folksong dating back to the remote past of Chinese antiquity more than two thousand years ago, a poem included in the Confucian classic, *Shi jing* or the *Book of Poetry*, already gives expression to such a desire, the search for a "land of happiness." The first stanza of that poem reads:

> Big rat, big rat,
> Don't eat my grains.
> I've fed you three years,
> And nothing I've gained.
> I'll leave you and go
> To a land of happiness,
> Oh that happy, happy land
> Is where I long to rest.[2]

1. Ruth Levitas, *The Concept of Utopia* (New York: Philip Allan, 1990), p. 191.

2. "*Shuo shu*" [Big Rat], in *Maoshi zhengyi* [*The Correct Meaning of the Mao Text of the Book of Poetry*], in Ruan Yuan (ed.), *Shisan jing zhushu* [*Thirteen Classics with Annotations*], 1:359b.

The land of happiness, however, may be rather elusive and difficult to locate. It was with good reason that for his imaginary ideal society, Thomas More coined the term *Utopia*, which literally means "no-place." Like Uqbar, Jorge Luis Borges's fantasy land of ideal objects, utopia has only a textual existence, and it tends to change, to deteriorate really, when it gets outside the text.[3] In the nineteenth century, there was a more hopeful idea of reachable utopias in the social or socialist imaginary. Utopia is "the one country at which Humanity is always landing," says Oscar Wilde as an idiosyncratic Fabian socialist. Having landed there, humanity sets sail again toward a yet better one with optimistic anticipations. "Progress is the realisation of Utopias."[4] But at the same time, there was also a more pessimistic vision of a forever evading utopia, which conveys a sense of the futility of searching for the land of happiness, thus showing the dark and melancholic side of the romantic outlook. The wanderer in a famous song by Franz Schubert, based on a poem by G. P. Schmidt von Lübeck, roams from one place to another, always searching for the land of happiness and always asking, "Where?" The answer he finally gets from a ghostly voice is definitely depressing: "*Dort, wo du nicht bist, ist das Glück!*" ("There, where you are not, is happiness"). "The poignant music of those last whispered words of anguish," as Robert Schauffler comments, "came from the heart of a man who realized that for him a perfect love would always remain a will o' the wisp."[5] It would be more precise to say, however, that for Schubert and the romantic melancholia he expressed in this particular *Lied*, the search for a land of happiness "would always remain a will o' the wisp." Such a pessimistic outlook effectively negates the possibility of finding happiness wherever one goes, and reveals a rather gloomy view not only of the nature of happiness, but of human nature itself. In this pessimistic view we seem to detect a deeply religious theme of the omnipresence of evil, the impossibility of ridding oneself of evil because of the dark side of human nature that connects not with angels, but with the devil. As John Milton writes of Satan:

---

3. See Jorge Luis Borges, "Tlön, Uqbar, Orbis Tertius," trans. James E. Irby, in *Labyrinths: Selected Stories and Other Writings*, eds. Donald A. Yates and James E. Irby (New York: The Modern Library, 1983), pp. 3–4. Utopia turns into dystopia when a social engineering program becomes repressive political reality, and much of dystopian or anti-utopian writings, beginning with Yevgeny Zamyatin's *We*, arose in the twentieth century as a response to Soviet socialism as such repressive realities.

4. Oscar Wilde, *The Soul of Man under Socialism*, in *Plays, Prose Writings and Poems*, ed. Anthony Fothergill (London: J. M. Dent, 1996), p. 28.

5. Robert Haven Schauffler, *Franz Schubert: The Ariel of Music* (New York: G. P. Putnam's Sons, 1949), p. 319.

The Hell within him, for within him Hell
He brings, and round about him, nor from Hell
One step no more than from himself can fly
By change of place.

Paradise Lost, iv.20

From the brief discussion above we may already have some basic understanding of the utopian desire and related issues. Utopia, if we use More's work as our conceptual model, is textual and imaginary, a good society that exists nowhere but in a book; it is a fantasy, but it has the tendency to project itself on social reality and therefore, as Dominic Baker-Smith remarks, it is a "political fantasy."[6] Utopia articulates a basic human desire beyond reality, but at the same time it is opposite to the religious institution of a superhuman and supernatural paradise beyond the reach of human beings condemned in their natural, i.e., imperfect and fallen, condition. It is the existence of evil in the human world that gives rise to the utopian desire for a better way of life in the first place, but it is also the presence of evil in human nature—particularly from a Christian point of view—that makes utopia impossible. That is indeed the paradox of utopia and its prospect of realization. Krishan Kumar has argued eloquently that there is "a fundamental contradiction between religion and utopia," because "Religion typically has an other-worldly concern; utopia's interest is in this world."[7] The relation between utopia and a secular outlook is thus a crucial issue that needs further exploration.

The biblical paradise, one of the central myths in the utopian imagination of the West—the Garden of Eden—has but a brief appearance in the early part of Genesis, only to be forever closed to human beings when Adam and Eve committed the first disobedience and were driven out of the Garden. The point of the biblical paradise, at least since St. Augustine's reinterpretation of it, is its eternal loss. The primary message the early Christians and their Jewish predecessors drew from the story of Adam and Eve was concerned with human freedom and responsibility. "Its point is to show," as Elaine Pagels observes, "that we are responsible for the choices we freely make—good or evil—just as Adam was."[8] Like a good old fable, the story about Adam and Eve eating of the forbidden tree served as a warning against making wrong choices by abusing

6. Dominic Baker-Smith, *More's Utopia* (London: HarperCollins, 1991), p. 75.

7. Krishan Kumar, *Utopia and Anti-Utopia in Modern Times* (Oxford: Basil Blackwell, 1987), p. 10.

8. Elaine Pagels, *Adam, Eve, and the Serpent* (New York: Vintage Books, 1989), p. xxiii.

one's freedom to choose. In *The City of God*, however, Augustine completely changed that in his reinterpretation of the biblical story as he understood Adam not as an individual person, but symbolically as humanity as a whole. "In the first man," says Augustine, "there existed the whole human nature, which was to be transmitted by the woman to posterity, when that conjugal union received the divine sentence of its own condemnation; and what man was made, not when created, but when he sinned and was punished, this he propagated, so far as the origin of sin and death are concerned."[9] According to Augustine, then, the fall of man is not just Adam's fall as the consequence of one individual's mistake, but the entire fall of humanity with Adam at the moment of transgression.

This is the powerfully influential concept of the original sin that casts a dark shadow on human nature as inherently bad and, as such, incapable of producing anything good and free "as from a corrupt root."[10] In Augustine's reinterpretation, the original sin has made all human beings sinners. "It was human choice—Adam's sin," says Pagels in summarizing Augustine's view, "that brought mortality and sexual desire upon the human race and, in the process, deprived Adam's progeny of the freedom to choose not to sin."[11] Human nature is forever contaminated by the original sin, and Augustine's City of God is thus the opposite of the City of Man, and the only way one may leave the sinful City of Man to reach the glory of the City of God is through repentance guided by the Christian church. The centrality of the church in Augustine's theology not only proved "politically expedient," as Pagels puts it, "but also offered an analysis of human nature that became, for better and worse, the heritage of all subsequent generations of western Christians and the major influence on their psychological and political thinking."[12] That is to say, under the influence of Augustinian theology, there was no other way to salvation but through the Christian church, and no good society could be built on earth by human beings in this life, whose only hope was to have their souls saved and sent to heaven in afterlife. "Certainly that seems to have been the general attitude towards utopianism during the Christian Middle Ages, when Augustine's influence was paramount in orthodox theological circles," as Kumar remarks. "The *contemptus mundi* was profoundly discouraging to

9. St. Augustine, *The City of God*, trans. Marcus Dods (New York: The Modern Library, 1993), xiii.3, p. 414.

10. Ibid., xiii.14, p. 423.

11. Pagels, *Adam, Eve, and the Serpent*, p. 130.

12. Ibid., p. xxvi.

utopian speculation; as a result, the Middle Ages are a conspicuously barren period in the history of utopian thought."[13]

Things started to change during the Renaissance when humanism introduced a more positive understanding of human nature and put man at the center of critical attention, even though the power and authority of the church still prevailed. The humanistic strategy is to argue that man is made in the image of God (*imago Dei*) and therefore has the capacity of developing freely. "We have made you a creature neither of heaven nor of earth, neither mortal nor immortal, in order that you may, as the free and proud shaper of your own being, fashion yourself in the form you may prefer," God told Adam in an imagined conversation in the Garden of Eden in Giovanni Pico della Mirandola's famous *Oration on the Dignity of Man* (1486). "It will be in your power to descend to the lower, brutish forms of life; you will be able, through your own decision, to rise again to the superior orders whose life is divine."[14] This seems to be a Renaissance commonplace shared by many humanists. Shakespeare's Hamlet also sees man in such dual possibilities or perspectives: "What a piece of work is a man, how noble in reason, how infinite in faculties, in form and moving, how express and admirable in action, how like an angel in apprehension, how like a god! The beauty of the world; the paragon of animals." These are certainly among the most famous words in praise of the dignity of man in the spirit of Renaissance humanism. Hamlet, however, immediately follows with the other view: "and yet to me what is this quintessence of dust?" (*Hamlet*, II.ii.303–09). The duality of man's potentials was fully acknowledged, but the general tendency of Renaissance humanism was to give hope to man's ability to change and improve, to recognize the sacred in the secular.

Man has the freedom and capacity to move either upward toward the divine, or downward to the brutish forms of life. Pico della Mirandola of course argued for the upward movement, and the way up was through the study of philosophy and theology, by abandoning the sensual and bodily desires and living the contemplative life of a philosopher. In Pico's formulation, education is at the core of man's effort to move toward the divine. As an exceptionally erudite scholar of his time, Pico not only appealed to the authority of the Christian religion, but also to the teachings of the Hebrews, the Chaldeans, Arabic thinkers, Greek philosophers, and even some occult mystics. His *Oration on the Dignity of Man*, as Richard Norman observes, is "an explicit statement

13. Kumar, *Utopia and Anti-Utopia*, p. 11.

14. Giovanni Pico della Mirandola, *Oration on the Dignity of Man*, trans. A. Robert Caponigri (Washington, DC: Regnery Publishing, Inc., 1956), pp. 7–8.

of the programme of reconciling the literature and thought of the ancient world with Christian religious belief."[15] Renaissance humanism is thus closely related to the idea of liberal education, the disciplines of *humanitas*, i.e., the study of man as different from the study of pure divinity or theology, from the study of pure nature or natural philosophy, and from vocational studies like law and medicine. The classical concept of "liberal education" was revived as an effort that would free the mind from all repressive dogmas. As Martha Nussbaum argues, liberal education followed "Greek and Roman Stoic notions of an education that is 'liberal' in that it liberates the mind from the bondage of habit and custom, producing people who can function with sensitivity and alertness as citizens of the whole world. This is what Seneca means by the cultivation of humanity."[16] The critical mind gradually set human beings free from the orthodoxy of Christian doctrine that dominated medieval Europe, and thereby laid the foundation of a notion of human nature as essentially good or at least ameliorable. The Reformation and the religious wars that ensued split up the Christendom into Catholics and Protestants, weakened the power of the church, and, as a result, European social and political life began to be secularized. With such tremendous changes and a positive understanding of man and human nature, it finally became possible to imagine a good society built by human beings on their natural strength without the divine aid or intervention.

That was also the time of the so-called discovery of the New World, when European explorers' voyages aroused much interest and excitement in Europe about faraway lands, and created a favorable condition for the popularity of travelogues and reports on *terra incognita*, real or imaginary. It was in that historical context that Marco Polo's thirteenth-century book about his travel to the East became famous in the fifteenth and the sixteenth centuries. "It was, perhaps surprisingly," as John Larner observes, "with the humanists that the Book of Marco Polo first gained stature." In *Fons memorabilium universi*, an early fifteenth-century encyclopedic work, the humanist Domenico di Bandino of Arezzo "describes Marco as 'the most diligent investigator of eastern shores' and includes very large citations from the Book in his own work."[17]

15. Richard Norman, *On Humanism* (London: Routledge, 2004), p. 9.

16. Martha C. Nussbaum, *Cultivating Humanity: A Classical Defense of Reform in Liberal Education* (Cambridge, MA: Harvard University Press, 1997), p. 8. The idea of the humanities as the core of liberal education as distinct from the study of natural science and vocational training is much emphasized in Cardinal Newman's classic, see John Henry Newman, *The Idea of a University* (New Haven, CT: Yale University Press, 1996 [1873]).

17. John Larner, *Marco Polo and the Discovery of the World* (New Haven, CT: Yale University Press, 1999), p. 136.

In his discussion of utopia and its literary form, Kumar sees "a direct causal connection between the voyages of discovery and the invention of utopia," because "These travellers' tales were, many of them, the raw material of utopias—almost incipient utopias."[18] It was certainly not fortuitous that More's *Utopia* takes the literary form of a travelogue, in which the narrator, Raphael Hythloday, claims to have chanced upon the secluded ideal society of Utopia after following Amerigo Vespucci four times in search of new lands, and moving even further on his own in the last voyage. The difficulty of accessibility is a typical feature of utopia, which is always hidden from the rest of the world by high mountains and dense forests, surrounded by a deep river or the sea. The literary form of utopia thus bears certain resemblance to the narrative of discovery, the Renaissance travelogue literature that speaks of new and exotic land found in faraway, unknown places.

The birth of utopia in the European tradition can therefore be best understood in the historical circumstances of the Renaissance and the Reformation, and its literary form relates to the travelogue literature made popular at the time by the discovery of the New World. Because of such close relations and the intelligibility of utopian narratives in those particular historical circumstances, many scholars regard utopia as uniquely European. For example, having situated More's work in such historical circumstances, Kumar argues that "utopia is *not* universal. It appears only in societies with the classical and Christian heritage, that is, only in the West."[19] "In the strictest sense of the word, utopia came into being at the beginning of the sixteenth century," Roland Schaer also says, and he declares that "the history of utopia necessarily begins with Thomas More."[20] For Kumar, utopia emerged only in modern times; even the Platonic Republic and the Christian notion of the millennium are mere prototypes of utopias, but not real utopias. He regards secularization as the necessary condition for the rise of utopia, but secularization understood in terms of European history. "One reason why it is difficult to find utopia in non-Western societies is that they have mostly been dominated by religious systems of thought," says Kumar. "It is this that also makes problematic the idea of a Christian utopia. Utopia is a secular variety of social thought. It is a creation of Renaissance humanism."[21] Here historical contextualization functions

18. Kumar, *Utopia and Anti-Utopia*, p. 23.

19. Ibid., p. 19.

20. Roland Schaer, "Utopia, Space, Time, History," trans. Nadia Benabid, in Roland Schaer, Gregory Claeys, and Lyman Tower Sargent (eds.), *Utopia: The Search for the Ideal Society in the Western World* (New York: The New York Public Library, 2000), p. 3.

21. Krishan Kumar, *Utopianism* (Minneapolis: University of Minnesota Press, 1991), p. 35.

as a powerful explanatory tool, but there is an obvious tension between the specific formulation of utopia as an ideal society in Western political thought and the universality of the utopian desire for a land of happiness beyond any given historical time and place. Even though contextualization is indispensable for understanding a text or an event, contexts, as Martin Jay argues, "are themselves preserved only in textual or documentary residues, even if we expand the latter to include nonlinguistic traces of the past."[22] A context is not a set of unquestionable historical givens, but is itself a prerequisite condition built up or constructed through interpretation. To me, however, the interpretive act involved does not necessarily diminish the explanatory power of contextualization, because it all depends on the cogency and persuasive power of a particular interpretation. Meaning is always contextual; so is understanding.

Kumar's contextualization of utopia in European social and intellectual history is extraordinarily persuasive, and his emphasis on secularism has captured the essence of all utopias. It becomes problematic, however, to confine utopia to the modern West because a secular outlook is neither necessarily modern nor uniquely Western. I would argue that under the influence of Confucianism, the Chinese cultural tradition is largely secular from the very beginning and deeply ethical in its belief in an innately good human nature. In fact, it was this largely secular tradition and a society with no dominant church in China as reported by Jesuit missionaries that had inspired philosophers like Leibniz and Voltaire to think of China as a model for Europe, a country built on reason and perfect morality rather than religious doctrines. Kumar's understanding of utopia as essentially secular is insightful, and what we need to do is to extend that insight beyond the scope of modern Europe. In ancient China, Confucius always put emphasis on moral and political issues in the cultivation of a gentleman (*junzi*) to serve society with appropriate knowledge and ethical values, while he dismissed any inquiry about the superhuman and supernatural world. His students recorded his teachings in the *Analects*, in which we find Confucius a rational thinker quite unconcerned with what we would call spiritual values or religious beliefs. We are told that "the Master did not talk about uncanny things, violence, disorder, or deities."[23] His skeptic attitude toward religious rituals is quite revealing when he remarked that in attending rituals and making offerings to the gods or ancestors, one should

22. Martin Jay, "Historical explanation and the Event: Reflections on the Limits of Contextualization," *New Literary History* 42:4 (Autumn 2011), p. 559.

23. Liu Baonan, *Lunyu zhengyi* [*The Correct Meaning of the Analects*], vii.21, in *Zhuzi jicheng* [*Collection of Master Writings*], 1:146.

"sacrifice as if ancestors were present, and sacrifice to the gods as if the gods were present."[24] The phrase "as if" (*ru*) in Confucius's remark is rather revealing, indicating a fundamentally skeptic attitude toward the existence of gods and spirits. When his student Ji Lu asked about how to serve gods and the spirits, Confucius dismissed the question altogether, posing a counter question instead of an answer: "How can you serve the spirits, when you are not even able to serve human beings?" Ji Lu went on to ask about death, and the Master replied, again with a counter question: "How can you know anything about death, when you don't even understand life?"[25] In most religious discourses, questions of gods, spirits, death, and afterlife are all major issues, but Confucius was singularly not interested. It is not that he had no notion of gods or the divine, for he did mention heaven several times as some sort of a supernatural power beyond the human world, but he was definitely more concerned with moral and political life in this world rather than afterlife in the world beyond.

About human nature Confucius was reticent and only said that "people are close to one another in nature, but their customs and habits set them apart."[26] He acknowledged that people do differ from one another because of their different customs and habits, their separate social conditions, but he did not specify whether people are good or bad by nature. In the Confucian tradition, it is Mencius—often considered the most important thinker second only to Confucius himself—that argued strongly for an inherently good human nature. In a debate, his rival Gaozi held that human nature is neither good nor bad, just like water is not predisposed to flow in any particular direction. Dig a channel in the east, water will flow east; dig a hole in the west, it will flow west. Taking up the water analogy, Mencius agreed that horizontally water may indeed run east or west depending on the condition of the terrain, but vertically, he ingeniously pointed out, the nature of water is such that it always runs downward. "Human nature is as necessarily good as water necessarily comes down," says Mencius. "There is no man who is not good, just as there is no water that does not run downward."[27] Of course there is evil in the human world, but he insists that evil is the distortion of human nature by harsh environment and unfortunate circumstances, just as it is possible to force water to move upward against its nature by mechanical means. Human

24. Ibid., iii.12, p. 53.

25. Ibid., xi.12, p. 243.

26. Ibid., xvii.2, p. 367.

27. Jiao Xun, *Mengzi zhengyi* [*The Correct Meaning of the Works of Mencius*], xi.2, in *Zhuzi jicheng* [*Collection of Master Writings*], 1:433–34.

nature is good, says Mencius, because human beings have "four beginnings" or four innate potentialities to be compassionate, to feel shame, to behave in modesty and courtesy, and to know what is right and what is wrong.[28] That is to say, human beings have the roots of goodness in their nature, and the whole purpose of the Confucian education is to cultivate these good potentials and bring them out to full fruition. Mencius is convinced of the perfectibility of man when he declares that "all men can become sages like Yao and Shun."[29] When we compare this with the Augustinian view of human nature as "a correct root," nothing can be more strikingly different. "Whatever else the classical utopias might say or fail to say," as Kumar observes, "all were attacks on the radical theory of the original sin. Utopia is always a measure of the moral heights man can attain using only his natural powers 'purely by the natural light.'"[30] This concept of utopia fits very well with the Confucian ideal of man and of society at large, because such an ideal depends on man's natural powers only, on his moral strength and perfectibility, without the divine intervention of gods or the spiritual guidance of an institutionalized church.

With such a positive view of human nature and a strong desire for a land of happiness already expressed in ancient time, that is to say, under the influence of a Confucian secular outlook, the literary manifestation of an ideal society in China appeared very early, more than a thousand years before Thomas More's *Utopia*. Tao Yuanming (365–427), one of China's greatest poets, wrote an exemplary utopian piece in classical Chinese literature, *The Peach Blossom Spring*, in which a fisherman discovered a secluded community of peace and harmony quite different from the world of war and suffering to which the fisherman belonged. Typical of a utopian narrative of discovery, the fisherman first found and entered a cave through a very narrow passage, and then he suddenly saw "an expanse of level land with rows and rows of houses. There were fertile farm fields, clear ponds, mulberry trees, bamboo groves and the like. Roads and thoroughfares crossed one another, and one could hear cocks crowing and dogs barking in the neighborhood. Men and women moving around or working in the fields all dressed the same way as people outside. The elderly and the young enjoyed themselves alike in leisure and contentment."[31] Tao's poem describes a tranquil agrarian society where people led a simple but happy life:

28. Ibid., iii.6, p. 139.

29. Ibid., xii.2, p. 477.

30. Kumar, *Utopia and Anti-Utopia*, p. 28.

31. Tao Yuanming, "Narration and a Poem on the Peach Blossom Spring," in Lu Qingli (ed.), *Tao Yuanming ji* [*Tao Yuanming's Works*] (Beijing: Zhonghua, 1979), p. 165.

Together they engaged in farming the land,
And retired to rest when the sun had set.
Mulberry and bamboo offered cool shadows;
Beans and grains all grew in accord with time.
Spring silkworms produced long threads,
No royal taxes were levied on autumn crops.[32]

For a fourth-century Chinese poet, it was quite unusual to conceptualize a peaceful society that paid no tax to the king's coffers, but as the inhabitants of the Peach Blossom Spring told the fisherman, it was in escape of the tyranny of the first Emperor of Qin (third century BCE) that their ancestors had found this inaccessible place and created the self-sufficient and self-governed society. Ever since then, the Peach Blossom Spring had remained unchanged, and the good folks "asked what dynasty it was now, and had no idea that there had been Han, let alone Wei and Jin."[33] That is to say, history and dynastic change had no effect on this secluded society, and the sense of timelessness is an important indication of utopia's perfect condition that admits neither decline nor improvement. As an outsider, the fisherman represents a connection with the real world of change and finitude in sharp contrast to this perfect and timeless utopia. Indeed, that may explain why, when the fisherman took leave after a couple of days, his hosts told him not to mention the place to anyone outside. When he got out and found his boat, however, he marked the route carefully and reported his discovery to the local magistrate. This breach of trust constitutes an intrusion of reality into utopia and also a threat, but the mysterious Peach Blossom Spring simply vanished without a trace and was never to be found again. In the Chinese tradition, then, the Peach Blossom Spring is indeed a fictional no-place, a utopia.

Compared with More's *Utopia* and Western utopian fiction in general, Tao Yuanming's piece is much shorter and simpler, without elaborate narrative details. "Since Confucianism did not show much interest in political and economic details," says Douwe Fokkema in his study of utopian fiction in China and the West, "it is not surprising that Chinese utopian fiction lacked that interest as well and restricted itself to the representation of pastoral, virtuous, or mystical bliss. The continuous predominance of Confucianism restrained any deviation from the *Peach Blossom Spring* model. If More's *Utopia* is the prototype of European utopian fiction, 'The Story of Peach Blossom Spring' is

32. Ibid., p. 167.

33. Ibid., p. 166.

that of the Chinese utopian narratives."[34] In fact, other than some variations on the theme of the Peach Blossom Spring and a few isolated pieces, there is no consistent literary tradition of utopian narratives in classical Chinese literature. Not until the late nineteenth century and the early twentieth did utopian fiction in a recognizably modern form start to appear in Chinese writings, and works like Kang Youwei's *Da tong shu* or *Book of Great Unity* assimilated many utopian elements from Western works.

As "political fantasy," however, utopia has particular relevance to social reality, and therefore the utopian vision is to be found not just in literature, but in moral and political philosophies. As Roland Schaer argues, utopia brings literature and politics together in an especially close relationship: "On the one hand, utopia is an imaginary projection onto a fictitious space created by the text of the narrative; on the other hand, the project it sets forth assumes implementation and as such it veers toward the side of history while simultaneously drawing its sustenance from fiction."[35] The significance of the utopian works by Thomas More, Francis Bacon, Tommaso Campanella and many others lies, after all, much more in social and political ideas they articulate than the literary values and artistic ingenuity they display. For Kumar, it was not literature, but political movement that constituted the main stream of utopianism in the nineteenth century, for he acknowledges that "socialism was the nineteenth-century utopia, the truly modern utopia, *par excellence*."[36] Likewise in the Chinese tradition, it is not just in literary works like the *Peach Blossom Spring*, but also in the many political ideas and imaginary constructs of a perfect society that we should look for manifestations of utopian desires. Utopia may exist in non-Western traditions not so much as fictional narratives, but as expressions of the desire for an ideal place, a land of happiness beyond reality.

That seems to be the case with what Aziz Al-Azmeh describes as utopia in Islamic culture, because it is not so much in literature as in legal and religious discourses that we may find something similar to utopia in a broad sense. Al-Azmeh first acknowledges that it is difficult to identify utopian elements in the Islamic tradition, for there is no coherent and consistent tradition of utopian literature, not even a "coherent, deliberate and disciplined body of investigation and inquiry" that can be called political theory as such. What can

34. Douwe Fokkema, *Perfect Worlds: Utopian Fiction in China and the West* (Amsterdam: Amsterdam University Press, 2011), p. 24.

35. Schaer, "Utopia, Space, Time, History," in *Utopia: The Search for the Ideal Society*, p. 5.

36. Kumar, *Utopia and Anti-Utopia*, p. 49.

be found is "rather an assembly of statements on topics political, statements dispersed in various discursive locations."[37] It is primarily in legal discourse that utopian ideas manifest themselves in Islamic culture, particularly in terms of *sharī'a* as a legal and conceptual model, for "*sharī'a* in this context is a remote ideal, unrealizable and therefore, in the banal sense, utopian."[38] Like the Confucian idealization of the rule of ancient sage kings in the remote past, the ideal of *sharī'a* becomes a measurement against which the present is to be judged and found lacking, thus playing the political role of social critique. Like King Wen and Duke of Zhou in ancient China, the idealized Medinan regime set up a standard and offers a rich resource for legal discourse concerning public affairs. "The Medinan regime is the true Golden Age which should be approximated in so far as this is possible in an imperfect world," says Al-Azmeh. It is "a moral, didactic utopia," "a utopia in terms of the here and now: an elsewhere, some examples from which can be made into legal statutes for the here and now."[39] Among Muslims, as Jacqueline Dutton also explains, the Golden Age or Medinan regime of the seventh century "is remembered as the period of 'pure Islam,' when Muslims were blessed with military, economic, and cultural dominance," but when that dominance and the influence of the Muslim community gradually became eroded, "the Medinan regime became more intimately associated with the ideal of return to a primordial state of harmony and grace through conservative religious practice of the Qur'an."[40] It is thus the idea of a Golden Age that can be seen as utopian in the Islamic culture, an idea with a deeply humanizing tendency in its understanding of Islam, a tendency Al-Azmeh elegantly describes as "divine accommodation to human reality."[41] Religion is interpreted in terms of human desires, "the Koran and the prophetic example are woven together into a systematic and integralist utopia. This utopia constitutes the type of which the desired future will, by political voluntarism, become a figure."[42]

The Islamic discourse on paradise offers an extraordinary example. By the ninth century, there is already a tradition (*hadīth*) on paradise that

37. Aziz Al-Azmeh, *Islams and Modernities*, 3rd ed. (London: Verso, 2009), p. 143.

38. Ibid., p. 146.

39. Ibid., p. 150–51.

40. Jacqueline Dutton, "'Non-western' utopian traditions," in Gregory Claeys (ed.), *The Cambridge Companion to Utopian Literature* (Cambridge, MA: Cambridge University Press, 2010), p. 234.

41. Aziz Al-Azmeh, *The Times of History: Universal Topics in Islamic Historiography* (Budapest: Central European University Press, 2007), p. 121.

42. Ibid., p. 127.

describes various pleasures the blessed one can hope to enjoy in heaven, and such descriptions tend to connect religious discourse and desires with strong secular implications. If Augustine considered mortality and sexual desire as the curse brought upon the human race by the fall of man, and if Christian asceticism condemns bodily pleasures, Islamic culture has a very different attitude toward legitimate desires and pleasures, including sexual ones. "The repudiation of pleasure characteristic of Christian traditions in general is almost entirely absent," says Al-Azmeh, "and monastic life with its various forms of physical self-immolation was frequently the object of derision by Muslim authors, who often regarded it as something contrary to what God intended for, and by, nature."[43] The carnal and the spiritual are here connected: "sexual pleasure in this world, within the confines of a legitimate union (marriage or concubinage), no matter how intense, is merely a pale foretaste of pleasure to come in Heaven, so that earthly sexual pleasure becomes a two-fold enjoyment: the actual sense of gratification, and the pleasure accruing to the imagination from the promise of indescribable sexual intensity to come, of which actual worldly gratification is merely an act of anticipation."[44]

This is exemplary of what may be called a proportionate imagination of the joy of religion in the Muslim world, that is, the anticipation that gratification of earthly pleasure will be multiplied numerous times when the blessed one comes to enjoy the pleasures promised in heaven. "Paradise is thus a grand utopian spectacle in which impeccability is articulated in terms of scale," says Al-Azmeh. "It is in keeping with this fundamental nature of things paradisiacal that every man in Paradise be optimally conceived: he will have the height of Adam (60 cubits), the age of Jesus (33 years), the beauty of Joseph, and he will speak Muhammad's language, for each of these descriptions is in itself consummate." In the same proportionate way, "the sexual capacity of every man in Paradise is the equal of that of one hundred men of the world, capable of deflowering and copulating with one hundred virgins every day, an optimal potency which is a consummate maximum like the impeccable expression in terms of prophets that was encountered above."[45] If paradise in Christian or Augustinian understanding is a lost possibility, the Islamic paradise is very much a future attraction to be hoped for and enjoyed. In the Islamic paradise, however, the most intense pleasure is that of beholding the face of Allah, which is, as Al-Azmeh puts it, "also a spectacle, that of the vision of God's Face which,

43. Ibid., p. 165.

44. Ibid., pp. 165–66.

45. Ibid., p. 172.

it has been rightly pointed out, is in continuity with the sexual pleasures of Paradise in which the sexual and the sacred are integrated."[46] Such an Islamic paradise is so closely intertwined with religious imagination that it is, strictly speaking, not secular; but neither is it sharply opposite to the secular, and therefore one may understand it as essentially utopian as the site of human desire, including sexual desire and pleasure, and its constant gratification.

About any discourse of pleasure or happiness, a fundamental question needs to be asked: whose happiness? Is it that of each individual in an ideal society, or that of the society as a whole? The question is central to all social ideals and has much to do with the degree of success—or failure—of particular utopias. "There is a kind of permanent dialogue among writers of utopian fiction about whether individual or collective happiness is to be preferred," says Fokkema. "Plato focused on the latter, and so did More, and to some extent also Bacon. In modern times the emphasis shifts to individual happiness with Huxley's *Island* and Houellebecq's *Possibility of an Island*. H. G. Wells, in his various novels, tried to steer a middle course. The political organization of collective happiness under Communist rule called for a dystopian reaction motivated by a search for individual freedom."[47] Chinese utopias seem to present a somewhat different model, in which, says Fokkema, "the distinction between the collective and the individual appears to be expressed in less sharp tones."[48] But generally speaking, utopia as a social imaginary tends to put more weight on the collective, and that is precisely the seed of its own negation, contained in the very concept of utopia itself. In More's *Utopia*, individual rights and freedom are already curtailed to facilitate the collective way of life and social engineering. For example, the Utopians are not allowed to travel freely and individually, but they "travel in groups, taking a letter from the governor granting leave to travel and fixing a day of return. . . . Anyone who takes upon himself to leave his district without permission, and is caught without the governor's letter, is treated with contempt, brought back as a runaway, and severely punished. If he is bold enough to try it a second time, he is made a slave."[49] As literary fiction, such curtailment of individual freedom remains a dark cloud in the blue sky of a utopian imagination, but when utopianism becomes an ideology and political theory in the modern world, not just as

46. Ibid., p. 175.

47. Fokkema, *Perfect Worlds*, p. 27.

48. Ibid., pp. 27–28.

49. Thomas More, *Utopia: Latin Text and English Translation*, eds. George M. Logan, Robert M. Adams, and Clarence H. Miller (Cambridge: Cambridge University Press, 1995), p. 145.

literary fiction but materialized as social movement and political reality, utopia's tendency to favor social order at the expense of individual freedom turns out to be unbearably repressive.

Writing in Soviet Russia in 1920, Yevgeny Zamyatin gave us not only one of the earliest and most influential anti-utopian or dystopian novels, but profoundly revealed the major problem with all utopias, "the problem uppermost" as he puts it, "of the individual personality versus the collective," and he claims that his novel *We* "was the first to expose this problem."[50] *We*, the collective, plural pronoun that erases the identity of each individual person, is significant as title of this novel, in which all characters remain nameless, identified only as numbers, mere statistics in a totalitarian "OneState." The substitution of personal names by nameless numbers in a collective *We* not only expresses Zamyatin's presentiment of the Stalinist dictatorship soon to come, but his profound insight into the very logic of totalitarianism. The story of *We* is a kind of science-fiction fantasy, a story of control and manipulation of individuals by the OneState in the name of the collective. The story is told by D-503, a technician trained to believe in the superiority of science, of mathematical calculations and equations, which dictate each and every move of all the numbers with a regulatory "Table of Hours," what the narrator calls "a system of scientific ethics—that is, one based on subtraction, addition, and multiplication."[51] Anything not regulated and prescribed—anything free—is considered unscientific, irrational, primitive, even criminal. "Freedom and criminality are just as indissolubly linked as . . . well, as the movement of an aero and its velocity," writes D-503 in his diary. "When the velocity of an aero is reduced to 0, it is not in motion; when a man's freedom is reduced to zero, he commits no crimes. That's clear. The only means to rid man of crime is to rid him of freedom."[52] The twisted logic seems mathematically correct, according to which the individual "I" has no weight against the collective "We," for "to assert that 'I' has certain 'rights' with respect to the State is exactly the same as asserting that a gram weighs the same as a ton," says D-503. "That explains the way things are divided up: To the ton go the rights, to the grams the duties. And the natural path from nullity to greatness is this: Forget that you're a gram and feel yourself a millionth part of a ton."[53] That is indeed how indoctrination works in the world of dystopias. By giving up one's rights and

50. Yevgeny Zamyatin, *We*, trans. Clarence Brown (Harmondsworth, UK: Penguin, 1993), p. xxvii.

51. Ibid., p. 14.

52. Ibid., p. 36.

53. Ibid., p. 111.

freedom to become part of a nebulous collectivity, as Renata Galtseva and Irina Rodnyanskaya comment, "the individual prepares for the namelessness—for becoming identical with a numbered place in a collective formation."[54] The insignificance of the individual vis-à-vis the all-important collective has always been the core of totalitarian thinking, the core idea of the propaganda and indoctrination in all dystopias.

From Zamyatin's *We*, Aldous Huxley's *Brave New World*, and George Orwell's *Nineteen Eighty-Four* to Ray Bradbury's *Fahrenheit 451* and Margaret Atwood's *The Handmaid's Tale*, all great works of anti-utopian literature in modern times issue a warning to alert readers about the horror of the loss of freedom, the danger of corruption of social ideals into nightmarish realities. "We are faced here with societies in the throes of a collective nightmare," as Erika Gottlieb argues. "As in a nightmare, the individual has become a victim, experiencing loss of control of his or her destiny in the face of a monstrous, superhuman force that can no longer be overcome or, in many cases, even comprehended by reason."[55] Interestingly, Zamyatin gives an ironic reinterpretation of the biblical story of the fall of man, in which happiness is equated with non-freedom. Through the mouth of R-13, the official poet of the OneState, whose job is to sing encomia to the OneState and the Benefactor on execution days and other such occasions, freedom is said to be the Devil's work, because it was the Devil who "pushed people to break the commandment and taste freedom and be ruined." By getting rid of freedom, R-13 declares: "We helped God finally overcome the Devil." The mindless numbers are now "simple and innocent again, like Adam and Eve," while the omnipotent OneState and the Benefactor protect them from thinking on their own, thus protect "our non-freedom, which is to say, our happiness."[56] How could freedom be rendered incompatible with happiness in this twisted logic? How could the perfect world of utopia degenerate into the nightmarish bondage of a dystopia? Gottlieb offers an answer by pointing to the betrayal of utopian expectations in the twentieth century: "Throughout the nineteenth century the world awaited a secular Messiah to redress the ills created by the Industrial Revolution in a double incarnation: first as science, which was to create the means to end all poverty, and second as socialism, which was to end all injustice. By eagerly awaiting the

54. Renata Galtseva and Irina Rodnyanskaya, "The Obstacle: The Human Being, or the Twentieth Century in the Mirror of Dystopia," in Thomas Lahusen with Gene Kuperman (eds.), *Late Soviet Culture: From Perestroika to Novostroika* (Durham. NC: Duke University Press, 1993), p. 80.

55. Erika Gottlieb, *Dystopian Fiction East and West: Universe of Terror and Trial* (Montreal: McGill-Queen's University Press, 2001), p. 11.

56. Zamyatin, *We*, p. 61.

fulfillment of these promises, the twentieth century allowed the rise of a false Messiah: state dictatorship."[57] The actual historical transformations from the nineteenth to the twentieth century surely involved more than waiting for a Messiah that turned out to be false, and the betrayal of utopian promises had more to do with a structural problem in the very conceptualization of utopia than mere historical accidents.

What is of particular interest here is the intertwining of the language of religion—incarnation, awaiting the fulfillment of promises or the coming of a Messiah—with the secular concepts of utopia and its degeneration into dictatorship. This is particularly noteworthy as it brings us back to the complicated relationship between utopia as by and large a secular notion and religion as a belief system predicated on the superhuman power of the divine. Utopianism in Islamic culture, as we have seen in Al-Azmeh's discussion above, may not clearly differentiate itself from religious discourses, but that may only put that notion of utopia in a somewhat ambiguous light. And yet, if utopia is indeed relentlessly secular, then the utopian vision seems to have failed miserably in the largely secular world of the twentieth century, and the optimistic belief that human nature and human reason are good enough to design and make a perfect and ideal society has turned to ashes in the political reality of modern times. What can we say about the failure of utopia? Is the concept doomed from the very start as human hubris? Is the failure due to the blind and misplaced trust in human rationality, in the power of science to solve all problems in our lives? Or perhaps more importantly, does it reveal an insufficient acknowledgment of the dark side of human nature itself? All these questions pose a serious challenge to utopia and its basis in secularism, and the political reality in modern times should make us humble in recognizing the limitations of utopian desires and promises. Without thinking through the many problems besetting the idea of utopia, the search for a land of happiness will most likely lead to failure and bitter disillusionment.

A major problem that needs to be thought through with regard to utopia, as I mentioned earlier, is the delicate balance between the individual and the collective. It is very important to realize that collectivity is but an abstract notion, which in social and political reality is always concretized in the person of a representative of the collective, that is to say, in the person of an individual or a group of elite individuals. That is the essential problem of political representation and power distribution: when the ruling elite claims to represent the collective good of the society as a whole and rules in the name of collectivity without a check-and-balance system to safeguard equality and

57. Gottlieb, *Dystopian Fiction East and West*, p. 5.

justice, you end up with a society of hypocrisy and deception, a nightmarish OneState with its dictator pretending to be the Benefactor. The dictator's "ton" outweighs all individual "grams," his huge ego suppresses all individual selves, and the collective becomes a repressive regime with one voice and one mind—that of the dictator. That is the reason why utopia seems to have a nasty tendency to turn into a totalitarian dictatorship. As Frédéric Rouvillois argues: "Utopia and totalitarianism are both engaged in a mirroring game, tirelessly sending the same image back and forth as if utopia were nothing more than the premonition of totalitarianism and totalitarianism the tragic execution of the utopian dream."[58] Utopian or dystopian fiction, however, cannot speak in just one voice, because the novel as a literary form, as Mikhail Bakhtin argues, is by nature polyphonic, containing "a diversity of social speech types (sometimes even diversity of languages) and a diversity of individual voices, artistically organized," thus speaking a social and ideological "heteroglossia."[59] Dystopian novels are therefore deeply ironic and subversive, for they all describe the gradual but inevitable collapse of the control of the one voice, the disintegration of the OneState, however powerful and unchallenged it might look at the beginning. "The novel is the expression of a Galilean perception of language, one that denies the absolutism of a single and unitary language," says Bakhtin.[60] That may explain why all great dystopian novels in modern literature, from Zamyatin's *We*, Huxley's *Brave New World*, Orwell's *Nineteen Eighty-Four* to Bradbury's *Fahrenheit 451* and Atwood's *The Handmaid's Tale*, all present a story of dynamic change, a story of resistance and rebellion, the collapse of totalitarian control, even if the story strikes a tragic note and refuses to close with a false sense of happy ending. A dystopian novel may end with the depressing nightmare still continuing, but it also shows that the nightmare is not totally unbreakable. The very form of the novel and its multiplicity of voices make the dystopian novel an essentially subversive genre.

At the same time, it is also important to realize that collectivity is necessary, that social order and communal good are as important as individual rights and freedom for human beings to live together in peace and harmony, while rampant self-interest and egotism may bring about tremendous damage to society as a whole. We hardly need fiction to show us how the insatiable greed

58. Frédéric Rouvillois, "Utopia and Totalitarianism," trans. Nadia Benabid, in Roland Shaer et al. (eds.), *Utopia: The Search for the Ideal Society*, p.316.

59. Mikhail M. Bakhtin, *The Dialogic Imagination: Four Essays*, trans. Caryl Emerson and Michael Holquist (Austin: University of Texas Press, 1981), pp. 262, 263.

60. Ibid., p. 366.

of few individuals can create a huge discrepancy in the distribution of wealth, and how financial crises arise from individual greed and systematic corruption in social reality. Unfortunately, human nature is such that all individuals tend to be self-centered, and when individuals claim endless rights and form alliance as small interest groups without a cohesive social vision, the community disintegrates and falls apart. That is, in a nutshell, the dilemma of utopia and dystopia, to which numerous political theories and social experiments are still trying to find an appropriate solution.

The twentieth century has witnessed two World Wars, the Holocaust, genocide, the Cold War, and the collapse of socialism which was closest to the realization of utopia on earth. Having gone through all these, as Kumar recently argues, utopia as a literary genre has declined, "writers no longer turn to the utopian form or genre for imagining a better or more perfect future," while "utopia's cousin—or alter ego—the dystopia, continues to flourish."[61] More importantly, utopia as social theory has proven highly questionable and has "gone out of fashion," and any effort to revive the idea without thinking through its problems "is likely to result in the creation of ungainly and highly unattractive forms."[62] Humanity as a whole, if we can be allowed to speak in a fairly abstract manner and on that global level of abstractness, has grown tired of political hypocrisy and deception, and does not welcome the coming of a false Messiah to announce the realization of God's kingdom on earth. Sufferings and miseries have made people more realistic and sober-minded than dreamy and gullible. And yet, has humanity completely lost the hope for a better way of being? Is it at all possible for humanity to lose hope completely, to give up the search for a land of happiness in spite of, or perhaps because of, sufferings and miseries? Unable to find happiness anywhere, the wanderer still goes on searching, and the utopian desire, even though temporarily dormant and unexpressed, may rise up and manifest itself yet again at certain moments of a more propitious time. Living in the present with the bitter aftertaste of dystopian realities, we should perhaps try to expedite the advent of precisely such a time. Though cautious about utopian claims to reality, we should perhaps encourage the writing of fiction, the imagining of a more persuasive utopia, a more tangible land of happiness. Without the hope and imagination of a better way of life and a better society, the world would not have the motivation and energy to move on, but the world must move on to a better future. Utopia, or at least some better version of the expression of utopian desires, is still to come in our literary and social imagination.

61. Krishan Kumar, "The Ends of Utopia," *New Literary History*, 41: 3 (Summer 2010), p. 555.

62. Ibid., p. 564.

8

Qian Zhongshu and World Literature

In twentieth-century China, Qian Zhongshu (1910–1998) is probably the most learned scholar with a wide scope of knowledge of traditional Chinese literature and culture on the one hand, and on the other, a familiarity with, and deep understanding of, the Western tradition that few Chinese scholars could match. "His knowledge of Chinese literature, of the Western tradition, and of world literature is immense," Pierre Ryckmans observed in as early as 1983. "There is no one like Qian Zhongshu today in China, not even in the world."[1] In 1985, Qian was elected an honorary member of the Modern Language Association of America, together with such stellar figures as Jacques Derrida, Umberto Eco, Gérard Genette, Wolfgang Iser, and Robert Weimann. Despite such high prestige, however, Qian Zhongshu remains largely unknown in the West, particularly in comparison with the other MLA honorary members elected in the same year as listed above. In the West, as I wrote elsewhere, "so far there has been very little critical assessment of Qian's scholarship to give it the credit and appreciation it deserves. Now that we are embracing a truly global concept of world literature beyond the familiar grounds of the European tradition, we should know what a great comparatist and humanist Qian Zhongshu was and how exemplary and significant his works are for anyone interested in world literature and East-West comparative studies."[2] In this chapter, my purpose is not only to introduce Qian Zhongshu as a distinguished comparatist and humanist to a wider audience outside China, but also to argue for the importance of a truly global perspective in the study of world literature.

More than thirty years ago, in early June 1980, the eminent Dutch scholar and comparatist Douwe Fokkema visited Qian Zhongshu in his home

1. Pierre Ryckmans, "Fou de chinois," *Le Monde*, June 10, 1983, p. 15.

2. Zhang Longxi, "Qian Zhongshu as Comparatist," in Theo D'haen, David Damrosch and Djelal Kadir (eds.), *The Routledge Companion to World Literature* (London: Routledge, 2012), p. 81.

at Sanlihe in Beijing, and at his request, I accompanied him and thus had the opportunity to meet Mr. Qian for the first time. During the visit, their conversation touched upon many subjects in the comparative study of literatures and cultures East and West, and at one point Fokkema praised Qian for making great contributions to comparative literature through his numerous discoveries of comparables between Chinese and European traditions in his many publications. Mr. Qian, however, politely declined the high compliment. "What I did is not comparative literature at all," he said with a smile, "but mere eclecticism." I was amazed by this very modest gesture, so when I wrote to him after that visit, I expressed my deep respect for his unassuming modesty and humility. In his almost immediate reply, which marked the first of several dozens of letters Qian Zhongshu wrote to me over the years, he disclosed that what he had said was, quite characteristically, more complicated than what the surface meaning might suggest. The word "eclecticism" had become almost a "dirty word" since the nineteenth century, he explained, so "syncretism" came to be a preferred term in modern usage. Instead of following the current usage, however, he chose to use the term in its earlier sense. "Eclectic," says Mr. Qian, "is my word that sounds 'modest' but in fact shows my proud nonconformity; so I spoke of the definition given in the French Encyclopedia, actually given by Voltaire and Diderot, that is, a bold, independent spirit that 'refuses to be bound by any theoretical system, but dares to think by itself (*ose penser de lui-même*) in assimilating the best of all the different schools of thought.'"[3] In a way that best describes Qian Zhongshu the man and the scholar, for his approach to knowledge is to work through all the rich textual materials and traditions by himself, and his principle in life as well as in scholarship is to think independently and critically, without subjecting oneself to the external pressure of authorities against one's own conviction and critical understanding. He took pride in being an "eclectic" so defined because he would rather go against the grain, so to speak, by refusing to accept blindly the authority of any particular "theoretical system." He was fully aware of the trend in contemporary time for such systems to dominate the mind by an orthodoxy, be it political, ideological, intellectual, and otherwise, which denies the critical mind its independence, its "eclectic" gathering of the best of human thinking and knowledge regardless of its provenance or affiliation. Such a nonconformist attitude and independent spirit may have particular relevance and significance in China in his time, but they are just as

3. Personal correspondence dated June 11, 1980. See Zhang Longxi, *Zouchu wenhua de fengbi quan* [*Out of the Cultural Ghetto*] (Beijing: Sanlian, 2004), pp. 223–24.

valuable to us today in what we do as scholars in our intellectual endeavors and as citizens in our lives.

Born in an intellectual family in Wuxi near Shanghai in 1910, Qian Zhongshu (1910–1998) had a solid education in classical Chinese at home. His father, Qian Jibo, was a well-known professor of Chinese, "a Confucian scholar with strict self-discipline, who had a significant influence on Qian Zhongshu."[4] The early twentieth century was a time of rapid and tremendous changes in China. After humiliating defeat in the Opium Wars and many unequal treaties in the nineteenth century, the last imperial dynasty was overthrown, the traditional Sinocentric notion that China stood at the center of "all under heaven" surrounded by less cultured barbarians quickly collapsed and was replaced by a brand-new concept of a world of many nations. In that "forest of nations," China was weak under the threat of Western powers, and most Chinese intellectuals were trying their best to look for ways to rejuvenate China. Translation of Western works became crucial in their search for new knowledge and power. Yan Fu (1854–1921), who studied at the Royal Navy College in Greenwich, England, in the late 1870s, became most influential for his translation of major works of European political and social thought, such as Adam Smith's *Wealth of Nations*, Thomas Huxley's *Evolution and Ethics*, John Stuart Mill's *On Liberty*, and several others. In the area of literature, translations of European and American novels by the ingenious Lin Shu (1852–1924) enjoyed a sweeping popularity, even though Lin himself did not know any foreign language. Working with collaborators knowledgeable in the originals, he was nonetheless successful in transforming what must have been rough oral renditions into graceful written Chinese with the elegance of a classical style. At a time when Chinese mandarins and bureaucrats had very little knowledge about the West, Lin Shu's translations of Western novels offered Chinese readers an enchanting world of different characters with different customs in very different social environments.

As a school boy, Qian Zhongshu had a passion for novels and stories. He was already familiar with traditional Chinese novels of historical adventures and heroic deeds, but reading Lin Shu's translation of Western novels was quite an exhilarating experience, which he described many years later as his "great discovery at the age of eleven or twelve" that led him to a completely new world outside that of the familiar traditional Chinese literature. In reading Lin's translations, he reminisces, "I came to know that Western novels

4. Tang Yan, *Qian Zhongshu: Minguo diyi caizi* [*Ch'ien Chung-shu: Oppressed Genius*] (Taipei: Taipei Times, 2001), p. 28.

could be so fascinating! I was never tired of reading Rider Haggard, Dickens, Washington Irving, Walter Scott, and Jonathan Swift time and again. If I had any conscious motivations for learning English at the time, one of them was that one day I could indulge myself in reading all the adventure stories by Haggard and other writers"[5] He commented on the effect of literary translation that was almost ironically self-defeating. "Translation is meant to save people the trouble of learning foreign languages and reading the originals," says Qian, "but all of a sudden it may change to tempt some to learn foreign languages and read works in the original. It may stir their curiosity and make them long for the original, as if whetting their appetite with a tasty morsel without satisfying their hunger and craving." Goethe in his *Maximen und Reflexionen*, he goes on to add, "compared translators rather impolitely to lowly and pushy matchmakers (*Übersetzer sind als geschäftige Kuppler anzusehen*)," who "show a half-concealed beauty (*eine halbverschleierte Schöne*) of the original, leaving readers desperate to see the beauty in their fevered imagination."[6] Good translations, in other words, may lead some readers to abandon translation for the original work. Translation, says Qian, may "entice" readers to the original, and that was what Lin Shu's translation did to him.

The early twentieth century was a time when the traditional and the new, classical Chinese learning and modern Western education all became available in China, so it was possible for that generation of scholars, or at least some lucky ones growing up in such an environment, to have both classical training and Western-style modern education. Qian Zhongshu was certainly one of those who benefitted tremendously from such available opportunities, for after home schooling in classical Chinese, he went to a secondary school in Suzhou, established by American Episcopal missionaries with a particular emphasis on English. "In Chinese, he was rigorously disciplined by his father and read many ancient books," as one of his biographers remarks, "in English, because of his own interest and also because his school was managed by Christian missionaries, he read many Western books in the original; thus he made rapid progress in both Chinese and English, which laid a very good foundation for his further development."[7] When he reached the age for college, Qian Zhongshu was admitted to one of China's best, Tsinghua University, and quickly became an outstanding student with some kind of a legendary aura around him. He actually failed the entrance exam in mathematics, but he was given special

5. Qian Zhongshu, "Lin Shu's Translation," in *Qi zhui ji* [*Collection of Seven Essays*], p. 70.

6. Ibid., pp. 68–69.

7. Tang Yan, *Qian Zhongshu*, pp. 38–39.

permission to matriculate by the president of the university on the strength of his extraordinarily good scores in both Chinese and English; when he arrived, therefore, "he already had a reputation as a talented one at Tsinghua."[8] Wu Mi, a famous scholar and at the time Dean of the College of Arts at Tsinghua, once put Qian Zhongshu, an undergraduate student, together with Chen Yinke, a renowned professor, and compared them to "dragons among humans," while seeing all the rest, including himself, as "just average fellows."[9] Qian Zhongshu thus already stood out as a learned scholar even when he was a young college student. After Tsinghua, he went to Oxford for two years and received a B. Litt. degree in 1937 with a thesis on "China in the English Literature of the Seventeenth and the Eighteenth Centuries"; and from Oxford he moved on to Paris and studied at the Sorbonne for another year.

That was a most difficult time in twentieth-century history. Nazi Germany, Fascist Italy, and Imperial Japan formed the alliance of the Axis, and Japan started a full-scale war with China in 1937. The terrible situation in China made it impossible for Qian to stay in Europe, and he left Paris for home in September 1938. As Peking, Shanghai, and much of the northern territories and the Chinese eastern coast had fallen under Japanese occupation, Qian went to Kunming to join the National Southwestern Associated University, which was formed by merging Peking University, Tsinghua University, and Nankai University during the Sino-Japanese war. Like all other Chinese intellectuals of his generation, Qian lived in a time of uncertainties and turmoil, and there was hardly a quiet and peaceful place for his scholarly pursuits during the war against Japan and then the civil war between the Kuomingtang and the Communists. And yet, Qian Zhongshu managed to teach in several universities and started to publish his influential works. A collection of essays, *Written on the Margins of Life*, came out in 1941, followed by *Humans, Beasts, and Ghosts*, a collection of short stories, in 1946. *Fortress Besieged*, his only novel, appeared in 1947, which is considered by many as the finest modern Chinese fiction, highly praised "for its delightful portrayal of contemporary manners, its comic exuberance, and its tragic insight," as C. T. Hsia remarks.[10]

Unlike his essays and stories written in the modern vernacular, a volume of literary criticism written in the classical language, *Tan yi lu* or *Discourses on the Art of Literature*, came out in 1948. This book is exemplary of Qian

8. Ibid., p. 66.

9. Ibid., p. 80.

10. C. T. Hsia, *A History of Modern Chinese Fiction*, 2nd ed. (New Haven, CT: Yale University Press, 1971), p. 434.

Zhongshu's scholarship that draws on incredibly rich textual sources in Chinese and European languages for comparisons, intertextual connections, and mutual illuminations. Though this is a volume of literary appreciation, Qian writes in the Preface, "it is in fact a book produced in sorrow and anxieties," for he was attending to his parents and taking care of his family during a time of war, and he described his situation "as precarious as swallows building their nest on a hanging curtain, or as ants gathering together on a withered locus tree." In that book, he continues to say, he often takes from works of the West as reference points in discussing Chinese works, and he justifies his comparative methodology by alluding to an old saying that "from the eastern sea to the western sea, the minds and principles are the same; in the teachings of the south and the north, the way and the means are not separate."[11] That saying comes from a Confucian thinker Lu Xiangshan (1139–1192) of the Song dynasty, who famously said that "there are sages emerging from the eastern sea with the same mind and principles; and there are sages emerging from the western sea with the same mind and principles."[12] Since the late sixteenth century, when Matteo Ricci (1552–1610) and the other Jesuit missionaries came to China and started the intellectual contacts between China and Europe, this saying had often been used to legitimize the mutual understanding and interaction between the "eastern sea" and the "western sea." By alluding to Lu Xiangshan's saying, Qian Zhongshu not only positions himself in a native intellectual tradition that justifies the assimilation of ideas from the West, but also lays down the grounds for his effort always to combine Chinese and Western literary works and philosophical ideas for better understanding and mutual illumination.

As a critical work, the *Discourses* offers insightful discussions of classical Chinese poetry, and typical of Qian's work, those discussions are not just limited in the classical tradition of Chinese commentaries, but always reach out to the West by quoting works in English, French, German, Italian, Spanish, and/or Latin. The wide range of reference is not just an extraordinary display of the author's knowledge and erudition, but opens new ways to look at old texts or old ideas. For example, a conventional view of Chinese literary history often relates a particular genre to a particular dynasty; thus, poetry is supposed to reach its peak during the Tang, *ci* or lyric poetry emerged in the Song, followed by the rise of drama in the Yuan and Ming, and novels in the Ming

11. Qian Zhongshu, Preface to *Tan yi lu* [*Discourses on the Art of Literature*], p. 1.

12. Lu Xiangshan, *Lu Xiangshan quanji* [*Lu Xiangshan's Complete Works*] (Beijing: Zhongguo shudian, 1992), p. 317.

and Qing dynasties. By presenting textual evidence of copious quotations, Qian Zhongshu disproves such a simplistic view of complex historical continuities and transformations, and proposes his own view that "the way literature evolves and develops is nothing but taking in what was not literary to be literary, and taking what was prosaic to be poetic. What used to be considered not suitable for literature is admitted as stuff for literature, and what used to be considered vulgar expressions are taken to be materials for the weaving of an elegant text."[13] The great Tang writer Han Yu (768–824) provides a convincing example, for he was particularly noted for turning phrases fit for prose into innovative poetic expressions. In his discussion of Han Yu's use of prosaic expressions in poetry, Qian opens the question up to a more general discussion of world literature. He points out the same tendency in William Wordsworth, who in his preface to *Lyrical Ballads* dismissed "poetic diction" in favor of ordinary language; in Victor Hugo, who in his preface to *Les Orientales* argued that anything can be a suitable literary subject (*Tout est sujet*); and in Friedrich Schlegel, who in *Athenäumfragmente*, no. 116, considered poetry as the culmination of all forms, "a progressive universal poetry (*eine progressive Universalpoesie*)." Then, as a rule in all literary histories, Qian reminds us with Victor Schklovsky that "[n]ew forms are simply canonization of inferior genres."[14] By putting Han Yu in the company of Wordsworth, Hugo, and Schlegel and by referring to Schklovsky's theoretical argument, Qian Zhongshu makes it clear that the development of literary genres and the changing concept of literature is a process of constant expansion, the assimilation of elements of prose in poetry, and the integration of what was considered non-literary into the legitimate sphere of literature. Thus what is taken to be a particular feature, even a feature of a particular writer within limits of Chinese literature, is now better understood as an exemplification of a general tendency in world literature, a rule in the unfolding of the history of literature.

It is worth noting that Qian Zhongshu cited Schklovsky in 1948, more than twenty years before Russian Formalism and Schklovsky became well-known among Western literary scholars. That shows how well read he was and what an acute sense he had to anticipate the new and important in the study of literature and critical theories. For the study of world literature, Qian's work is valuable for making connections between very different traditions on the basis of detailed textual evidence of comparable ideas and concrete expressions. For example, in commenting on a famous line by the Tang poet Li Ho (790–816),

13. Qian Zhongshu, *Tan yi lu* [*Discourses on the Art of Literature*], pp. 29–30.

14. Ibid., pp. 34–35.

"My writing brush amends where nature amiss without heaven's work," Qian Zhongshu not only quotes classical Chinese writers on the idea of man's work as separate from nature and heaven, but also opens this up to a discussion of the relationship between nature and art in a much larger context. He observes that there are two main trends of thought on this issue. One puts emphasis on the imitation of nature, which in the West originated in Plato (*Republic*, 339–97, 595–607; *Laws*, 669–74, etc.), developed by Aristotle (*Poetics*, I:5, II:2, IV:9, V:1, VI:2–6, etc.), reiterated by Cicero (*Orator*, II–III), became predominant from the sixteenth to the eighteenth centuries, and remains influential even today. Shakespeare's well-known phrase sums it all up when Hamlet claims that the end of art is "to hold, as 'twere, the mirror up to nature" (*Hamlet*, III.ii.22). In Chinese poetry, Han Yu's line, "words become marvelous, seeing the shape of heaven," articulates a similar idea. "This school of thought maintains," says Qian, "that nature, though containing all beauties, is not perfect and completely beautiful, and so the poet must adopt a selective imitation in his work."[15] The other school of thought, he continues, puts emphasis on human creativity above nature, and in the West it first appeared in Dio Chrysostom (*Oratio*, XII: "De dei cogitatione"), expounded by Plotinus (*Enneads*, I.vi), and understood by various writers from Francis Bacon (*Advancement of Learning*, Bk. II) to the brothers Edmond and Jules de Goncourt (*Journal*, jeudi jan. 1861; 8 juin 1862; 3 juillet 1865), Charles Baudelaire (Curiosités esthétiques: "Salon de 1859"), and James McNeill Whistler (*Ten O'Clock*). Qian quoted Dante as representing the Western view: "*Ma la natura la dà sempra scema, / similemente operando all'artista / c'ha l'abito dell'arte e man che trema*" (*Paradiso*, XIII, 76–8). In this context, Li Ho's line, "My writing brush amends where nature amiss without heaven's work," becomes extremely significant as an epitome of the idea of artistic creativity. "This school of thought," says Qian, "not only regards beauty created in art far superior to nature, but deems nature as containing no beauty, only raw materials to be made into beautiful things through artistic work and transformation. That is why nature needs to be 'amended' by the artist 'without heaven's work.' But in my view," Qian continues, "these two schools of thought, though seemingly opposite, are in fact complementary to one another; they look different, but they share the same mind." Again, Shakespeare provides a suitable expression to sum up the relationship: "This is an art / Which does mend nature, change it rather, but / That art itself is Nature" (*The Winter's Tale*, IV.iv.95). Qian praises Shakespeare for his "completely persuasive and

15. Ibid., p. 60.

marvelous words."[16] The intertextual weaving of Chinese and European sources is typical of Qian's writing, which effectively presents the point he is making in a convincing manner, for it is always richly illustrated by concrete examples and buttressed by textual evidence from several traditions. What is often discussed within limits of Chinese literature is thus brought to a much wider scope, in which the Chinese text engages in a cross-cultural dialogue with texts of many other traditions, and a particular idea or insight becomes more relevant and revealing in the larger context of world literature.

The novel *Fortress Besieged* (1947) and the critical volume *Discourses* (1948) mark an important point of Qian's career as he was reaching the prime of his creativity as a writer and critic, but that was also the time when the political situation in China underwent tremendous changes and the intellectual milieu quickly deteriorated. From the early 1950s until the end of the Cultural Revolution in the late 1970s, intellectuals in China were constantly subjected to ideological control and even persecution in the numerous political campaigns, in which many writers and scholars were condemned as "rightists," lost their freedom or their voice, as they were intimidated into coercive silence. For example, Shen Congwen (1902–1988), one of the best and most prolific writers in modern China, who had published dozens of novels and short stories and cut a very prominent figure from the 1920s to the 1940s, completely stopped his creative writing and never published a single work of fiction after 1949. Likewise, Qian Zhongshu never wrote the second novel he had planned and kept a very low profile. In more than 30 years, as he told me in a private communication, "of all the planned works, not one out of ten was completed."[17] The condition in Mao's China was certainly not propitious for literary creativity or critical thinking, and other than a selection of Song dynasty poetry, Qian hardly published anything in those years. The *Selection of Song Dynasty Poetry with Annotations* (1958), however, is an excellent piece of work. Given the political milieu at the time of its compilation and publication, the selection of poems could not have deviated much from the permissible lines of literary orthodoxy with its emphasis on "critical realism" in dealing with traditional literature, but Qian's annotations show his profound understanding of the entire tradition of classical Chinese poetry, and his introduction constitutes a wonderful essay that subtly challenges the critical orthodoxy of the time. The introduction begins with a brief discussion of the history of the Song dynasty as background of

16. Ibid., p. 61.

17. Personal correspondence dated June 11, 1980. See Zhang Longxi, *Zouchu wenhua de fengbi quan* [*Out of the Cultural Ghetto*], p. 223.

much of its poetic creation, which seems to endorse the Marxist doctrine of literature as a mirror reflection of its social and historical conditions, but Qian immediately moves away from such a mechanical reflection theory. “A work of literature is produced in the author’s historical milieu and takes root in the reality in which he lives,” says Qian, “but the ways in which it reflects the milieu and gives expression to the reality can be multifarious and varied.”[18] He goes on to argue that poetry may realistically describe the social condition of a time, but realism cannot be the sole criterion to judge the value of poetry. He thus dismisses the idea of “history in verse” and considers it a “prejudice,” for “poetry is a living being with flesh and blood; history may well be its bone structure, but to judge the value of a poem by solely considering whether its content can be verified in historical records would be as if the beauty of a human body created by a painter or a sculptor is to be testified through an X-ray examination.” He then differentiates poetry from history by identifying their different functions and efficacies, putting poetry eventually above history:

> The reality in literary creation is not equivalent to the factuality in historical scholarship; therefore it is just as inappropriate to mechanically use evidential scholarship to test the reality of a literary work, as to naively ask literary works to provide historical facts. Historical evidential scholarship only focuses on the appearance of things, which constitutes its virtue of self-discipline, otherwise it loses its precision and identity, and turns into something prone to overreach and exaggerate, and to make far-fetched connections. A literary work, on the other hand, may probe into the hidden essence of things and bring out the protagonist’s unexpressed psychological intricacies, otherwise it would have failed to fulfill its task as an art work and abdicated its responsibilities and prerogative to create. Evidential scholarship only ascertains what has happened, but art can imagine what should have happened and conjecture why it has so happened. In that sense, we may say that poetry, fiction, and drama are superior to history.[19]

The argument is of course unmistakably Aristotelian; in fact Qian Zhongshu refers to Aristotle’s *Poetics* in a footnote, supported by textual

18. Qian Zhongshu, *Song shi xuan zhu* [*Selection of Song Dynasty Poetry with Annotations*] (Beijing: Renmin wenxue, 1958), p. 3.

19. Ibid., pp. 4–5.

evidence drawn from Chinese literature and history. The historical book *Zuo zhuan*, says Qian, "has records of Chu Ni's monologue before he committed suicide, which many readers since ancient times have found hard to believe, or at least unclear on the part of the historian, because, since it was a monologue, 'who heard it and who recounted it?' (See Li Yuandu, 'On Chu Ni,' in vol. 1 of *Writings from the Tianyue Mountain Studio*). But about 'the lovers' whispers in a quiet midnight' as described in the *Song of Everlasting Sorrow*, no one seems to have asked dull-wittedly, 'who heard it and who recounted it?' Nor has anyone played the killjoy to accuse the 'Taoist from Linqiong' of lying."[20] Both the historical book *Zuo zhuan* and the *Song of Everlasting Sorrow*, a famous poem by Bo Juyi (772–846) of the Tang dynasty, contain implausible records of private speech that no one could have overheard, but the poet's description has never been blamed for its improbability, whereas careful readers have questioned the veracity of *Zuo zhuan* as historical records. This clear distinction among Chinese readers in their reactions toward historical narrative and poetic imagination effectively points to the distinction of the two kinds of discourse, thus consolidating the view Aristotle articulated in *Poetics* and also Qian's oblique critique of the Maoist doctrine of literature as a mechanical copying or reflection of reality.

The death of Mao and the end of the Cultural Revolution in 1976 marked the turning point of China's destiny as well as the fate of millions and millions of Chinese. In 1979, *Guan zhui bian* or *Limited Views*, Qian Zhongshu's *magnum opus* written under difficult conditions during the Cultural Revolution, came out from the prestigious publisher Zhonghua shuju and won immediate acclaim, and an expanded second edition was published in 1986. His novel, *Fortress Besieged*, was republished in 1980 and adapted for a popular television serial in 1990, which made Qian Zhongshu a household name in China far beyond intellectual circles. The second and much enlarged edition of *Discourses on the Art of Literature* was published in 1984, and *Qi zhui ji* or the *Collection of Seven Essays* came out in 1985, the same year when he was elected an honorary member of the MLA. Qian Zhongshu was "rediscovered" and a trend of "Qian studies" started in earnest among some Chinese scholars and students. Forty years after his return to China from Europe, he was allowed to join Chinese delegations and visited America (1979) and Japan (1980), and was made a Deputy President of the Chinese Academy of Social Sciences in 1982. In a letter he wrote to me at the time, he said he "never dreamed of" being placed in such an office, which he described in a self-mocking tone by deliberately

20. Ibid., p. 5.

misquoting Shakespeare (*Twelfth Night*, II.v.145): "Some are born mandarins, some become mandarins, some have mandarinate thrust upon them."[21] Even for his election to the MLA honorary membership, he told me that he had no choice but to accept because "the Academy ordered me to accept; having to wear that mandarin hat on my head and thus lost the autonomy of my body, I am not able to emulate what Valéry said in praise of Mallarmé that '*Pauvre et sans honneurs, la nudité de sa condition avilissait tous les avantages des autres*.' "[22] He knew so deeply the ways of the world and had such cool-minded observations of men's vanity and folly that he could not be tempted by fame or the title of some revered office. He refused to be lionized and turned down invitations to interviews or television appearances. He wanted to be left alone to do his work, for the five volumes of the *Limited Views* are only part of a much larger work he had planned. Unfortunately, he never had time enough to bring his planned work to completion, and he passed away on December 19, 1998, leaving behind a great volume of unfinished manuscripts and notes, which were later published in their original, unedited form as facsimile reproductions.

Written in classical Chinese like his earlier work *Discourses on the Art of Literature*, *Guan zhui bian* or *Limited Views* as Qian Zhongshu's most major work of scholarship covers much more than just literature. It is an ambitious work of commentary on some of the most important ancient Chinese books, and again like the earlier *Discourses*, it always brings the Chinese text into intriguing dialogues with Western texts of various languages. It evinces the author's encyclopedic knowledge and offers an excellent model for Chinese-Western comparative studies. The very first entry, a commentary on the meaning of *yi* in the title of the great Chinese classic, *Yi jing* (*I Ching* or the *Book of Changes*), lays the ground for East-West comparative studies. Qian begins by quoting the Han dynasty commentator Zheng Xuan (127–200), who explained that "the word *yi* has one name but three meanings: first, 'easy,' second, 'change,' and third, 'no change.' " It is remarkable that of the three meanings, two are contradictory. Qian goes on to cite the examples of some other Chinese words, such as *shi* or poetry, *lun* as in *Lun yu* or the Confucian *Analects*, *wang* or king, and *ying* or response, and shows how all of these have different and sometimes contradictory meanings. Then, he turns to G. W. F. Hegel's ill-informed view of the Chinese, particularly Hegel's pride

21. Personal correspondence dated June 28, 1982. See Zhang Longxi, *Zouchu wenhua de fengbi quan* [*Out of the Cultural Ghetto*], p. 231.

22. Personal correspondence dated May 3, 1982. See ibid., p. 232.

over the German word *Aufheben* as containing contradictory meanings in one and the same name:

> Hegel once denigrated our language and thought it unfit for philosophizing (*Wissenschaft der Logik*, Reclams "Universal-Bibliothek," I, 19); while he praised the German language as suitable for expressing the subtlety of metaphysical meanings, as exemplified by the word *Aufheben* that contains in one and the same word two contradictory meanings (*ein und desselbe Wort für zwei entgegengesetzte Bestimmungen*), which, he claimed, not even Latin has a word to match in depth and subtlety (Ibid., 124–25). We need not blame Hegel for his ignorance of the Chinese language; neither should we be surprised at his careless high-sounding argument based on such ignorance, for that is not uncommon with those learned master-savants; but as scholars we do feel it a shame that he has turned what is the same in minds and principles from the eastern sea to the western sea into the proverbial incomparable apples and oranges.[23]

The mention of "the eastern sea" and "the western sea" recalls what we have seen in the preface to the *Discourses*, where the phrase serves to legitimate the cross-cultural illumination of Chinese and Western traditions. The refutation of Hegel's denigration of Chinese is necessary for the entire project of East-West comparative studies in Qian's work, so the discussion of the bisemy of words with contradictory meanings in Chinese makes an important point that *Aufhebung* is not the only word that contains two opposite meanings. In fact, Stephen Ullmann pointed out long ago that there is "a special case of bisemy," where we find "*antonymous senses* attached to the same name," and his examples include such words as the Latin *sacer* and the French *sacré*, meaning both "sacred" and "accursed."[24] We realize that the refutation of Hegel is strategically placed at the very beginning of this monumental work so that the reader can be prepared to enter the intricate and enchanting world of comparisons East and West, and be guided in an exciting intellectual adventure that takes one beyond the limitations of one's myopic, monolingual, narrow-minded, self-centered, and self-enclosed parochialism, to

23. Qian Zhongshu, *Guan zhui bian* [*Limited Views*], pp. 1–2.

24. Stephen Ulmann, *The Principles of Semantics* (Oxford: Basil Blackwell, 1963), p. 120.

a much expanded horizon and a wide scope of knowledge probably the reader has never experienced before.

Quite apart from the difficulty of the classical Chinese language in which Qian Zhongshu's two major scholarly works are written, another difficulty lies, particularly for a Western reader, in the very form of Qian's work. It is the traditional form of commentaries almost randomly put together without a particular logical order. These loosely connected fragments of insights embody a deeply personal conviction of the author that what matters is the detailed knowledge of ideas and things, rather than systematic structures and abstract theories. All philosophical systems will collapse eventually, Qian argues, and when they do, they will lose all their impressive structural complexity and organization, but bits and pieces of their original ideas may retain their value and validity, just like bricks and timbers may still be useful when huge buildings crumble to dust. "Remnant ideas that are dislodged from systems and nascent ideas that are not yet assembled into systems are all fragmented," says Qian. "It is therefore a shallow and vulgar view—if not an excuse for laziness and sloppiness—to take notice only of big volumes and long treatises but look down upon terse expressions and pithy phrases, or to be so intoxicated by quantity as to discard a gram of seemingly insignificant words in favor of a ton of nonsense."[25] With such a suspicion of systems, Qian writes his commentaries not to systematically explicate the philosophical, literary, or some other aspect of ancient Chinese books, but always focused on specific points in particular words in a particular text, and always put them in comparison with concrete words in different texts Chinese and Western. His commentaries are mostly short entries ranging from a few lines to a few pages, with no apparent connections among them, and they always begin with textual details and proceed to develop freely, touching on any number of diverse realms of knowledge, such as philosophy, history, literature, psychology, philology, and so on. He always cites a wealth of materials in classical Chinese and several Western languages, weaving a rich intertextual tapestry of quotations that bear on one another in unexpected ways, making the idea under discussion clear and convincing, as it is illustrated by a great number of examples and supported by a remarkable amount of textual evidence that reveals surprisingly enlightening connections. "To readers with a habitual urge for logical connections and clear boundaries of scholarly 'fields' or academic 'disciplines,'" as I said elsewhere, the short, apparently fragmented commentaries in Qian's work "may appear overwhelmingly rich and waywardly exuberant. But once we surrender

25. Qian Zhongshu, "Reading *Laokoon*," *Qi zhui ji* [*Collection of Seven Essays*], p. 30.

our usual expectation of a linear argument and let ourselves be guided by the seemingly erratic turns of a great mind, Qian's erudition, the dazzling brilliance of his insights, the apposite quotations, the revelation of deep affinities and connection of ideas in a wealth of texts, and the knowledge and wisdom released from ancient works through his commentaries will reward us with a special kind of pleasure, a deep sense of intellectual gratification." Indeed, Qian Zhongshu's works "represent the very best of Chinese scholarship in our time that will immensely improve our understanding of Chinese culture, and let readers appreciate the rich legacy of that culture not as something alien, exotic, and mysterious, but fully accessible in a rational discourse and the mutual illumination of the East and the West."[26] Fortunately, we now have at least a partial translation of Qian's major work, *Limited Views*, expertly rendered into English by Ronald Egan and published by Harvard.[27]

The short fragments of commentaries in Qian's work, however, are not without their order and connection, after all. I have put together Qian's commentaries on the *Laozi*, or the famous *Tao de ching*, to show his major points on this important book of Taoist philosophy. To showcase just one aspect of those commentaries, allow me to point to his commentary on the one phrase in chapter 40 of the *Laozi*: "Turning back (*fan*) is the way the *tao* moves." Here the word "turn back" or *fan*, says Qian, is a case of bisemy with opposite meanings, just like Hegel's favorite *aufheben*, for "the first is the *fan* as in *zheng fan* (positive and negative), that is, negation; the second is the *fan* as in *wang fan* (go out and come back), that is, return."[28] According to Qian, the best description of the way the *tao* moves is Laozi's remarks in chapter 25: "I would constrainedly name it 'Great.' Being great, it is said to vanish. Vanishing, it is said to move far away. Being far away, it is said to return." Comparing this movement of the *tao* with the syllogistic movement of opposites in Hegel's dialectics, Qian says:

> "Great" is the positive (*zheng*); to "vanish" is to depart from it, to run counter to Great in self-alienation, and that is the negation. "To move far away" is the end result of departure, the extreme

26. Zhang Longxi, "Qian Zhongshu on Philosophical and Mystical Paradoxes in the *Laozi*," in Mark Csikszentmihaly and Philip J. Ivanhoe (eds.), *Religious and Philosophical Aspects of the Laozi* (Albany: SUNY Press, 1999), p. 98.

27. See Qian Zhongshu, *Limited Views: Essays on Ideas and Letters*, trans. Ronald Egan (Cambridge, MA: Harvard University Asia Center, 1998).

28. Qian Zhongshu, *Guan zhui bian* [*Limited Views*], p. 445.

> of negation, and it is said to "return" because moving far away will reverse the course, that is, the negation of the negation (*dé-négation*), and the "ultimate conformity" will "harmonize" (*he*) with the positive. Therefore, the word *fan* means both countering (*weifan*) in its negative sense, and return (*huifan*) in its positive sense. What Hegel calls "the negation of the negation" (*Das zweite Negative, das Negative des Negation, ist jenes Aufheben des Widerspruchs*) characterizes the same principle.

Here we see Qian makes another jibe at Hegel's Eurocentric dismissal of the Chinese language and philosophy by showing how the Taoist philosopher has laconically expressed the same principle of dialectics and how Chinese words like *fan*, no less significant than Hegel's favorite term *Aufhebung*, also contain opposite meanings in the same name as both "counter" or "going against" and "return" or "coming back." Qian Zhongshu thus continues to argue that Laozi's concise expression adumbrated what in Hegel was to develop into an elaborate system of philosophical discourse:

> The word *fan* in "Turning back is the way the *tao* moves" thus means both "negation" and "return" or "the negation of negation," and the phrase contains both sides of the movement: to move against the positive, and also to move against negation and harmonize with the positive. It is my humble opinion that among all our ancient writings, these five characters from the *Laozi* epitomizes the principles of dialectics . . . Hegel remarks that contradiction is the root of all movement and liveliness (*die Wurzel aller Bewugung und Lebendigkeit*), that dialectics can be conceived of as a circle that winds up in itself (*als einen in sich geschlungen Kreis*), that its moving forward (*ein Vorwärts*) is also moving backward (*ein Rückwarts*), and that the true (*das Wahre*) manifests itself in an opposite doubling (*die entgegensetzende Verdopplung*); he also describes the process of thinking as a circle that turns back to itself (*ein Kreis, der in sich zurückgeht*). All his hundreds of words are nothing but the unfolding and expansion of what is meant by the one phrase in the *Laozi*.[29]

---

29. Ibid., p. 446. Qian gives references to Hegel's *Wissenschaft der Logik*, Reclams "Universal-Bibliothek," III, 365; II, 80; III, 373, 375; *Aesthetik*, Aufbau, 69; *Phänomenologie des Geistes*, Berlin: Akademie Verlag, 20; *Geschichte der Philosophie*, Felix Meiner, I, 118, cf. 109.

Of course, Qian Zhongshu is not saying that systematic theorizing has little or no value, for he is himself a voracious reader of major Western works of philosophical systems, and his familiarity with them indicates that he not only pays attention to these systematic works, but also holds them in high regard. There are obvious differences in the expression of ideas in systematic or epigrammatic forms between China and the West. From Plato and Aristotle to Vico, Kant, Hegel, and contemporary philosophers, Western philosophy often manifests itself in a systematic discourse and is written down in huge volumes, but in China, great thinkers like Confucius, Laozi, Zhuangzi, and numerous others throughout the centuries did not construct theoretical systems, and many of their ideas and insights are found in pithy expressions, in fragmented commentaries, even in short poetic lines or observations in notes. The point is that the quality of writing and the insight contained in a particular idea have little to do with the form of expression, be it systematic or otherwise. We cannot dismiss the value of systems, and we certainly should not give up reading voluminous works under the pretense of considering only concrete, fragmented ideas, but Qian's emphasis on concrete, textual units of ideas and insights is important, and it is in the weaving of different texts from China and the West, in the concrete words and phrases as numerous quotations put together in an intertextual and cross-cultural dialogue, that Qian Zhongshu sets up an excellent example for East-West comparative studies.

Other than the two works written in classical Chinese, Qian Zhongshu has also a collection of critical essays written in the modern vernacular with lots of quotations in classical Chinese as well as in several European languages, which make more sustained arguments on a number of important themes in comparative studies. *Qi zhui ji* or *A Collection of Seven Essays* was published in 1984 and represents some of the best work in modern Chinese scholarship. The first essay in that collection deals with Chinese painting and Chinese poetry, with an emphasis on the difference in the criteria or standards for evaluating painting and poetry in traditional Chinese criticism. This becomes a significant issue because there have been critical opinions in China that regard painting as "poetry with shape" and poetry as "painting without shape," or painting as "voiceless poetry" and poetry as "speaking picture." Such opinions suggest that poetry and painting almost share the same origin and can be judged by the same criteria. Qian immediately brings this into comparison with similar Western views: "Simonides of Cleos has long held that 'painting is speechless poetry, while poetry is painting with a voice.' The fourth example of *commutatio* in a book on rhetoric attributed to Cicero states that 'just as a poem is a speaking picture, a picture should be a silent poem' (*Item poema loquens pictura, pictura tacitum poema debet esse*). Da Vinci puts it directly when he says that painting is 'a mute poem' (*una poesia muta*), while poetry is 'a blind picture' (*una pittura cieca*)."[30] That is exactly the traditional view Gotthold Lessing tried to refute in his famous work *Laokoon*. "The idea that poetry and painting are sister arts forms a cornerstone of ancient Western theories of the arts," says Qian, "but that is also the stumbling block Lessing wanted to remove, for in his view, poetry and painting have their own features and appearances, and they are 'no jealous sisters' (*keine eifersüchtige Schwester*)."[31] The task Qian sets up for his essay is to examine whether this popular view in both China and the West can stand the test of critical practice.

"In the history of Chinese painting," Qian Zhongshu argues, "the Southern School of painting is most representative and the most important." He then goes on to quote the Ming dynasty writer and calligrapher Dong Qichang (1555–1636) as saying that "Chan Buddhism has the Southern and the Northern Schools, which started to diverge during the period of Tang. The Southern and the Northern Schools of painting also diverged during the Tang, but they are not divided by the painters' provenances in the south or the north."[32] Qian points out that such division of regional manners or styles related to the south or the north is an old tradition that can be traced back not just to the Tang in the eighth and the ninth centuries, not even to the Six Dynasties in the fourth and the fifth centuries, but much earlier, already existent in the pre-Qin antiquity. "In fact, in the 'Doctrine of the Mean' section of *Li ji* or the *Record of Rites*, it is said that 'the strong in the south' was tolerant and peaceful, 'not seeking revenge of the unjust,' which was quite different from 'the strong in the north' that loved to fight, 'not abhorring even death.' That already differentiated moderation and impetuosity as characteristic of the 'south' and the 'north.'" But that is not just a Chinese habit, but can be found in the West as well. "Pascal divided two kinds of spirits (*deux sortes d'esprit*): one 'strong and narrow,' the other 'broad and weak' (*l'esprit pouvant être fort et étroit, et pouvant être ample et faible*). In his analysis of rationality, Kant identified two basic tendencies, of which one takes interest in multiplicity on the principle of specification (*das Interesse der Mannigfaltigkeit, nach dem Princip der Specification*), while the other takes interest in unity on the principle of aggregation (*das Interesse der Einheit, nach dem Princip der Aggregation*). The differentiation of the Southern and the Northern Schools in Chan Buddhism may be said to be a

30. Qian Zhongshu, "Chinese Poetry and Chinese Painting," *Qi zhui ji* [*Collection of Seven Essays*], p. 5.

31. Ibid., p. 6.

32. Ibid., p. 7.

manifestation of the two kinds of spirits or the two tendencies of rationality in Buddhist thought."[33] The two tendencies may coexist, but in the tradition of Chinese painting, the Southern School started with Wang Wei (699–759) gradually became the mainstream and the orthodoxy, whereas in the tradition of Chinese poetry, those poets whose style was close to Wang Wei's and the Southern School of painting never occupied high positions in the mainstream or the orthodoxy. Wang Wei happens to be also a famous poet but, as Qian comments, "Wang Wei is certainly a major poet; his poetry and his painting can be said 'to have the same interest, though expressed in different forms,' and he has secured the place to occupy the first chair in the tradition of old painting. And yet, when it comes to ranking in the tradition of old poetry, the first chair is not to be assigned to Wang Wei. Ever since the mid-Tang, the greatest poet revered by all has always been Du Fu. To borrow Croce's words, Wang Wei in comparison with Du Fu can only be counted as 'a small-great poet' (*un piccolo-grande poeta*), while his confederate Wen Tingyun can be called a 'great-small poet' (*un grande-piccolo poeta*)."[34] In summing up, Qian argues that "the position generally accorded the Spiritual Resonance School in the tradition of Chinese poetry is not the same generally acknowledged to be occupied by the Southern School in the tradition of Chinese painting, for traditional literary criticism refused to acknowledge the Spiritual Resonance School as representing the standard poetic style, while traditional art criticism recognized the Southern School as representing the standard painting style. So on the issue of 'mainstream' and 'orthodoxy,' Chinese traditional poetry and traditional painting are not governed by the 'same rule.'"[35] That is to say, in traditional Chinese criticism, poetry and painting do not share the same criteria or standard despite the often heard opinions to the contrary.

What is important for our appreciation of world literature is Qian's reference to many works in the Western tradition that help illuminate the discussion of traditional Chinese poetry and painting. In the second essay in the collection, Qian continues to explore the relationship between poetry and plastic arts through his critical reading of Lessing's *Laokoon*. Qian begins by explicating his view that critical insights are sometimes expressed in fragments and quick glimpses of the essential rather than systematic discourse on the obvious, so we should not "discard a gram of seemingly insignificant words in favor of a ton of nonsense." He substantiates this point by referring to

33. Ibid., pp. 9–10.

34. Ibid., pp. 18–19.

35. Ibid., p. 14.

Diderot's much discussed *Paradoxe sur le comédien*, in which the "paradox" lies in Diderot's argument that "actors must keep calm in order to represent the characters and their strong emotions convincingly, it is the lack of emotions inside that makes the best of actors to act out passions (*c'est le manqué absolu de sensibilité qui prépare les acteurs sublimes*); thus to represent a character's fury realistically (*jouer bien la fureur*), the actor himself should not be really furious (*être furieux*)." In eighteenth-century Europe, Qian continues to say, "Diderot was not the only one who held such a view, and Don Quixote had already adumbrated the idea when he said that 'the cleverest character in a comedy (*la más discreta*) is the foolish clown (*el bobo*), for the one playing the fool is definitely not a simpleton (*es simple*).'" Qian then turns to Chinese sources and says:

> The wisdom of the Chinese populace in ancient time also realized this and gave it a concise expression: "First learn how not to feel before you learn how to act in a play." Diderot's theory makes us look back at this old Chinese saying with respect and realize how profound its meaning is; at the same time, this old Chinese saying also seems to send its support to Diderot from millions of miles away and makes us realize that his theoretical argument is not just a foreigner's prejudice or casuistry. Such looking back in a new perspective is the crucial turning point in the process of understanding that Hegel has repeatedly talked about, namely, turning from "perceiving" (*bekannt*) to "knowing" (*erkannt*), from old acquaintance to real understanding. I dare say that as a theoretical discovery, that popular Chinese saying is not inferior to Diderot's argument.[36]

To find theoretical discoveries and insights in unexpected connections of Chinese and European texts is the basic way in which Qian Zhongshu makes his argument. There are numerous examples of such unexpected connections in his reading of *Laokoon*, but let me mention here just a few. The ancient Chinese had long realized a major point Lessing made in his book, namely that poetry as a temporal art can depict actions in a sequence, which painting as a spatial art cannot. An old record from the Tang period has it that a man showed Wang Wei a painting of a group of music players, Wang said, "this is the scene of playing the first bit of the third section of the *Rainbow Robe*

36. Qian Zhongshu, "Reading *Laokoon*," ibid., p. 30.

Song." At first the man did not believe him, but later he was convinced when he asked musicians to play the song and matched the scene with the painting. In the eleventh century, Shen Kuo (1031–1095), one of ancient China's best scientific minds, debunked this old legend as totally absurd, "made up by those who loved unusual curiosities, for in painting music performance, one can only paint one sound." Qian comments that "we can see from that simple phrase that he had realized that spatial art was constrained to depict the scene of only one particular moment."[37] Another memorable example is a painter's realization of the difficulty of representing temporal movement. A poem by Ji Kang (223–263) has these lines: "My eyes send off the flying geese, / And my hand swipes at the five strings." When the famous painter Gu Kaizhi (344–405) heard this, he acknowledged that "it is easy to paint 'my hand swipes at the five strings,' but it is difficult to paint 'my eyes send off the flying geese.'" The difficulty Gu Kaizhi felt, says Qian, can be understood in the light of Lessing's theory. "The scene of 'eyes sending off the flying geese' is quite different from 'eyes looking at the flying geese,' for it is not an instantaneous scene, but a progressive continuing action. 'Sending off' and 'flying' back to their nest indicate that the geese are flying to their destination, gradually getting closer and closer, while the man following their flight and watching, gradually getting farther and farther away. Here we do have a problem of temporal sequence Lessing spoke of."[38] That is to say, in those seemingly simple fragments we can see that the ancient Chinese understood very well the distinction between poetry as temporal art and painting as spatial art, which Lessing discussed in *Laokoon*.

Lessing did not provide an exhaustive discussion, however, because there are many other things the ancient Chinese knew as difficult to paint; these include many images, subtle emotions and feelings described in Chinese poetry that are impossible to depict in plastic arts, "such as the sense of smell ('fragrance'), of touch ('moist,' 'chilly'), of hearing ('choked sound of sobbing,' 'the bell ringing'), and inner psychological conditions ('missing one's home') that are, unlike sorrow, joy, anger, or worries, not easily expressed outwardly; all these are 'difficult to paint' or 'cannot be depicted,' but that is not just a problem of time and space."[39] Moreover, Qian goes on to argue, colors in poetry can be literal depiction of colors, but they can also be symbolic suggestions,

37. Ibid., p. 31.

38. Ibid., p. 33.

39. Ibid., pp. 33–34.

which are sometimes impossible for pictorial representation. Poets can combine darkness and light together, as Li Ho wrote: "The will-o'-the-wisp shines black on the pine leaves," or Xu Lan described the same as "There's other fire pitch-black, / Hidden in the valley with ghostly whispers." Such fire is "black" but can "shine" with a dim light, something poetry can describe but painting can hardly represent. Qian then turns to Western poetry and quotes Milton and others, for Milton describes the phosphorus burning in the hell as "no light but rather darkness visible," and he also spoke of Satan as shooting a "black fire" at heaven. Victor Hugo described "a terrible black sun lit up the night" (*Un affreux soleil d'où rayonne la nuit*). All these are difficult to represent pictorially. Indeed, as Qian Zhongshu remarks, "a rather common metaphor is hard enough to represent in a painting, but metaphor is precisely what literary language is especially good at."[40] Many poetic metaphors, such as comparing a mountain to a camel's hump, are all based on partial likeness, not total identity, and thus easy for the art of literature to describe, but very difficult or simply impossible for a painter to portray. Lessing did not delve into these in any depth, so Qian Zhongshu broadens Lessing's insights by bringing many such examples from Chinese and European literatures.

The most important point Qian makes toward the end of his essay, however, is to confirm that Lessing has made a significant contribution to critical theory with his concept of the suggestive "moment" (*Augenblick*), which Hegel appropriated and many later theoreticians also accepted. "The richly pregnant moment," says Qian, "is a very useful concept."[41] Not only do painters and sculptors choose such a moment that leads to, but not quite reaches, the climax, thus containing the possibilities of what is still unfolding, but poets and story tellers also make use of such a device. "Narratives in verse or prose are continuous and unfolding, capable of representing the entire 'action' completely from beginning to end, without the limitation of paintings that can only represent the scene of a single moment," Qian argues. "And yet, sometimes they choose to appear in bits and pieces, and end at a point close to the climax, leaving the rest to the reader to imagine. In other words, the principle of 'the pregnant moment' can also be used in the art of letters."[42] Qian draws many examples from Chinese and Western literatures that make ingenious use of Lessing's concept of *Augenblick*, and in traditional Chinese criticism, he particularly singles out Jin Shengtan (1610–1661) for "putting the

40. Ibid., p. 37.

41. Ibid., p. 42.

42. Ibid., p. 43.

greatest emphasis on this narrative method." He then quotes Jin Shengtan on the writing of narratives: "The art of writing consists in looking at the point without writing about it directly, but rather, leading to this from far away. After some twists and turns, at the point of getting close to this, stop again. Repeat several times, always start from somewhere far away, make twists and turns, and stop when it gets near, never write about what is being looked at directly, but let the reader catch a glimpse of it himself outside the text."[43] Jin Shengtan was indeed very close to Lessing's idea without knowing Lessing or any other European critical work, and he discussed novels and plays rather than painting and sculpture. And yet, as Qian remarks, "his commentaries enable us to realize that 'the pregnant moment' can be useful not only for the ending of short stories, but also for the chapter transitions in novels. The conventional formula in episodic novels, the common phrase that 'if you want to know what happens later, you have to listen to our continuation in the next chapter,' purports to keep the reader interested and not let his attention slacken off."[44] That is to say, when the narrative is about to reach its climax, the author suddenly stops there, leaving the reader filled with expectations and anticipations, eager to read on. Not just Chinese episodic novels use this trick, but Qian draws examples and critical comments from George Sand, Alfred de Vigny, Otto Ludwig, to Ludovico Ariosto and Corneille, and come to the conclusion through such cross-cultural comparisons. "Though Lessing spoke of the 'pregnant moment' with regard to plastic arts, he unintentionally offered a useful concept for the art of letters."[45] Thus Qian singles out the most brilliant idea and insight in Lessing's *Laokoon*, and helps us better understand this important concept equally useful in painting, sculpture, and literature.

Two other pieces in the *Collection of Seven Essays*, "Synaesthesia" and "Our Sweetest Songs," are thematic studies on a critical concept or idea, richly illustrated by works from different traditions. "Synaesthesia" begins with a discussion of several comments on the famous line from a poem by Song Qi (998–1061): "On the branch of a red apricot tree, spring is clamorous." By quoting from many texts, Qian shows that the word "clamorous" is often used in the works of Song dynasty poets. "The word 'clamorous,'" says Qian, "describes the condition of things that is soundless as if it were a waving motion with sound, thereby giving what is seen a sense of what is heard."[46]

43. Ibid., p. 44.

44. Ibid., p. 45.

45. Ibid., p. 48.

46. Qian Zhongshu, "Synaesthesia," ibid., p. 55.

There are examples in the West as well, as Qian says, "Western languages use words meaning 'crying loud' or 'making a bang' (*loud, criard, chiassoso, chillón, knall*) to portray too bright or too strong colors, while light colors are said to be 'deaf' (*la teinte sourde*); aren't these helpful in understanding the word 'clamorous' in ancient Chinese poetry? In psychological or linguistic terms, these are all examples of 'synaesthesia' or 'empathy.'"[47] It is characteristic of Qian Zhongshu's writings to have a wealth of textual examples from China and the West to help mutual explication. From a rich pool of quotations in different languages, he enables us to see that "synaesthesia" exists everywhere and is used widely in various languages. From daily language to poetic diction, from Aristotle to ancient Chinese classics, from Homer to Ezra Pound, from Western mysticism to Chinese Taoism and Buddhism, the many examples Qian draws make us realize that synaesthesia and empathy are ubiquitous, something we can easily notice if we have the mind and the sensibility. But just as Qian points out, such a commonly seen device in Chinese poetry and prose "seems to have escaped understanding and recognition by ancient critics and rhetoricians."[48] In the West, "though Aristotle mentioned synaesthesia in *De Anima*, he never touched on it in his *Rhetoric*."[49] Once synaesthesia is put forward as a critical concept for discussion, however, Qian is able to reveal its ubiquity and usefulness in literature and art, and give us a much deeper understanding of its significance.

Likewise, as a literary theme, "poetry can give vent to grievances" never received the attention it deserves in traditional critical theories. In the *Analects*, Confucius specified four functions for poetry—that poetry can be used to inspire, to observe social conditions, to form a sense of community, and to give vent to grievances—of which the last is only one of the four functions. But by quoting many examples from Chinese and Western literary texts, Qian Zhongshu proves that the idea that "poetry can give vent to grievances" is a universally effective principle, namely, that the most effective and moving works of literature are produced from sorrow and miseries, while works writing about sorrow and miseries are also most powerful in moving and affecting readers. "Pain can give rise to poetry better than pleasure, and good poems mainly express unhappy, sorrowful or depressed feelings. In ancient China, this idea was not just a commonplace in critical theory on poetry, but became a

47. Ibid., pp. 55–56.

48. Ibid., p. 54.

49. Ibid., p. 62.

convention in the practice of writing."[50] Of the numerous examples, let me just pick up a particularly impressive one. The fifth-century Chinese critic Liu Xie (465?–522) argues in his famous work, *The Literary Mind or the Carving of Dragons*, that a great work of literature is often the product of the author's painful lived experience and sorrow, just "like pearls that come out of the disease of suffering oysters." That interesting metaphor is borrowed from an earlier work, *Huainan zi*, where it is said that "the pearl as bright as the moon is for the oyster a disease, though for us a benefit." Applied to literary creation, the metaphor perfectly conveys the idea that poetry gives vent to grievances. Interestingly, as Qian points out, this metaphor is not just a Chinese one, but can be found in Western texts as well:

> When Western writers talk about literature, their use of metaphor is remarkably coincidental with that of the Chinese. Franz Grillparzer remarks that poetry is like a pearl, the product of a sick and silent shell-fish (*die Perle, das Erzeugnis des kranken stillen Muscheltieres*); Flaubert observes that a pearl is formed in the illness of the oyster (*la perle est une maladie de l'huître*), while the style of a writer flows out of a deeper sorrow (*l'écoulement d'une douleur plus profounde*). Heine wonders whether poetry is to man what the pearl is to the poor oyster, the stuff of illness that makes it suffer (*wie die Perle, die Krankheitsstoff, woran das arme Austertier leidet*). A. E. Housman maintains that poetry is a sort of "secretion; whether a natural secretion, like the turpentine in the fir, or a morbid secretion, like the pearl in the oyster." Apparently such a metaphor is found everywhere and used by all writers independently of one another, because it expresses precisely the idea that "poetry gives vent to grievances," and that it is "produced under the pressure of suffering or misfortune."[51]

Reading this passage, we cannot but marvel at the affinities of the poetic minds Chinese and Western, and also we cannot but admire Qian Zhongshu's erudition and extraordinary memory that he was able to pinpoint exactly where to look for textual examples and collect the metaphors of "pearl in a suffering oyster" from different works in different languages, presented as

50. Qian Zhongshu, "Our Sweetest Songs," ibid., p. 102.

51. Ibid., p. 104.

textual evidence to support the universal applicability of the idea that "poetry can give vent to grievances." Once given a persuasive explication, the phrase from Liu Xie's *Literary Mind or the Carving of Dragons* and the poetic function identified in the Confucian *Analects* are combined to form a significant concept meaningful in both literary creation and literary criticism. Future critics can no longer neglect this important critical concept and insight, but need to explore its depth in the works of world literature. Qian Zhongshu's essay is always wide in scope and rich in details, it is always crossing over boundaries, "speaking of the Western and the modern, but wittingly or unwittingly moving far to China and antiquity," as he says in describing his own style.[52] Knowledge of the ancient and the modern, Chinese and Western, is in fact interconnected, and it is the task of comparative studies to go beyond disciplinary boundaries and to seek understanding and comprehension by working out these interconnections.

The seven essays in Qian's collection may be divided into three groups. The first two discuss the critical tradition in China and the West on painting and poetry, the next two propose important critical concepts, and the remaining three are concerned with literary translation and reception. The essays on Lin Shu's translation and on the translation of Longfellow's *Psalm of Life* not only discuss translation of literary works, but lead us into the historical world of the late imperial China to have a vivid sense of the social milieu and intellectual ambience of the twilight years of the Qing dynasty. Lin Shu, as I mentioned in the beginning part of this chapter, did not know any foreign language but produced very popular translations of more than 170 Western novels in collaboration with those who knew the originals. In such indirect translations, there are certainly mistakes and infelicities that provide stuff for a good laugh, and Qian does point out some of them to make his essay a delightfully humorous reading. He makes it clear, however, that not just Lin Shu's translation, but translation in general, is prone to such mistakes. "Westerners have this proverb: 'translators are traitors' (*Traduttore traditore*). Our Chinese ancestors also held that the *fan* (trans-) in *fanyi* (translation) is equivalent to the *fan* or 'turning' as in 'turning to the backside' when looking at an embroidered piece of silk, showing its backside: '*fan* (turn) is like to turn over a piece of brocade; there are flowers on both sides, but the flowers are all in reverse' (Monk Zanning [919–1002] on translating Buddhist sutras). This metaphor," says Qian, "reminds us of Don Quixote's remark that reading translation is like looking at Flemish tapestries from the reverse side (*es como*

52. Ibid., p. 113.

quien mira los tapices flamencos por el revés)." But translation also plays the role of match-making, it is, says Qian, "a go-between or liaison officer, introducing all to make acquaintance with foreign works, and entice us to fall in love with foreign texts, as if a match-maker, leading to a kind of 'literary marriage' between countries, the only 'marriage' between countries with very little danger of turning against each other, quarrel, separation, and brawl."[53]

At the time, however, i.e., at the end of the last imperial dynasty of Qing and the beginning of the Republican period in China, old-fashioned literati had little understanding of the importance of translation and even doubted there was any literature in foreign countries. Qian Zhongshu depicts the intellectual climate at the time by drawing on his own experience. In 1931 or 1932, he went to see Mr. Chen Yan, a famous poet and a respected senior scholar, with whom he had a long conversation in Suzhou. Though he knew that Qian Zhongshu was studying abroad and could understand foreign languages, Mr. Chen thought he "must have been studying some practical subjects like science and engineering, or law and administration, or economics." What ensued in the conversation turned out to be rather interesting:

> On that day, he finally found out, and he said with a sigh: "for literature, why would you learn in a foreign country? Isn't it true that our Chinese literature is good enough?" I dared not to argue with him, but could only dodge behind his friend's name, so I said that reading novels translated by Lin Shu had got me interested in foreign literature. Mr. Chen said, "This is all messed up! If Qinnan [Lin Shu] knew this, he may not be pleased. Having read his translations, you should go further to study his classical style prose, how come you turned to look for foreign countries instead? Isn't Qinnan 'pushing fish to the deep waters'?"[54]

Here Qian Zhongshu attaches a long footnote to describe the prejudice against foreign literature among many old-fashioned men of letters at the time. "Many men of letters of an old generation hold such a view," says Qian, "of which a poem by Fan Zengxiang (1846–1931) is exemplary: 'We have boundless learning in addition to classis and histories, / What poetry there is to read among the Europeans?' They had to admit that China was behind the West in terms of science, but they made literature the basis of their sense of

53. Qian Zhongshu, "On Lin Shu's Translation," ibid., p. 68.

54. Ibid., p. 87.

national superiority." But this is not just the prejudice among Chinese literati, for "it looks like men in other ancient Eastern countries also held similar views. Edmond de Goncourt reported that the Persians also questioned: 'the Europeans can make watches and all kinds of machines and are indeed quite clever, but the Persians are still superior; do the Europeans have writers and poets (*si nous avons des littérateurs, des poètes*)?'" Even though Lin Shu did not think much of his own translation in comparison with his prose writings, he at least knew that there were foreign novels worthy of translation. So Qian praised Lin Shu and says, "on that point, Lin Shu's perception surpassed that of his more talented and learned contemporaries."[55]

In his essay on the translation of Longfellow's *Psalm of Life*, Qian Zhongshu mentions Zhang Deyi (1847–1918), a top student graduated from the Interpreters' College set up by the Qing government in 1862, who later went to Europe several times on diplomatic missions. Though he was said to have an "excellent command of English," Zhang Deyi was quite ignorant of Western literature, mistaking *Gulliver's Travels* for factual records, thus completely missing the point of its social satire. At precisely the time when Zhang was traveling in England and writing down some naively imbecile comments on this famous work of English literature, says Qian, "Lin Shu, who knew not a single word of a foreign language and had never in his life gone abroad, and Wei Yi, who never graduated from any college, were translating *Gulliver's Travels*." Comparing Zhang Deyi's wrong ideas about this work with Lin Shu's view, Qian remarks that "I don't think it is difficult to judge who of the two had a better understanding of Western literature."[56]

When two cultures make the first encounter, translation, even inadequate translation, constitutes the necessary step toward mutual understanding, like a bridge across huge linguistic and cultural gaps. Thomas F. Wade (1818–1895), interpreter, diplomat, and the first holder of the Chair of Chinese at Cambridge University, once translated H. W. Longfellow's *A Psalm of Life* into Chinese, which was then polished by Dong Xun (1810–1892), minister in charge of foreign affairs in the late Qing government. Dong wrote the poem on a fan and entrusted it with Anson Burlingame (1820–1870), Envoy Extraordinary sent by the Qing government to the United States, who delivered it to Longfellow himself. Wade's Chinese was limited, and as a result his translation was infelicitous, even at times incomprehensible; Dong Xun, on the other hand, did not know any foreign language and could only work with a half-intelligible translation and relying on his own guess and conjecture. Not surprisingly, the

55. Ibid., note 60, p. 98.

end result is quite unfaithful to the original. By analyzing the translation in detail, Qian Zhongshu shows how the linguistic problems reveal the lack of understanding between China and the West at the time, and how ignorant the Chinese then were concerning anything foreign.

Like the ancient Greeks, the ancient Chinese were culturally self-centered and regarded anyone unable to speak their language as a barbarian, who supposedly shared the language with birds and animals. Such a traditional view remained strong even in the late Qing period, and can be seen in a hilarious passage of the diary entry kept by a conservative-minded Weng Tonghe (1830–1904). Weng went to the office in charge of foreign affairs near the Chinese New Year's Day, and soon after, "upon seeing ambassadors of various countries coming for New Year greetings," he wrote, "I went to the western side to avoid the crowd and looked from afar at the main hall. About twenty or so people gathered there around the table, with whom Lord Zheng talked in the barbarian language, chirping from time to time." Lord Zheng or Zheng Jize (1839–1890) was a famous diplomat who was known to speak a fluent, if grammatically flawed, English. As Qian Zhongshu comments, it is a commonplace in old Chinese texts to describe the language of foreigners as the chirping of birds; therefore "to the ears of Weng Tonghe, who always ran to avoid rubbing shoulders with foreign ghosts, any foreign language, be it English or French, would all sound like endless chirping and twittering."[57] In the late nineteenth century, Chinese elites would still fall back on their unshakable sense of cultural superiority in spite of, or perhaps because of, China's defeat in the Opium Wars. "They all admitted that the West was more advanced in natural sciences and in some areas of social sciences, and that China should learn from it," says Qian in describing the general consensus among the late Qing elites; "but at the same time, insofar as literature and moral philosophy were concerned, ours were the best and there was no need to import these from foreign countries. Moreover, once foreigners realized the wonder and superiority of those things Chinese, they would probably 'come to us' for enlightenment."[58] That was indeed the mentality and attitude of most Chinese literati elites in the late nineteenth century and the early twentieth, shortly before the last imperial dynasty was to collapse. At that time, Chinese

56. Qian Zhongshu, "The First English Poem Translated into Chinese, *Psalm of Life*, and Several Related Matters," ibid., p. 135.

57. This is Weng's diary entry for the 10th day of the first month, the 13th year of Guangxu (1887); quoted ibid., p. 122.

58. Ibid., p. 121.

elites only had very vague ideas about foreign countries and knew precious little about foreign affairs; very few of them had any knowledge of a foreign language, let alone engaging in anything like translation of foreign literature.

Under such circumstances and in such an intellectual climate, it is quite unusual for Longfellow's *A Psalm of Life* to appear in a Chinese translation. The translated poem was written on a Chinese fan and brought to America by Anson Burlingame, presented to Longfellow himself, which the poet recorded in his diary, but only said it was sent as a gift from "a Chinese mandarin" without mentioning the translator's name. One of Longfellow's biographers later wrote that the "mandarin" was a certain "Jung Tagen," which Qian Zhongshu was able to establish, after careful scrutiny, that it should have been "Tung Tajen" or *Dong daren*, namely, His Excellency Lord Dong. The official Lord Dong must have been Dong Xun, who was Minister of Foreign Affairs at the time, but was the poem written by Dong Xun the same as written on the fan, which Longfellow mentioned in his diary? "It should be easy to find the answer," Qian Zhongshu wrote in 1981, "by anyone who has the opportunity to visit the United States and also has the interest to examine things left by Longfellow."[59] In the 1990s, that Chinese fan reappeared in the Longfellow House in Cambridge, Massachusetts, and it turned out exactly as Qian had anticipated, a fan with Longfellow's *A Psalm of Life* written in Chinese in graceful calligraphy, dated spring 1865 with the signature of none other than Lord Dong Xun. Therefore, fortunately in the future, "anyone who has the opportunity to visit the United States and also has the interest to examine things left by Longfellow" would be able to look at that legendary fan, an object that has an interesting story inscribed in it as a testimony to the literary encounter between China and the West.

What Qian Zhongshu does best is discovering the connection of ideas and themes in Chinese and Western literatures and cultural traditions, the revealing of surprising affinities and the interconnectedness of the human mind and imagination through wide-ranging comparisons. His extraordinary erudition and vast scope of knowledge, and his example as a scholar, are always encouraging and most inspiring. He is always looking beyond all kinds of boundaries and has a low opinion of those who pride themselves of being experts and specialists, because, he says:

> Objects of humanistic studies are connected with one another and can mutually illuminate, not only crossing boundaries of nations

59. Ibid., p. 119.

> and time periods, but running through different fields and disciplines. Because of the severe limitations of our lives and intellect, we can only reduce our research areas in increasingly narrower circles and divide our specialties into increasingly smaller subfields. That is for the sake of convenience and we have no other choice. Therefore, to become a specialist in a particular field, even though subjectively one may feel proud of it, is objectively something one cannot help but have to live with.[60]

That grand vision of always transcending the limitations of a "special field" to achieve a more inclusive and broad horizon is essential for humanistic studies, as it is an appropriate guidance for the study of world literature. It is difficult to emulate the kind of encyclopedic knowledge we find in Qian Zhongshu's works, but it should be a goal for anyone devoted to a global perspective to aim at and try to achieve.

---

60. Qian Zhongshu, "Our Sweetest Songs," ibid., p. 113.

9

The Poetics of World Literature

In a study of tragedy in relation to Aristotle's *Poetics*, F. L. Lucas argues that poetics, i.e., a philosophical treatment of the nature and elements of literary representation, could have emerged only in ancient Greece because, among all the peoples in the ancient world, the Greeks alone had the intellectual curiosity and capability of raising questions. "Other races have fashioned into art and story dreams as lovely; but it is from the Greeks that Europe has learnt, so far as it has learnt, to question as well as to dream, to take nothing on earth, or in heaven, for granted—that unfaith, in a word, which has also removed mountains."[1] The philosophical inquiry into the origin and ultimate elements of things was supposedly a unique Greek predilection, for "the other ancient nations" did not question the world they lived in. "They loved, as most men do still, certainty better than truth."[2] We may not expect Lucas to know anything about Qu Yuan (339?–277? BCE), a poet in ancient China, who began his *Asking Heaven* with such questions:

> Who passed on and told us about the beginning of earliest ancient time?
>
> How could one make inquiry before the sky and the earth took their shape?
>
> Who could see through the gloom when night and day were undivided?

1. F. L. Lucas, *Tragedy: Serious Drama in Relation to Aristotle's Poetics*, rev. ed. (London: The Hogarth Press, 1957), p. 12.

2. Ibid., p. 13.

> How could one know the world when all appeared full of formless air?[3]

He then followed with nearly 180 questions consecutively to inquire about the why and how of the universe, about ancient myths and human history. It is true that this poem is not well-known except to students of ancient Chinese literature, but the point is that today, when we discuss *poetics* in relation to a truly global concept of *world literature*, we need a much broader frame of reference than Lucas's that begins and ends with Europe. We need to go beyond the Greek and the Aristotelian tradition even as we fully acknowledge Aristotle's *Poetics* as a classic example of the kind of work we need to do.

The horizon opened up is truly immense, if poetics is to address the infinitely vast body of literature in all the world's languages and cultures, but David Damrosch has offered a more manageable, though still daunting, concept that includes "all literary works that circulate beyond their culture of origin, either in translation or in their original language."[4] Circulation and translation are thus defining factors, and world literature is literature read in the multicultural world, beyond its original home in a national language and culture. Thus world literature "is not an infinite, ungraspable canon of works but rather a mode of circulation and of reading."[5] Likewise we may define the poetics of world literature as a set of fundamental questions about the nature, qualities, values, and components of literature so understood, rather than an infinite, ungraspable conglomeration of all the critical views in the world's different traditions. As world poetics, it must cross over national and regional boundaries. As Earl Miner points out in a pioneer work, "to consider [poetics] of but one cultural tradition is to investigate only a single conceptual cosmos, however intricate, subtle, or rich that may be. To consider the other varieties of poetics is by definition to inquire into the full heterocosmic range, the full argument from design, of literature."[6] What matters for poetics is not so much comprehensiveness as relevance and representativeness: the poetics of world literature must be comparative, encompassing more than one national or regional

3. Qu Yuan, *Tian wen* [*Asking Heaven*], in Jin Kaicheng (ed.), *Chu ci xuanzhu* [*Selected Songs of Chu with Annotations*] (Beijing: Beijing chubanshe, 1980), p. 59. For an English translation, see Qu Yuan et al., *The Songs of the South: An Ancient Chinese Anthology of Poems by Qu Yuan and Other Poets*, trans. David Hawkes (Harmondsworth, UK: Penguin, 1985).

4. David Damrosch, *What Is World Literature?* p. 4.

5. Ibid., p. 5.

6. Earl Miner, *Comparative Poetics: An Intercultural Essay on Theories of Literature* (Princeton, NJ: Princeton University Press, 1990), p. 7.

tradition, and should lead us to a better understanding of world literature with depth and appreciation. It is an open concept expandable to accommodate new examples, a poetics that develops as the very notion of world literature does.

From the comparative and global perspective, then, it is worth noting that despite its central importance in the Western critical tradition, Aristotle's *Poetics*, as Stephen Halliwell reminds us, "never became at all readily available or widely known" in ancient or medieval Europe.[7] For Europe, the *Poetics* of the Stagirite was a "rediscovery" during the Renaissance in the late sixteenth century. When it was lost in Europe, however, the *Poetics* was studied by Arabic scholars, notably Abū al-Walīd Muhammad Ibn Ahmad Ibn Rushd (1126–1198), known in the West as Averroes. His commentary on the *Poetics* offers an opportunity to open up Aristotle's work to other, rather different traditions. For instance, Aristotle makes this distinction between tragedy and comedy that "the latter tends to represent people inferior, the former superior, to existing humans."[8] In his commentary, Averroes renders these two terms as "satire" for discouraging vices and "eulogy" for encouraging virtues. "Since every comparison and narrative representation is concerned only with the noble and the base," says Averroes, "it is clear that in comparison and narrative representation only praise and blame are sought."[9] To substitute "satire and eulogy" for Aristotle's "comedy and tragedy" may seem a moralistic misreading, but that is linked, as Charles Butterworth explains, to Averroes's "understanding that poetry focuses either on praise or on blame," which "derives more from the rank he ascribes to poetry in the hierarchy of knowledge than from his misapprehension of what Aristotle means by tragedy and comedy."[10] Averroes may have overemphasized the pedagogic and moral functions of tragic and comic drama, but that only shows that poetry plays quite different roles in different cultures and societies.

By an intriguing coincidence, "praise" and "blame" are exactly the two functions Confucian commentators assigned to poetry in ancient China, particularly in the commentaries on the *Book of Poetry*. To each poem in that ancient anthology, the commentator would attach a "preface" to specify whether that poem is meant to "praise" the moral influence of ancient sage kings or

---

7. Stephen Halliwell, "Aristotle's poetics," in George A. Kennedy (ed.), *The Cambridge History of Literary Criticism*, vol. 1, *Classical Criticism* (Cambridge: Cambridge University Press, 1989), p. 149.

8. Aristotle, *Poetics* 48a, ed. and trans. Stephen Halliwell, in Aristotle, *Poetics*, Longinus, *On the Sublime*, and Demetrius, *On Style* (Cambridge, MA: Harvard University Press, 1995), p. 35.

9. Averroes, *Averroes' Middle Commentary on Aristotle's Poetics*, trans. Charles E. Butterworth (Princeton, NJ: Princeton University Press, 1986), p. 66.

10. Ibid., pp. 13–14.

to "blame" the decadence of a morally fallen state under a wicked ruler. With irony and satire as textual possibilities, "the same poem can offer either praise or blame, depending on how you take it," as Haun Saussy observes, "since the indeterminacy arises from the assumption that the poem may say something quite other than what it means, *if* it is a 'decadent' poem and *if* it blames while appearing to praise."[11] In many cases, particularly to love poems with erotic implications, such a moralistic hermeneutics of "praise" or "blame" imposes rather strained interpretations in total disregard of the literal sense. Let us just take one example, a short poem from the *Book of Poetry*, "Crafty Boy," which has these two stanzas:

O that crafty boy,
He does not talk with me.
All because of you,
It makes me unable to eat.

O that crafty boy,
He does not eat with me.
All because of you,
It makes me unable to rest.

In our "naive" reading, we may understand the poem as a lover's complaint, but the traditional "minor preface" guides the reader to a very different meaning: "The poem 'Crafty Boy' is a satire to blame Hu, who was unable to work with good aids and thus allowed a wicked minister to usurp power and prevail."[12] By putting the poem in a historical context, the Confucian commentator changes the way the speaker in the poem can be identified, and thus the poem can be read not as a young woman's complaint about her unrequited love, but as a loyal minister's remonstration with his lord, Count Zhao of Zheng, named Hu, that by alienating his loyal advisors, the Count was creating a disaster in his court. There is nothing in the text itself to support such a moral and political reading, but by a sort of historical contextualization, the Confucian commentator effectively changed the direction of reading and thus the meaning of the poem. Such interpretations may remind us of the rabbinic and Christian exegeses of

11. Haun Saussy, *The Problem of a Chinese Aesthetic* (Stanford, CA: Stanford University Press, 1993), p. 96.

12. *Mao shi zhengyi* [*The Correct Meaning of the Mao Text of the Book of Poetry*], in Ruan Yuan (ed.), *Shisan jing zhushu* [*The Thirteen Classics with Annotations*], 1:342.

the "Song of Songs" and can only be called allegorical, which operate, as I have argued elsewhere, "to displace the controversial textual elements with ideologically acceptable alternatives, and to change the genre of the text from a poem about love to a canonical text about moral virtue or spiritual truth."[13] As an interpretive method, allegorical interpretation first arose in the sixth century BCE with philosophical readings of Homer, and was later adopted by Philo of Alexandria and Christian exegetes to interpret the Bible. By arguing that the Homeric or the scriptural text, or the text of a poem in the Confucian classic, means something different from what it literally says, allegorical interpretation mainly serves to justify the canonicity of texts that may otherwise be charged of untruth or immorality. Why allegorize? How does allegorical interpretation come about? What implications does it have for the reading of literature? These are the type of questions we should ask in the poetics of world literature.

One major critical question concerns the origin of poetry. Aristotle sees poetry as arising naturally from the human instinct of mimesis, which "distinguishes them from other animals: man is the most mimetic of all, and it is through mimesis that he develops his earliest understanding."[14] Poetry as an art of mimesis can be analyzed in logical terms, but an earlier concept of poetic inspiration emphasizes the irrational, even "mad," and certainly unconscious dimensions of poetic creation. Plato claims that poets cannot explain their own works because "it was not wisdom that enabled them to write their poetry, but a kind of instinct or inspiration, such as you find in seers and prophets."[15] He portrays the poet as "a light and winged thing, and holy, and never able to compose until he has become inspired, and is beside himself and reason is no longer in him."[16] He also mentions the prophetess at Delphi and the priestesses at Dodona, and admits that "the greatest blessings come by way of madness, indeed of madness that is heaven-sent."[17] Obviously, Plato recognizes the mysterious side of artistic creation that cannot be fully explained in logical terms, though as a philosopher, he certainly prefers the logical and the rational to the poetic, the irrationally inspired.

The ideas of inspiration and unconscious creation exist in many cultures, and they exist, for example, in Sanskrit poetics of ancient India, where poetry

13. Zhang Longxi, *Allegoresis: Reading Canonical Literature East and West* (Ithaca, NY: Cornell University Press, 2005), p. 110.

14. Aristotle, *Poetics* 48b, p. 37.

15. Plato, *Socrates' Defense (Apology)* 22c, trans. Hugh Tredennick, in *The Collected Dialogues*, p. 8.

16. Plato, *Ion* 534b, trans. Lane Cooper, ibid., p. 220.

17. Plato, *Phaedrus* 244a, trans. R. Hackforth, ibid., p. 491.

was thought to come spontaneously, as "the outpouring of the intense *emotion with the ease and spontaneity of water* overflowing a jar."[18] Inspiration, says Rajendran, was thought to be "a phenomenon of unpredictable occurrence," and critics such as the ninth-century Ānandavardhana held that "when the poet is rapt in contemplation, his imagination is flooded by genuine poetic figures without the least amount of conscious effort."[19] The inspirational idea locates the origin of poetry in the poet's subjective condition rather than the imitation of an external action, while the ancient Chinese *Book of Documents* presents yet another alternative that "poetry speaks of one's intent, and song prolongs the spoken words." Emperor Shun had just ordered his minister Kui to teach the royal princes poetry and music, and when Kui struck the stone instruments and poetry was chanted in total harmony, "gods and men were at peace," and "all the hundred animals danced in accordance."[20] This almost immediately calls to our mind the Greek myth of Orpheus, whose powerful song, as Pierre Somville puts it, "capable of charming all the realms of the living, from craggy rocks to the wildest beasts, suffices to ensure the cohesiveness of the cosmos and universal harmony."[21] The Orphic myth reveals a pre-Socratic notion of art before the separation of language from music and dance. "Myth, language and art," says Ernst Cassirer, "begin as a concrete, undivided unity, which is only gradually resolved into a triad of independent modes of spiritual creativity."[22] This is verified by both the Chinese and the Greek myths, and in discussions of world poetics, we may rethink such basic questions as the relationship between speech and music, the oral origin of earliest poetry, the connection of early drama with religious rituals and with music and dance in theatrical performance.

These connections are made very clear in the "Great Preface" to the *Book of Poetry* in ancient China (second century BCE), where poetry is the manifestation of one's intent and closely related to singing and dancing as expressions of one's emotions:

18. C. Rajendran, *Studies in Comparative Poetics* (Delhi: New Bharatiya Book Co., 2001), p. 11.

19. Ibid., p. 10.

20. *Shangshu zhengyi* [*The Correct Meaning of the Book of Documents*], in Ruan Yuan (ed.). *Shisan jing zhushu* [*The Thirteen Classics with Annotations*], 1:130.

21. Pierre Somville, "Poetics," trans. Catherine Porter and Dominique Jouhaud, in Jacques Brunschwig and Geoffrey E. R. Lloyd (eds.), *The Greek Pursuit of Knowledge* (Cambridge, MA: Harvard University Press, 2003), p. 303.

22. Ernst Cassirer, *Language and Myth*, trans. Susanne K. Langer (New York: Dover Publications, 1953), p. 98.

> Poetry is where one's intent goes. In the mind, it is intent, and coming out in words, it becomes poetry. Emotions are stirred within and are manifested in the form of words. When words alone are not enough, one heaves a sigh. When sighing is not enough, one sings out. When singing out is not enough, without knowing it, one waves one's hands and stamps one's feet in dancing.[23]

In such an understanding, poetry does not arise from imitation of an external action, but issues forth as the expression of one's inner thoughts and emotions, as articulation rather than imitation. The term "intent" (*zhi*) can be understood in different ways, as James J. Y. Liu notes, "those critics who understood it as 'heart's wish' or 'emotional purport' developing expressive theories and those who understood it as 'mind's intent' or 'moral purpose' often combining the expressive concept with the pragmatic."[24] In another important work of Chinese criticism, Liu Xie (465?–522) proposes yet another origin of literature when he claims that *wen* or literature was "born together with heaven and earth."[25] Some have interpreted this as presenting a natural or cosmological origin of literature, but this should be better understood as the critic's strategy to bestow on literature the borrowed authority of nature or the entire universe. To the question of the origin of poetry, then, we have several answers from different perspectives, each revealing a different dimension of poetry as a creative art.

Art as the inspired creation of poetic genius is quite common in different literary traditions. In Sanskrit poetics, genius is the result of good dharma accumulated in previous life circles. As the seventh-century critic Dandin puts it, "*Kaviprathibhā*, the poetic genius is a miraculous faculty inherited from the previous birth."[26] Genius is indeed a natural and inborn talent, without which artistic creation is impossible. Even the neo-classicist Boileau warns the would-be poet at the beginning of *L'Art poétique* that if he does not feel heaven's mysterious influence and was not born under the star of a poet's genius, he will never be good at writing poetry: "*S'il ne sent point du Ciel l'influence secrète, / Si son astre en naissant ne l'a formé poète, / Dans son génie étroit il est toujours captif; / Pour lui Phébus est sourd, et Pégase est*

23. *Mao shi zhengyi* [*The Correct Meaning of the Mao Text of the Book of Poetry*], in Ruan Yuan (ed.), *Shisan jing zhushu* [*The Thirteen Classics with Annotations*], 1:269–70.

24. James J. Y. Liu, *Chinese Theories of Literature* (Chicago: University of Chicago Press, 1975), p. 70.

25. Liu Xie, *Wenxin diaolong zhu* [*The Literary Mind or the Carving of Dragons with Annotations*], 1:1.

26. Rajendran, *Studies in Comparative Poetics*, p. 10.

rétif."[27] The Platonic idea of inspiration became crucial for the concept of genius in nineteenth-century romantic literature as well as in post-Kantian aesthetics. Kant himself considers poetry as the highest of arts, which "owes its origin almost entirely to genius and is least open to guidance by precept or examples."[28] For Kant, however, what is essential in aesthetic judgment is taste, not genius, and in case the two are in conflict and one must be sacrificed, "then it should rather be on the side of genius."[29] In post-Kantian aesthetics, as H. G. Gadamer explains, "the Kantian ideas of taste and genius completely traded places. Genius had to become the more comprehensive concept and, contrariwise, the phenomenon of taste had to be devalued."[30] From Friedrich von Schelling to Sigmund Freud, the individual came to be the focus of contemplation, and art and the unconscious became increasingly linked to each other in aesthetics and psychoanalysis, in which poetry or art in general was understood either as the unconscious creation of genius or as the sublimation of an unfulfilled wish or a repressed desire.

In literary creation, however, any emphasis on the unconscious must be balanced by conscious effort, and this is acknowledged almost without exception in all critical traditions. The nineteenth-century romantic idea of the unconscious creation of genius led to the rise of hermeneutics as an art of interpretation to bring the unconscious creation to the level of conscious understanding, hence Friedrich Schleiermacher's famous definition of the hermeneutic task as "to understand the text at first as well as and then even better than its author."[31] The creative, inspirational, and mysterious dimension needs to be supplemented by the critical, logical, and interpretive dimension. Poetic genius must be supplemented by learning and hard work. Thus we may understand why Yan Yu (1192?–1245?), an influential critic in China of the Song dynasty, would make the following statement that would otherwise sound preposterous: "Poetry needs a different kind of talent and has nothing to do with books; it has a different kind of interest and has nothing to do with reasoning. Yet one cannot become an accomplished poet without reading many

27. Nicolas Boileau, *L'Art poétique* (Paris: Bordas, 1963), p. 47.

28. Immanuel Kant, *Critique of Judgment*, trans. Wener S. Pluhar (Indianapolis, IN: Hackett, 1987), p. 196.

29. Ibid., p. 188.

30. Gadamer, *Truth and Method*, p. 56.

31. Friedrich Schleiermacher, *Hermeneutics: The Handwritten Manuscripts*, trans. James Duke and Jack Forstman (Missoula, MT: Scholars Press, 1977), p. 112.

books and doing lots of reasoning."[32] Here the two sides, genius and learning, are equally important for poetic creativity.

The natural gift of a poetic genius, often symbolized by the mythological Pegasus, always needs grooming, i.e., diligent study and learning, in order to bring out its full potential to real power. In *An Essay on Criticism*, Alexander Pope tells the young poet: "First follow Nature, and your judgment frame / By her just standard, which is still the same."[33] But later he gives a quite different advice through the example of Virgil: "But when t'examine every part he came, / Nature and Homer were, he found, the same"; so he concludes: "Learn hence for ancient rules a just esteem; / To copy nature is to copy them."[34] Here again, the advice is to imitate nature with one's inborn talent, but also to learn from the exemplary works of one's predecessors. Genius and tradition, natural giftedness and hard work, spontaneity and careful planning, all these are necessary for an accomplished poet and a successful work of literature.

Genius is an individual talent, and it needs to be balanced by the richness of a literary tradition. When T. S. Eliot declares in "Tradition and the Individual Talent" that "No poet, no artist of any art, has his complete meaning alone. His significance, his appreciation is the appreciation of his relation to the dead poets and artists," the romantic concept of the individual is obviously devalued in modernist poetics.[35] Insofar as literature has its own path to follow in development, literary forms, exemplary works, and generic conventions become extremely important. "Poetry can only be made out of other poems; novels out of other novels," as Northrop Frye puts it. "Literature shapes itself, and is not shaped externally: the *forms* of literature can no more exist outside literature than the forms of sonata and fugue and rondo can exist outside music."[36] The emphasis further shifted from individual talent to language and literary conventions as a system in modern literary theory. As Jonathan Culler argues, "conventions are the constituents of the institution of literature," in which a poem is not autonomous and self-complete, but "an utterance that has meaning only with respect to a system of conventions which the reader

32. Yan Yu, *Canlang shihua jiaoshi* [*Canlang's Remarks on Poetry with Annotations*], ed. Guo Shaoyu (Beijing: Renmin wenxue, 1983), p. 26.

33. Alexander Pope, *An Essay on Criticism*, ll. 68–69, *Selected Poetry and Prose*, 2nd ed., ed. William K. Wimsatt (New York: Holt, Rinehart and Winston, 1972), p. 69.

34. Pope, *An Essay on Criticism*, ll. 134–35, 139–40, ibid., p. 71.

35. T. S. Eliot, "Tradition and the Individual Talent," *Selected Prose of T. S. Eliot*, ed. Frank Kermode (New York: Harcourt Brace Jovanovich, 1975), p. 38.

36. Northrop Frye, *Anatomy of Criticism: Four Essays* (Princeton, NJ: Princeton University Press, 1957), p. 97.

has assimilated."[37] Literature is here seen as almost an impersonal institution, but it is of course also the collected body of works by individual authors. How to balance the genius and tradition, the unique quality of individual talent and the exemplariness of the classics, all these are again important questions in world poetics.

As critical analysis of literature, poetics necessarily concerns itself with the literary language and the components of the literary work. In *Poetics*, Aristotle analyzes six elements of the tragic drama—"plot, character, diction, thought, spectacle, and lyric poetry."[38] Much of traditional Indian literature, as Barbara Miller says, "is characterized by a preoccupation with the nature of language." The very name of Sanskrit means "put together, codified, classified."[39] Sheldon Pollock also notes that Sanskrit is an elevated language " 'put together' by means of phonological and morphological transformations."[40] Sanskrit poetics makes an important contribution in the notion of *vakrokti* or oblique, indirect language as essential to poetry. "Indian thinking on poetry, which is largely centered around language," says R. S. Pathak, "regards poetry primarily as a linguistic organization, and, according to it, the language of poetry is *vakrokti* par excellence."[41] The Indian idea of oblique, indirect, or suggestive language has also some significant influence in traditional Chinese poetics. Yan Yu, a twelfth-century critic mentioned before, whose *Canlang's Remarks on Poetry* is famous for introducing the Buddhist term of Chan into the critical discourse on poetry, was instrumental in making the idea of poetic suggestiveness systematic and influential in traditional Chinese criticism. The best kind of poetry, he argues, should be "like music in the air, color in the features, the moon reflected in water, an image in the mirror, with meaning reaching out to infinitude when words have come to an end."[42] Jiang Kui (1155?–1221), Yan Yu's contemporary and a fine poet, also remarks that "language is valuable for its implicitness," and quotes the great poet Su Shi as saying that "the

37. Jonathan Culler, *Structuralist Poetics: Structuralism, Linguistics and the Study of Literature* (London: Routledge & Kegan Paul, 1975), p. 116.

38. Aristotle, *Poetics* 50a, p. 49.

39. Barbara Stoler Miller, "The Imaginative Universe of Indian Literature," in B. S. Miller (ed.), *Masterworks of Asian Literature in Comparative Perspective: A Guide for Teaching* (Armonk, NY: M. E. Sharpe, 1994), p. 5.

40. Sheldon Pollock, "Sanskrit Literary Culture from the Inside Out," in S. Pollock (ed.), *Literary Cultures in History: Reconstructions from South Asia* (Berkeley: University of California Press, 2003), p. 62.

41. R. S. Pathak, *Comparative Poetics* (New Delhi: Creative Books, 1998), p. 99.

42. Yan Yu, *Canlang shihua jiaoshi* [*Canlang's Remarks on Poetry with Annotations*], p. 26.

word that has an end but an endless meaning is the supreme word."[43] Qian Zhongshu argues that such an aesthetic sense of suggestiveness is important in both painting and poetry, for "in portraying a scene in painting, there is no need to attend to all the minute details, and in writing about feelings and events in poetry, there is no need to describe everything exhaustively, but some room should be left for the audience to savor it, to contemplate on what is not depicted from what is depicted, and recognize what is unsaid from what is said." Qian further observes that "in speaking of poetry, the ancient Indians also had a school with emphasis on 'tone' (*dhvani*, sound, echo, tone), and what is 'tone' is *vyaṅgya*, or suggested sense."[44] Questions of poetic language and its use are certainly essential for the poetics of world literature, and the ways poets use suggestive, indirect language to express what is more than words can express certainly merit careful discussion.

Poetry and drama have close relations in very early time. Just as Aristotle's *Poetics* makes a great contribution to the study of tragic drama, the earliest treatise in Sanskrit poetics, Bharatamuni's *Nāṭyaśāstra* (ca. second century BCE), also offers a comprehensive discussion of the art of drama in terms of taste (*rasa*), emotion (*bhāva*), language, and bodily gestures that give expression to various emotions. Sanskrit drama is highly stylized, as Bharatamuni describes eight kinds of taste or emotions symbolically represented in eight colors and related to eight deities: "love is purple, buffoonery white, mercy gray, violence red, bravery orange, fear black, disgust blue, and surprise yellow."[45] In Sanskrit drama as in traditional Chinese theatre and some other traditions, it is common to use painted masks to symbolize emotions or characters by various colors. Compared with Greek tragedies, Sanskrit plays and, for that matter, traditional Chinese plays, often close with happy endings to satisfy the moral sense of poetic justice. Thus, whether there is tragedy in Indian or Chinese drama becomes an often asked question. This can be explored first by looking at Aristotle's opinion about the ending of tragedies. At one point (53a), Aristotle seems to prefer tragedies that "end in adversity," but in another place (54a), he considers the dramatic action "best" in which "when the person is on the point of unwittingly committing something irremediable, but recognises it before doing so."[46] Aristotle does not seem to have a decisive opinion as to whether

43. Jiang Kui, *Baishi daoren shishuo* [*The White-Stone Taoist's Discourse on Poetry*], in He Wenhuan (1732–1809) (ed.), *Lidai shihua* [*Remarks on Poetry from Various Dynasties*], 2 vols. (Beijing: Zhonghua, 1981): 2:681.

44. Qian Zhongshu, *Gui zhui bian* [*Limited Views*], pp. 1358–59.

45. Huang Baosheng, *Yindu gudian shixue* [*Classical Poetics of India*] (Beijing: Peking University Press, 1999), p. 41.

46. Aristotle, *Poetics* 53a, 54a, pp. 73, 77.

tragedy should end in sorrow or pain, even though it usually does, and Greek tragedies, unlike later, for example, Shakespearean tragedies, do not necessarily end in death or even disaster (e.g., Sophocles' Oedipus or Aeschylus's Orestes).

Related to this—and important to any consideration of justice—is Aristotle's idea that a tragic hero is someone "who falls into adversity not through evil and depravity, but through some kind of error."[47] Aristotle's original for "error" is *hamartia*, which many nineteenth-century critics understood as a tragic flaw or moral weakness, and thus the tragedy became a sort of just punishment. Georg Gottfried Gervinus, for example, tried to ferret out the moral weaknesses of Shakespearean tragic heroes and found them somehow deserving their fate because, says Gervinus, "if poetry does not exhibit the rule of moral justice, it degrades itself to a lower position than that of genuine history."[48] Such moralism is rejected by most modern critics, who consider *hamartia*, as Frye remarks, "not necessarily wrongdoing, much less moral weakness: it may be simply a matter of being a strong character in an exposed position."[49] Frye brings up a striking image: "Tragic heroes are so much the highest points in their human landscape that they seem the inevitable conductors of the power about them, great trees more likely to be struck by lightning than a clump of grass."[50] The image certainly alludes to the ancient fable about the oak tree struck down in the thunderstorm, but the bending reed survived unbroken. Interestingly, that image also appears in classical Chinese literature. Cao Zhi (192–232) wrote in a poem: "Tall trees wail in the strong wind, / The sea casts off the rising waves."[51] Li Kang, a writer of the same Three Kingdoms period, wrote in his *Treatise on Fate* that "the tree taller than the woods, the wind will break it off; the mound jutting out from the bank, the current will rush against it; and the man nobler than the average, the multitude will traduce him." Qian Zhongshu compares these words with many other texts, including La Fontaine's version of the fable, in which the reed says: "I bend and do not break (*Je plie et ne romps pas*)," and a Chinese proverb that "big trees call forth big wind."[52] If the quintessential tragic sense is the sense of a high and

47. Aristotle, *Poetics* 53a, p. 71.

48. Georg Gottfried Gervinus, *Shakespeare Commentaries*, 2 vols., trans. F. E. Bunnett (London: Smith Elder, 1863), 1:28.

49. Frye, *Anatomy of Criticism*, p. 38.

50. Ibid., p. 207.

51. Cao Zhi, "Song of the Yellow Bird in the Wild Fields," in Yu Guanying (ed.), *San Cao shi xuan* [*Selected Poems of the Three Cao's*] (Beijing: Writers Press, 1956), p. 27.

52. Qian Zhongshu, *Gui zhui bian* [*Limited Views*], p. 1082.

exposed position, where a noble hero has no choice but to bear the brunt in a clash of forces, then, such a sense can be said to permeate not only plays, but numerous poems in classical Chinese literature, even though the general tone of the Chinese plays, and particularly the endings, are different from a typical tragedy in the Greek or European tradition. It is perhaps not so much tragedy as a form of drama, but the tragic sense, i.e., a sense of the irresistible and incomprehensible fate, the unpredictable course of things and events, and the helplessness of men and women caught in an absurd human condition, that seems to be common in the world's various literary traditions.

Such critical issues are best explored comparatively in the poetics of world literature, for the global perspective will allow us to arrive at more adequate understanding than is possible within the limits of a national or regional literary tradition. Since George Lakoff and Mark Johnson's *Metaphors We Live By* (1980), for example, the cognitive approach to the study of metaphor, language, and literature has developed into a new field of "cognitive poetics," which, as Peter Stockwell defines it, is all about "the study of literary reading."[53] If such new approaches can develop beyond the Western boundary and be tested in the wider sphere of world literature, much is to be gained. World literature as a concept and as a body of literary works is still growing, and so is world poetics, which promises to provide us with critical perspectives more expansive than ever before and therefore the prospect of greater knowledge and deeper insights in literary theory and literary criticism.

53. Peter Stockwell, *Cognitive Poetics: An Introduction* (London: Routledge, 2002), p. 165.

10

The Changing Concept of World Literature

Most discussions of world literature mention, at some point or other, the German term *Weltliteratur* and trace the origin of the concept to Johann Wolfgang von Goethe. Though Goethe was not the first to use that term in German, given his great reputation and influence on the European cultural scene in the late eighteenth and the early nineteenth centuries, as John Pizer remarks, "it is Goethe to whom credit must be given for creating the paradigm that became a significant, widely debated element in critical and pedagogical literary discourse."[1] Pizer helpfully situates Goethe's concept in its historical context, in which Germany was not politically unified and all European nations, after the divisive Napoleonic Wars, were badly in need of mutual understanding and peaceful coexistence. In some sense, that was a situation not so very different from our world today, in which globalizing tendencies in economics, communication, and scientific and technological development coexist with many communities' intensifying grasp on ethnic or national identities, even the resurgence of a tenacious tribalism.

Theoretically speaking, the tension between two opposite forces has always resided in *Weltliteratur* as a concept, which stands poised between the local and the global, national specificities and cosmopolitan claims to literary universality. With regard to Goethe's own understanding, some have questioned whether his idea of *Weltliteratur* was actually limited to European literature only, or whether his cosmopolitan concept was contradictory to his emphasis on the important role Germans should play in its formation. To tip the balance of Goethe's concept to the side of German nationalism or Eurocentrism, however, not only ignores Goethe's own positive take on *Weltliteratur*, but

1. John Pizer, "Johann Wolfgang von Goethe: Origins and relevance of *Weltliteratur*," in D'haen, Damrosch and Kadir (eds.), *The Routledge Companion to World Literature*, p. 3.

is simply anachronistic and wrong. First of all, for Goethe, what was German was not national, but fragmented and divergent, tied together only by a shared language; and second, what was national was not opposed to what he thought to be universal. "It is evident that the best poets and writers of all nations have for some time been concentrating their efforts on universal human concerns," wrote Goethe in 1828 when commenting on Thomas Carlyle's *German Romance*, but "we increasingly see a writer's national and individual characteristics illuminated from within by these universal concerns."[2] In a letter to Count Stolberg, dated June 11, 1827, Goethe clearly stated that "Poetry is cosmopolitan, and the more interesting the more it shows its nationality."[3]

Interestingly, as Pizer shows in his discussion of the idea of world literature, it takes a critic from Africa, the Moroccan-born Germanist Fawzi Boubia, to recognize this and "establish the genuinely global dimensions of Goethe's Weltliteratur postulations and foreground their seminal and precocious embrace of alterity in the hermeneutic dialogue among the world's literatures."[4] In fact, almost thirty years ago, Claudio Guillén already said as much when he urged us to "remember that Goethe started from the existence of some national literatures—thus making possible a dialogue between the local and the universal, between the one and the many, a dialogue that from that day to this has continued to breathe life into the best comparative studies."[5] Earlier still, René Etiemble argued in 1974, that Goethe's "elevation of *Weltliteratur* implicitly condemns German nationalism and, with it, all nationalism."[6] The suspicion of Eurocentrism reveals a sensibility of our own time, but to Goethe's mind, the either/or dichotomy between the local and the global, or the national and the universal, would probably be quite alien. Great works of literature always take root in particular linguistic, cultural, and national traditions, but they are at the same time capable of transcending the limitations of the local and the parochial to reach readers beyond the boundaries of their provenance, either in original forms or in successful translations.

More importantly, as Boubia points out, it is in his conversation with Johann Peter Eckermann that "Goethe first developed his Weltliteratur paradigm

2. Johann Wolfgang von Goethe, *Essays on Art and Literature*, ed. John Gearey, trans. Ellen von Nardroff and Ernest H. Nardroff (Princeton, NJ: Princeton University Press, 1994), p. 207.

3. Ibid., p. 208.

4. John Pizer, *The Idea of World Literature* (Baton Rouge: Louisiana State University Press, 2006). p. 25.

5. Claudio Guillén, *The Challenge of Comparative Literature*, trans. Cola Franzen (Cambridge, MA: Harvard University Press, 1993), pp. 39–40.

6. René Etiemble, "Faut-il réviser la notion de *Weltliteratur*?" in *Essais de littérature (vraiment) générale*, 3rd ed. (Paris: Gallimard, 1974), p. 17.

in the context of reflecting on poetic production in Asia, and in considering that China in particular enjoyed a flourishing literary culture when Europeans were still wandering about in the forests."[7] Indeed, it was in talking about his reading of a Chinese novel in translation that Goethe made the famous announcement that "poetry is the universal possession of mankind. . . . National literature is now rather an unmeaning term; the epoch of world literature is at hand, and every one must strive to hasten its approach."[8] It is true that Goethe argued for returning to the ancient Greeks for patterns of European literature, but his concept of *Weltliteratur* did open up to non-Western literatures, and *that* constitutes the paradigmatic sense which renders Goethe's concept more relevant to our time than to his own. As Richard Meyer argued in 1900, Goethe's concept was "future-oriented," a concept that "had just dawned" in his time.[9] It is in our time, when literary scholars everywhere have a much stronger sense of the global connectedness of nations and peoples, a much greater need to open one's eyes beyond the tunnel vision of one's own group or community, and a much more readiness to embrace alterity beyond one's linguistic and cultural comfort zones, that Goethe's concept of *Weltliteratur* may have found a better condition than ever before to make a real impact on the ways we think globally about literature, culture, tradition, and ultimately about the world in which we live.

Goethe talked about *Weltliteratur* in the 1820s, and the term was picked up again by Karl Marx and Friedrich Engels in the *Communist Manifesto* of 1848, where, in describing the global tendencies propelled by the fast growth of world capitalism, they saw world literature as a cultural phenomenon inevitably superseding national literatures. If Goethe's vision was a humanistic one, Marx conceptualized world literature as part of a global tendency closely related with economic and political developments at the time. Goethe's and Marx's concepts of world literature have been understood differently by different scholars. "That phrase 'world literature,' and the vision that the creation of such a thing was desirable," says Aijid Ahmad, "Marx had taken from his favorite poet, Goethe," even though Marx "associated the creation of 'world literature' not with the self-activity of a high-minded intelligentsia or as a mode of exchange among the principal classicisms, which is more or less what Goethe had in mind, but

7. Pizer, *The Idea of World Literature*, p. 26.

8. *Conversations of Goethe with Eckermann and Soret*, trans. John Oxenford, rev. ed. (London: George Bell & Sons, 1883), pp. 212–13.

9. Monika Schmitz-Emans, "Richard Meyer's Concept of World Literature," trans. Mark Schmitt, in D'haen et al. (eds.), *The Routledge Companion to World Literature*, p. 50.

as an objective process inherent in other kinds of globalisation where modes of cultural exchange follow closely upon patterns of political economy."[10] In Mads Thomsen's understanding, however, Goethe's notion of world literature was an "idealistic vision of the symphony of the masterpieces from different nations," while Marx's concept was a "more cynical vision of global distribution of books as commodities."[11]

Goethe and Marx surely conceived of *Weltliteratur* differently, but given Marx's conviction that history is an evolutionary process of progress, a Hegelian kind of development from a lower to a higher form, his remarks on capitalism and the bourgeois production of world literature are not as negative as some contemporary commentators would have us to believe. For Marx, it was only to the extent that capitalism was to be superseded by a yet higher stage of social and historical development, i.e., socialism and communism, that capitalism was negative—but negative in the Hegelian sense of *Aufhebung*, i.e., negating the limitations of capitalism but preserving all it would have achieved as a necessary stage of human history and social progress. For Marx, capitalism in its own right was better than the feudalist medieval society and definitely higher than the Asiatic mode of production, the agrarian societies in China and in Asia at large, which in his view represented a more primitive stage of social development. So when Marx declared the demise of national literatures, he was very much in agreement with Goethe in looking at *Weltliteratur* as a new and progressive phenomenon: "National one-sidedness and narrow-mindedness become more and more impossible, and from the numerous national and local literatures there arises a world literature."[12] This famous statement from the *Communist Manifesto* is not at all a negative evaluation. On the contrary, Marx and Engels saw the globalizing tendency of world capitalism a necessary prerequisite condition for the socialist revolution, and hence the slogan, repeated later by all political publications in the Soviet Union and the other socialist countries: "Workers of all countries, unite!" The working class in their understanding was a global force of revolution, not bounded by national affiliations. The socialist movement was an international one, and the Communist International was based on that global idea. So in that sense, Marx's

10. Aijid Ahmad, "*The Communist Manifesto* and 'World Literature,'" *Social Scientist* 29:7–8 (Jul.–Aug. 2000): 13.

11. Mads Rosendahl Thomsen, *Mapping World Literature: International Canonization and Transnational Literatures* (London: Continuum, 2008), p. 13.

12. Karl Marx and Friedrich Engels, *The Communist Manifesto* (New York: The Seabury Press, 1967), pp. 136–37.

idea was not an antidote to Goethe's, though he understood world literature as the cultural aspect of the mode of production under global capitalism, rather than the humanistic appreciation of the major works of the world's different literary and cultural traditions.

Since Goethe's time, the concept of world literature has always been a somewhat flexible and changing idea, not a rigid fixation on a set of canonical works. There have been many changes and different understandings, and a number of questions become central to our rethinking of world literature at the present time. First, the scope or coverage of world literature must be significantly large. The importance of such cultural cartography is already prominent in Goethe's concept, for it was Persian poetry and a Chinese novel he read in translation that brought *Weltliteratur* to its global dimension. As a discipline, comparative literature also started out as an effort to break away from the constraints of national literatures and their attendant monolingual limitations, but in practice it remained largely a European operation. Franco Moretti puts it bluntly: "comparative literature has not lived up to" *Weltliteratur* as Goethe and Marx had in mind. "It's been a much more modest intellectual enterprise, fundamentally limited to Western Europe, and mostly revolving around the river Rhine (German philologists working on French literature)."[13] That was why Etiemble wanted to revisit Goethe's *Weltliteratur* as an alternative to comparative literature despite the latter's cosmopolitan intention and emphasis on polyglottism. "The time is over when the Hungarian savant Hugo von Meltzl, a disciple of Goethe and advocate of *Weltliteratur*, could still propose a *Dekaglottismus* as the languages of civilization: German, English, Spanish, Dutch, Hungarian, Icelandic, Italian, Portuguese, Swedish and French—to which he added Latin," says Etiemble, because outside these European languages, literatures in Sanskrit, Chinese, Japanese, Indian, Persian, and Arabic had produced masterpieces "when most of the literatures of the *Dekaglottismus* either did not exist, or were still in their infancy."[14]

13. Franco Moretti, "Conjectures on World Literature," *New Left Review* 1 (Jan.–Feb. 2000): 54.

14. Etiemble, *Essais de littérature (vraiment) générale*, p. 19. It is only fair to point out, however, that Meltzl was well aware of the problem of focusing purely on European literature, as he criticized August Koberstein for tracing the aubade to Wolfram von Eschenbach without knowing "the fact that Lieder of this type were sung eighteen centuries ago in China (as those contained in the *Shih Ching*) and are frequently found among the folksongs of modern peoples, for instance, the Hungarians." See Meltzl, "Present Tasks of Comparative Literature" (1877), in David Damrosch, Natalie Melas, and Mbongiseni Buthelezi (eds.), *The Princeton Sourcebook in Comparative Literature: From the European Enlightenment to the Global Present* (Princeton, NJ: Princeton University Press, 2009), p. 43.

Etiemble commented on a number of German and French anthologies and bibliographies of world literature and found them woefully ignorant of major works of non-Western literatures. Most of those early anthologies, as Sarah Lawall has observed, were predicated on the Darwinian theories of social and cultural evolution and "saw themselves as illustrating the rise of civilization to its current apogee in Western culture and transmitting the moral lessons of that rise."[15] The influential *Norton Anthology of World Literature* did not include more non-Western works until it came out in an "expanded" edition in 1995. Things have since changed dramatically, and the rise of world literature can be seen as coeval with changes in social, economic, and political spheres in an increasingly globalized world. By now we may assume that the "world" in world literature has to be truly global or, to borrow a term recently made popular, it should be planetary, in a geographical sense. That is to say, when discussing world literature, the sampling of literary works must cross over not only languages and cultures, but also regions and continents, beyond Eurocentrism or any other ethnocentrism.

The mere expansion of coverage, the conglomeration of different literatures, however, does not make a meaningful concept of world literature. The sheer quantity of works available makes it impossible for anyone to read even a small portion of the world's literatures, so world literature as a concept has to be a theoretical construct, rather than a mere juxtaposition of literatures as textual materials. As Moretti argues, simply reading "more" is not enough. "It has to be different. The *categories* have to be different." The solution he proposes is "distant reading," which "allows you to focus on units that are much smaller or much larger than the text: devices, themes, tropes—or genres and systems."[16] Many have responded to Moretti's theoretical model, but few have pointed out the similarity between the strategy of "distant reading" and Northrop Frye's archetypal criticism, which treats literature as a total structure or system rather than individual works randomly amalgamated together. Moretti's model, however, has a different political underpinning than Frye's. Drawing on Immanuel Wallerstein's "world-systems" theory and Fredric Jameson's "law of literary evolution," Moretti argues that the modern novel develops from European centers of metropolitan culture to non-European peripheries, "as a compromise between a western formal influence (usually French or English) and local materials."[17] Despite its remarkable explanatory power, the center-

15. Sarah Lawall, "The West and the Rest: Frames for World Literature," in David Damrosch (ed.), *Teaching World Literature* (New York: MLA, 2009), p. 21.

16. Moretti, "Conjectures on World Literature," pp. 55, 57.

17. Ibid., p. 58.

periphery model and, for that matter, the world-systems theory on which it depends, fail to recognize the resilience of local traditions that constitute crucial internal contexts, not just "local materials," for the development of the novel in the peripheries. In other words, the tension between the local and the global in the concept of world literature cannot be resolved by ignoring the local dimension, though as a *modern* form of literature, the novel in the peripheries is indeed under a heavy Western influence. In the case of the Chinese novel, for example, influential movers of the May Fourth new culture movement in the early twentieth century, radical iconoclastic figures like Lu Xun and Hu Shih, also looked to China's past in addition to the West. Lu Xun wrote one of the earliest histories of the classical Chinese fiction, and Hu Shih advocated the reexamination of China's classical tradition and revolutionized the study of the great eighteenth-century Chinese novel *Hong Lou Meng* (*Dream of the Red Chamber*, also known as *The Story of the Stone*), which remains a major influence on most modern Chinese writers.

Focusing on the modern form does create problems with implications not only of a historical, but also a theoretical nature. This is particularly evident in the case of Pascale Casanova's idea of the "world republic of letters." Describing the formation of the world's literary space "as the product of a historical process," she maintains that

> it appeared in Europe in the 16th century, France and England forming its oldest regions. It was consolidated and enlarged into central and eastern Europe during the 18th and especially the 19th centuries, propelled by Herderian national theory. It expanded throughout the 20th century, notably through the still-ongoing decolonization process: manifestos proclaiming the right to literary existence or independence continue to appear, often linked to movements for national self-determination.[18]

Such an account of the history of world literature is unabashedly Eurocentric and modernist, closely mapping on the European expansion in the colonialist era and the subsequent decolonization in the mid-twentieth century, but completely oblivious of the Hellenistic and Roman world and ignorant of the formation of literary constellations outside Europe, such as the Persian and the Ottoman empires, or the East Asian region with the Chinese written language and culture playing a pivotal role in pre-modern times. Casanova's Paris-centered model, as Alexander Beecroft remarks, "cannot account for the full range of

18. Pascale Casanova, "Literature as a World," *New Left Review* 31 (Jan.–Feb. 2005): 73–74.

literary production across all cultures and times. . . . Forms of literary circulation which predate French literary culture, or which exist outside it today, have no real place in Casanova's world-system."[19] Aamir Mufti also criticizes Casanova for missing the "philological revolution" in Oriental studies, when "non-Western textual traditions made their first entry *as literature*, sacred and secular, into the international literary space that had emerged in early modern times in Europe."[20] Because of such blind spots, Mufti continues, Casanova fails to see non-Western literatures in world literary space until the middle of the twentieth century, as a result of decolonization, when "such figures as Kateb Yacine, V. S. Naipaul, and Salman Rushdie and the psychology of *assimilation* into metropolitan languages and cultures typify the non-Western writer."[21] The formation of Casanova's world literary space thus looks like a process of radiation of European influence, and more specifically Parisian influence, onto the rest of the world, but it is important to realize that though Paris may have been the capital of the Western republic of letters at a certain period of time, such a mapping of world literary space is neither historically accurate nor theoretically productive. It may even smack of a kind of cultural narcissism known to be particularly strong in certain French intellectual circles.

The debate on the manifesto "*Pour une littérature-monde français*" is noteworthy in this regard, as it reveals the complex relationships of the French language and literature with colonialism and decolonization. Signed by 44 writers, mostly originated from outside France, and published in *Le Monde* on March 16, 2007, the manifesto announced "the end of 'francophone' literature—and the birth of a world literature in French."[22] It is an effort to destabilize the center and peripheries and calls for the equality of all writers writing in French, whether hexagonal or francophone. "With the center placed on an equal plane with other centers," the signatories conclude in an idealistic vein, "we're witnessing the birth of a new constellation, in which language freed from its exclusive pact with the nation, free from every other power hereafter but the powers of poetry and the imaginary, will have no other frontiers but those of the spirit."[23] As his response to the manifesto shows, the soon-to-be French President, Nicolas Sarkozy, began

19. Alexander Beecroft, "World Literature without a Hyphen: Towards a Typology of Literary Systems," *New Left Review* 54 (Nov.–Dec. 2008): 89.

20. Aamir Mufti, "Orientalism and the Institution of World Literatures," *Critical Inquiry* 36:3 (Spring 2010): 459.

21. Ibid., p. 460.

22. "Pour une 'littérature monde' en français," *Le Monde*, 19 Mars 2007.

23. Ibid.

his article in *Le Figaro* with the statement that "*La francophonie n'est pas morte.*"[24] He considers that francophonie is alive and well, a testimony to the influence of the French language from the center to the peripheries—a direct reversal of the direction celebrated in the manifesto in *Le Monde*. Yet Françoise Lionnet points out an irony in the fact that the manifesto, signed in Paris to destabilize the center in the very center itself, "reinforces by the same token the city's role as a site of cultural prestige that can grant distinction and visibility to writers in accordance to the regulatory principles of literary modernity with their well-established systems of coveted awards."[25]

Perhaps there is a yet deeper irony concerning another tension, briefly revealed in Sarkozy's defense of the francophone, namely, the rivalry between French and English as *lingua franca* for world literature. This seems to be an issue too embarrassingly sensitive to be discussed in much of the debate on the manifesto of *littérature-monde français*, but it leads toward what Casanova holds as the "primary characteristic of this world literary space," namely, "hierarchy and inequality."[26] Casanova's sober-minded, *realpolitik* view of the world literary space has the virtue of presenting the modern and contemporary world in a clear picture, not obscured by a sentimental moralism. "The unequal distribution of literary resources is fundamental to the structure of the entire world literary space, organized as it is around two poles."[27] For Casanova, the two poles are European metropolitan centers and non-European peripheries, but even within European centers, the distribution of cultural and symbolic capitals is likewise unequal, particularly between English and French competing for linguistic prestige. In a world that is increasingly globalized and also increasingly diversified, English has long evolved beyond England into a language widely used in social, economical, cultural, and all other aspects of contemporary life, and journals like *World Englishes* are published to discuss the legitimacy of diverse usages. The French language, in contrast, still retains its traditional prestige and centrality yet to be drastically diversified, and therefore the *littérature-monde* movement, as Dutton remarks, may be moving to "a new model that is potentially just as fraught with risk as francophonie."[28]

24. Nicolas Sarkozy, "Pour une francophonie vivante et populaire," *Le Figaro*, 22 Mars 2007.

25. Françoise Lionnet, "Universalism and francophonies," *International Journal of Francophone Studies* 12: 2&3 (2009): 206.

26. Casanova, "Literature as a World," p. 82.

27. Ibid., p. 83.

28. Jacqueline Dutton, "Francophonie and universality: the ideological challenges of *littérature-monde*," *International Journal of Francophone Studies* 12: 2&3 (2009): 429.

The question is: Is a world literature in French a real alternative to the center-periphery dichotomy with its dubious colonial implications?

The importance of translation as an affirmative force and not merely an unhappy necessity is certainly something new in the concept of world literature. In opening up to translations, world literature differs from comparative literature with its traditional disciplinary requirement of near-native proficiency in French, German, and Latin. Traditional elite comparative literature programs, as David Damrosch observes, "had a real distaste for translation."[29] Thomas Greene in his 1975 ACLA "Report on Standards" considered "the association of comparative literature with literatures in translation" as "the most disturbing" sign of the slackening of disciplinary rigor and standards. "Greene's critique hit home," says Damrosch. "No self-respecting program in his day could wish to be seen as the educational equivalent of the food court in 'the Mall of America.' "[30] Perhaps by pure serendipity, "the food court of a mall" is precisely the metaphor Stephen Owen used in his critique of "world poetry," which flattens out regional differences and offers different cuisines as national types, as representatives of food (or literature) that lack "distinct histories and distinct values."[31] As a Sinologist and specialist of classical Chinese poetry, Owen's critique a dozen years ago of the modern Chinese poet Bei Dao, who once wrote about democracy and oppression, proved to be misplaced and controversial, for he accused the Chinese poet of "using one's victimization for self-interest: in this case, to sell oneself abroad by what an international audience, hungry for political virtue, which is always in short supply, finds touching."[32] But when oppression and the struggle for democracy form part of the "distinct histories and distinct values" for the modern Chinese, Owen has no legitimate reason to dismiss these as inadmissible in modern Chinese poetry. In his essay reexamining the controversy of world poetry, however, Owen raises a pressing question about the "food court" of world literature, and articulates his worry about a non-Western poet writing for an international audience—which in practical terms means a European and American audience—under the "pressure for linguistic fungibility."[33] The question concerns both the authenticity of literary works,

29. David Damrosch in "Comparative Literature/World Literature: A Discussion with Gayatri Charkravorty Spivak and David Damrosch," *Comparative Literature Studies*, 48: 4 (2011): 458.

30. Ibid., p. 460.

31. Stephen Owen, "Stepping Forward and Back: Issues and Possibilities for 'World' Poetry," *Modern Philology* 100: 4 (May 2003): 535.

32. Stephen Owen, "The Anxiety of Global Influence: What Is World Poetry?" *New Republic* November 19, 1990, p. 29.

33. Owen, "Stepping Forward and Back: Issues and Possibilities for 'World' Poetry," p. 532.

particularly lyric poetry, deeply rooted in a particular language and a national tradition, and the ways in which these works may be understood beyond their historical and cultural contexts.

In a way, Owen's skepticism of poetry in translation may be related to what Gayatri Spivak emphasizes as "singularity," i.e., the need to "regionalize" a poet like Tagore in order to understand him in his specific linguistic and cultural background.[34] Spivak would certainly abhor the food court model of literary representation, and she is skeptical that students with special linguistic knowledge or cultural background in a multicultural class could speak of different literatures with any greater credibility than food court dishes could adequately represent different kinds of the world's cuisines. "Thinking of any international student as an authority on globality because of his/her identity is like thinking all Americans abroad are experts on Melville," says Spivak in a rare moment of absolute clarity out of her typically dense and difficult theoretical discourse.[35] But world literature is not taken hostage by translation or national literature specialists, and the idea is not to depend on translation with no knowledge of any foreign languages at all. In his response to Spivak, Damrosch proposes "a *sliding scale* of language study" as a solution, that is, "a near-native grasp of one language" plus "a range of competence in several others."[36]

The important step here is again to cross over the divide between European centers and non-European peripheries, and to acquire languages that are different not within one group, European, Asian, African, etc., but across linguistic groups. As world literature covers more than the usual ground in linguistic and cultural diversity beyond individual capacities, translation becomes necessary and extremely important, and the often debated issue of translatability brings the question of translation to a much deeper level than the usual kind of translation studies. As Susan Bassnett acknowledges, new and exciting ideas about translation are not coming from translation studies as such: "where we must turn today for the most innovative thinking about translation is to scholars who see themselves as comparatists, as postcolonialists, as world literature people."[37] The tension in the concept of world literature between the local and the global, the national and the universal, differences and affinities,

34. Gayatri Charkravorty Spivak in "Comparative Literature/World Literature: A Discussion with Gayatri Charkravorty Spivak and David Damrosch," p. 478.

35. Ibid., p. 467.

36. Damrosch, ibid., p. 461.

37. Susan Bassnett, "From Cultural Turn to Translational Turn: A Transnational Journey," in Cecilia Alvstad, Stefan Helgesson and David Watson (eds.), *Literature, Geography, Translation: Studies in World Writing* (Cambridge: Cambridge Scholars Publishing, 2011), p. 72.

pushes the discussion of translation to a level of conceptualization that involves fundamental issues of thinking and communication across vast linguistic and cultural boundaries, issues of the possibility and practice of cross-cultural understanding and communication. In that sense, world literature engages translation in much more complicated theoretical discussions than ever before.

From Goethe and Marx to Casanova, Moretti, and Damrosch, the concept of world literature has been theorized mostly in the context of Western literary studies. Today, in world literature's tendency to go beyond Eurocentrism and any other ethnocentrism, the question necessarily arises: Is world literature to expand not only its coverage or reading materials to a global dimension, but also its critical and theoretical horizon to embrace the entire world, beyond the great East-West divide? Revathi Krishnaswamy raised that question against "a widespread assumption that theory is the product of a uniquely Western philosophical tradition. From this perspective, the non-West may be a source of exotic cultural production but cannot be a site of theory."[38] He proposes the notion of "world literary knowledges" that "aims to go beyond inducting a few token non-Western greats into theory's hall of fame; rather, it asks us radically to re-vision the question of what counts as theory in the first place."[39] Drawing on India's rich literary and critical traditions not only of Sanskrit poetics, but also of Tamil/Dravidian linguistics and poetics, the popular multilingual *bhakti* or devotional literatures, and Dalit literatures of the lower castes, Krishnaswamy provides three examples of how literary knowledge may emerge to deal with theoretical questions in different ways and different formulations. It is in this connection that we may appreciate the different notions of world literature presented by Tagore and Zheng Zhengduo, the more recent contributions by Karen Thornber on East Asian literary relations, or Ronit Ricci on literary networks in the Arabic world; and also we may appreciate the works and critical insights provided by scholars like Qian Zhongshu from a truly global perspective. In considering world literature in theory, we need to build a level playing field where the West meets the East as equal contributors, and the poetics of world literature should be a set of questions that inquire into the nature of language and expression, meaning and understanding, interpretation and aesthetic values, the origin of poetry and literature, the relationship between art and nature, and so on and so forth. The ways in which these questions get asked and answered are surely different in different literary traditions, but it is

38. Revathi Krishnaswamy, "Toward World Literary Knowledges: Theory in the Age of Globalization," *Comparative Literature* 62: 4 (Fall 2010): 400.

39. Ibid., p. 401.

such basic questions and their answers that make up what literary theory is in world literature, with valuable insights richly elucidated by different examples and critical formulations.

Thus, theory has the tendency to travel, to move from one place to another so that linkages and comparisons can be made in "contrapuntal juxtaposition" of literary creations and cultural practices. Edward Said's classic essay on "Traveling Theory" has long pointed out the geopolitics in the transformations of literary theories in a globalized world that no longer conforms to the simple structure of European metropolitan centers and non-European peripheries. When theoretical concepts travel to a new cultural and political environment, Said argues, they will necessarily encounter resistance as "an inevitable part of acceptance."[40] Mechanical application of a theoretical notion in a new environment is thus always infertile; only adaptation and accommodation will bear fruits that are nurtured by the rich soil in which it has taken roots. In that sense, world literature will never be the same everywhere it is studied. As Lawall observes with regard to world literature anthologies, "it is unlikely that any global perspective can be truly decentered, providing equal representation and a neutral framework."[41] That is to say, world literature in practice is always localized, with different works selected for study and critical comment, different issues addressed in different cultural and theoretical perspectives and with different interests.

World literature is thus always a concept that changes in response to local needs and contexts. At the same time, the competiveness and highly selective nature of works that achieve a secure place within world literature yield a relatively stable set of canonical works from the world's different literary traditions. In that sense, world literature is also a productive way to go back to literature itself, a way to counter the moving away from literature in much of the discourse of literary theory and cultural studies in recent decades. The conceptual openness or flexibility of world literature, and the dynamic mix of new entries from previously neglected regions along with the ongoing relative stability of major literary works, constitute the strength and vitality of world literature as an exciting field with new possibilities for literary studies; and that may be the secret of the undeniable ascendance and success of world literature in our world today.

---

40. Edward Said, *The World, the Text, and the Critic* (Cambridge, MA: Harvard University Press, 1983), p. 227.

41. Sarah Lawall, "The West and the Rest: Frames for World Literature," in Damrosch (ed.), *Teaching World Literature*, p. 29.

Bibliography

Aaron, Daniel. "What Can You Learn from a Historical Novel?" *American Heritage* 43: 6 (Oct. 1992): 55–61.

———. *American Notes: Selected Essays*. Boston: Northeastern University Press, 1994.

Ahmad, Aijid. "*The Communist Manifesto* and 'World Literature.'" *Social Scientist* 29:7–8 (Jul.–Aug. 2000): 3–30.

Al-Azmeh, Aziz. *Islams and Modernities*, 3rd ed. London: Verso, 2009.

———. *The Times of History: Universal Topics in Islamic Historiography*. Budapest: Central European University Press, 2007.

Alvstad, Cecilia, Stefan Helgesson, and David Watson (eds.). *Literature, Geography, Translation: Studies in World Writing*. Cambridge: Cambridge Scholars Publishing, 2011.

Ankersmit, F. R. *Historical Representation*. Stanford: Stanford University Press, 2001.

Appiah, Kwame Anthony. *Cosmopolitanism: Ethics in a World of Strangers*. New York: W. W. Norton, 2006.

Apter, Emily. *The Translation Zone: A New Comparative Literature*. Princeton, NJ: Princeton University Press, 2006.

Aristotle. *Poetics*, trans. Richard Janko. Indianapolis: Hackett Publishing Co., 1987.

———. *Poetics*, ed. and trans. Stephen Halliwell, pp. 1–141 in Aristotle, *Poetics*, Longinus, *On the Sublime*, and Demetrius, *On Style*. The Loeb Classical Library 199. Cambridge, MA: Harvard University Press, 1995.

Augustine, St. *The City of God*, trans. Marcus Dods. New York: The Modern Library, 1993.

Averroes. *Averroes' Middle Commentary on Aristotle's Poetics*, trans. Charles E. Butterworth. Princeton, NJ: Princeton University Press, 1986.

Badiou, Alain. *Handbook of Inaesthetics*, trans. Alberto Toscano. Stanford, CA: Stanford University Press, 2005.

Baker-Smith, Dominic. *More's Utopia*. London: HarperCollins, 1991.

Bakhtin, Mikhail M. *Problems of Dostoevsky's Poetics*, ed. and trans. Caryl Emerson. Minneapolis: University of Minnesota Press, 1984.

———. *The Dialogic Imagination: Four Essays*, trans. Caryl Emerson and Michael Holquist. Austin: University of Texas Press, 1981.

Balzac, Honoré de. *Le Père Goriot*. Paris: Éditions Garniers Frères, 1961.

Barr, Michael D. *Cultural Politics and Asian Values: The Tepid War*. London: Routledge, 2002.

Baudet, Henri. *Paradise on Earth: Some Thoughts on European Images of Non-European Man*, trans. Elizabeth Wenthold. Middletown, CT: Wesleyan University Press, 1988.

Beecroft, Alexander. "World Literature without a Hyphen: Towards a Typology of Literary Systems." *New Left Review* 54 (Nov.–Dec. 2008): 87–100.

Benjamin, Walter. *Illuminations*, trans. Harry Zohn. Glasgow: Fontana, 1973.

Bennett, Enoch Arnold. *The Grim Smile of the Five Towns*. London: Penguin, 1946.

Berman, Antoine. *The Experience of the Foreign: Culture and Translation in Romantic Germany*, trans. S. Heyvaert. Albany: State University of New York Press, 1992.

Bermann, Sandra, and Michael Wood (eds.). *Nation, Language, and the Ethics of Translation*. Princeton: Princeton University Press, 2005.

Bloom, Harold (ed.). *Sophocles' Oedipus Plays: Oedipus the King, Oedipus at Colonus, & Antigone*. Broomall, PA: Chelsea House Publishers, 1999.

Boileau, Nicolas. *L'Art poétique*. Paris: Bordas, 1963.

Borges, Jorge Luis. *Labyrinths: Selected Stories and Other Writings*, eds. Donald A. Yates and James E. Irby. New York: The Modern Library, 1983.

Boynton, Percy H. (ed.). *American Poetry*. New York: Charles Scribner's Sons, 1918.

Brunschwig, Jacques, and Geoffrey E. R. Lloyd (eds.). *The Greek Pursuit of Knowledge*. Cambridge, MA: Harvard University Press, 2003.

Buck, David D. "Forum on Universalism and Relativism in Asian Studies: Editor's Introduction." *The Journal of Asian Studies* 50:1 (Feb. 1991): 29–34.

Carr, E. H. *What is History?* Harmondsworth: Penguin Books, 1964.

Casanova, Pascale. *The World Republic of Letters*, trans. M. B. DeBevoise. Cambridge, MA: Harvard University Press, 2004.

———. "Literature as a World." *New Left Review* 31 (Jan.–Feb. 2005): 71–90.

Cassirer, Ernst. *Language and Myth*, trans. Susanne K. Langer. New York: Dover Publications, 1953.

Cauquelin, Josiane, Paul Lim, and Birgit Mayer-König (eds.). *Asian Values: An Encounter with Diversity*. Surrey: Curzon, 1998.

Chateaubriand, Viscount de. *The Genius of Christianity; or the Spirit and Beauty of the Christian Religion*, trans. Charles I. White. Baltimore: John Murphy and Co., 1856.

Chatier, Roger. *On the Edge of the Cliff: History, Language, and Practices*, trans. Lydia G. Cochrane. Baltimore, MD: Johns Hopkins University Press, 1997.

Clark, Katerina, and Michael Holquist. *Mikhail Bakhtin*. Cambridge, Mass.: Harvard University Press, 1984.

Cohen, Paul A. *Discovering History in China: American Historical Writing on the Recent Chinese Past*. New York: Columbia University Press, 1984.

———. *China Unbound: Evolving Perspectives on the Chinese Past*. London: RoutledgeCurzon, 2003.

Collingwood, R. G. *The Idea of History*, ed. Jan van der Dussen. Oxford: Clarendon Press, 1993.

Csikszentmihaly, Mark, and Philip J. Ivanhoe (eds.). *Religious and Philosophical Aspects of the Laozi*. Albany: SUNY Press, 1999.

Culler, Jonathan. *Structuralist Poetics: Structuralism, Linguistics and the Study of Literature*. London: Routledge & Kegan Paul, 1975.

Curd, Patricia (ed.). *A Presocratics Reader: Selected Fragments and Testimonia*, trans. Richard D. McKirahan, Jr. Indianapolis, IN: Hackett, 1996.

Damrosch, David, Natalie Melas, and Mbongiseni Buthelezi (eds.). *The Princeton Sourcebook in Comparative Literature: From the European Enlightenment to the Global Present*. Princeton, NJ: Princeton University Press, 2009.

Damrosch, David (ed.). *Teaching World Literature*. New York: MLA, 2009.

———. *What Is World Literature?* Princeton, NJ: Princeton University Press, 2003.

———. "Comparative Literature / World Literature: A Discussion with Gayatri Charkravorty Spivak and David Damrosch." *Comparative Literature Studies*, 48: 4 (2011): 455–85.

Davidson, Donald. *Inquiries into Truth and Interpretation*, 2nd ed. Oxford: Clarendon Press, 2001.

Derrida, Jacques. *Of Grammatology*, trans. Gayatri Chakravorty Spivak. Baltimore: Johns Hopkins University Press, 1976.

Dickens, Charles. *A Tale of Two Cities*. New York: The Modern Library, 1996.

Diderot, Denis. *This Is Not a Story and Other Stories*, trans. P. N. Furbank. Oxford: Oxford University Press, 1993.

Dong Zhongshu 董仲舒 (179–04 BCE). *Chun qiu fan lu* 春秋繁露 [*Exuberant Dews of the Spring and Autumn*], annotated by Ling Shu 凌曙. Shanghai: The Commercial Press, 1937.

Duara, Prasenjit. *Rescuing History from the Nation: Questioning Narratives of Modern China*. Chicago: University of Chicago Press, 1995.

Dutton, Jacqueline. "Francophonie and universality: the ideological challenges of *littérature-monde*." *International Journal of Francophone Studies* 12: 2&3 (2009): 425–38.

Eckermann, Johann Peter. *Conversations of Goethe with Eckermann and Soret*, trans. John Oxenford, rev. ed. London: George Bell & Sons,1883.

Egan, Ronald. "Narratives in *Tso chuan*." *Harvard Journal of Asiatic Studies* 37: 2 (Dec. 1977): 323–52.

Eliot, T. S. *Selected Prose of T. S. Eliot*, ed. Frank Kermode. New York: Harcourt Brace Jovanovich, 1975.

Emerson, Ralph Waldo. *Essays and Letters*, ed. Joel Porte. New York: Library of America, 1983.

Etiemble, René. *Essais de littérature (vraiment) générale*, 3rd ed. Paris: Gallimard, 1974.

Fabian, Johannes. *Time and the Other: How Anthropology Makes Its Object*. New York: Columbia University Press, 1983.

Fokkema, Douwe. *Perfect Worlds: Utopian Fiction in China and the West*. Amsterdam: Amsterdam University Press, 2011.

Foucault, Michel. *The Order of Things: An Archaeology of the Human Sciences*. New York: Vintage, 1973.

Freud, Sigmund. *Collected Papers*, 5 vols. New York: Basic Books, 1959.

Frost, Robert. *Selected Poems*. New York: Gramercy Books, 1992.

Frye, Northrop. *Anatomy of Criticism: Four Essays*. Princeton, NJ: Princeton University Press, 1957.

Fu Gengsheng 傅庚生 (ed.). *Guo yu xuan* 國語選 [*Selections from Discourses of the States*]. Beijing: Renmin wenxue, 1959.

Gadamer, Hans-Georg. *Truth and Method*, 2nd rev. ed., translation revised by Joel Weinsheimer and Donald G. Marshall. New York: Crossroad, 1991.

Ge Zhaoguang 葛兆光. *Gudai Zhongguo de lishi, sixiang yu zongjiao* 古代中國的歷史、思想與宗教 [*History, Ideas, and Religion in Ancient China*]. Beijing: Beijing Normal University Press, 2006.

Gernet, Jacques. *China and the Christian Impact: A Conflict of Cultures*, trans. Janet Lloyd. Cambridge: Cambridge University Press, 1985.

Gervinus, Georg Gottfried. *Shakespeare Commentaries*, trans. F. E. Bunnett. 2 vols. London: Smith Elder, 1863.

Ginzburg, Carlo. "Killing a Chinese Mandarin: The Moral Implications of Distance." *Critical Inquiry* 21: 1 (Autumn 1994): 46–60.

Goethe, Johann Wolfgang von. *Essays on Art and Literature*, ed. John Gearey, trans. Ellen von Nardroff and Ernest H. Nardroff. Princeton: Princeton University Press 1994.

Gottlieb, Erika. *Dystopian Fiction East and West: Universe of Terror and Trial*. Montreal: McGill-Queen's University Press, 2001.

Guillén, Claudio. *The Challenge of Comparative Literature*, trans. Cola Franzen. Cambridge, MA: Harvard University Press 1993.

Guo Qingfan 郭慶藩 (1844–1895). *Zhuangzi jishi* 莊子集釋 [*The Variorum Edition of the Zhuangzi*], in vol. 3 of *Zhuzi jicheng* 諸子集成 [*Collection of Masters Writings*].

Hamilton, Edith, and Huntington Cairns (eds.). *The Collected Dialogues of Plato, including the Letters*. Princeton: Princeton University Press, 1961.

Hayot, Eric. *The Hypothetical Mandarin: Sympathy, Modernity, and Chinese Pain*. Oxford: Oxford University Press, 2009.

He Wenhuan 何文煥 (1732–1809) (ed.). *Lidai shihua* 歷代詩話 [*Remarks on Poetry from Various Dynasties*], 2 vols. Beijing: Zhonghua, 1981.

Herodotus. *The History*, trans. David Grene. Chicago: University of Chicago Press, 1987.

Huang Baosheng 黃寶生. *Yindu gudian shixue* 印度古典詩學 [*Classical Poetics of India*]. Beijing: Peking University Press, 1999.

Huang Chun-chieh 黃俊傑. "The Idea of *Zhongguo* and Its Transformation in Early Modern Japan and Contemporary Taiwan." *Taiwan Dong Ya wenmin yanjiu xuekan* 台灣東亞文明研究學刊 [*Taiwan Journal of East Asian Studies*] 3: 2 (Dec. 2006): 91–100.

Huang Pumin 黃樸民. *Tian ren he yi: Dong Zhongshu yu Handai ruxue sichao* 天人合一:董仲舒與漢代儒學思潮 [*Unity of Heaven and Man: Dong Zhongshu and Confucian Thoughts in the Han Dynasty*]. Changsha: Yuelu shushe, 1999.

Iyer, Raghavan (ed.). *The Glass Curtain between Asia and Europe*. London: Oxford University Press, 1965.

Jakobson, Roman, and Morris Halle. *Fundamentals of Language*. The Hague: Mouton & Co., 1956.

Jay, Martin. "Historical explanation and the Event: Reflections on the Limits of Contextualization." *New Literary History* 42:4 (Autumn 2011): 557–71.

Ji Xianlin 季羨林 and Zhang Guanglin 張光璘 (eds.). *Dong Xi wenhua yilun ji* 東西文化議論集 [*Essays on Eastern and Western Cultures*], 2 vols. Beijing: Economics Daily Press, 1997.

Jiao Xun 焦循 (1763–1820). *Mengzi zhengyi* 孟子正義 [*The Correct Meaning of the Works of Mencius*], in vol. 1 of *Zhuzi jicheng* 諸子集成 [*Collection of Masters Writings*].

Jin Kaicheng 金開誠 (ed.). *Chu ci xuanzhu* 楚辭選注 [*Selected Songs of Chu with Annotations*]. Beijing: Beijing chubanshe, 1980.

Jullien, François. *La valeur allusive: Des catégories originales de l'interprétation poétique dans la tradition chinoise (Contribution à une réflexion sur l'altérité interculturelle)*. Paris: École française d'Extrême-Orient, 1985.

———. *Detour and Access: Strategies of Meaning in China and Greece*, trans. Sophie Hawkes. New York: Zone Books, 2000.

———, with Thierry Marchaissse. *Penser d'un Dehors (la Chine): Entretiens d'Extrême-Occident*. Paris: Éditions du Seuil, 2000.

———. "Did Philosophers Have to Become Fixated on Truth?" trans. Janet Lloyd. *Critical Inquiry* 28:4 (Summer 2002): 803–24.

Kant, Immanuel. *Critique of Judgment*, trans. Wener S. Pluhar. Indianapolis, IN: Hackett, 1987.

Kao, Yu-kung, and Tsu-lin Mei. "Meaning, Metaphor, and Allusion in T'ang Poetry." *Harvard Journal of Asiatic Studies* 38: 2 (1978): 281–356.

Kennedy, George A. (ed.). *The Cambridge History of Literary Criticism*, vol. 1, *Classical Criticism*. Cambridge: Cambridge University Press, 1989.

Krishnaswamy, Revathi. "Toward World Literary Knowledges: Theory in the Age of Globalization." *Comparative Literature* 62: 4 (Fall 2010): 399–419.

Kugel, James L. *The Idea of Biblical Poetry: Parallelism and Its History*. New Haven: Yale University Press, 1981.

Kuhn, Thomas S. *The Structure of Scientific Revolution*, 2nd enlarged ed. Chicago: University of Chicago Press, 1970.

———. *The Road since Structure: Philosophical Essays, 1970–1993, with an Autobiographical Interview*, ed. James Conant and John Haugeland. Chicago: University of Chicago Press, 2000.

Kumar, Krishan. *Utopia and Anti-Utopia in Modern Times*. Oxford: Basil Blackwell, 1987.

———. "The Ends of Utopia." *New Literary History*, 41: 3 (Summer 2010): 549–69.

Lahusen, Thomas, with Gene Kuperman (eds.). *Late Soviet Culture: From Perestroika to Novostroika*. Durham, NC: Duke University Press, 1993.

Lakoff, George, and Mark Turner. *More than Cool Reason: A Field Guide to Poetic Metaphor*. Chicago: University of Chicago Press, 1989.

Landau, Iddo. "To Kill a Mandarin." *Philosophy and Literature* 29 (April 2005): 89–96.

Langer, Lawrence L. *Holocaust Testimonies: The Ruins of Memory*. New Haven, CT: Yale University Press 1991.

Laozi. *Tao te ching*, trans. D. C. Lau. Harmondsworth, UK: Penguin, 1963.

———. *The Classic of the Way and Virtue: A New Translation of the Tao-te ching of Laozi as Interpreted by Wang Bi*, trans. Richard John Lynn. New York: Columbia University Press, 1999.

Larner, John. *Marco Polo and the Discovery of the World*. New Haven, CT: Yale University Press, 1999.

Levinas, Emmanuel. *Outside the Subject*, trans. Michael B. Smith. Stanford: Stanford University Press, 1994.

———. *Time and the Other [and Additional Essays]*, trans. Richard A. Cohen. Pittsburgh: Duquesne University Press, 1987.

Levitas, Ruth. *The Concept of Utopia*. New York: Philip Allan, 1990.

Li Gang 李綱. *Liangxi ji* 梁溪集 [*Li Gang's Collected Writings*], in vol. 1126 of *Siku quanshu* 四庫全書 [*Complete Collection of the Four Treasuries*]. Shanghai: Shanghai guji, 1987 reprint.

Li Meng 李猛. "Whose History to Rescue?" *Ershi yi shiji* 二十一世紀 [*Twenty-First Century*], no. 49 (October 1998): 128–33.

Lionnet, Françoise. "Universalism and francophonies," *International Journal of Francophone Studies* 12: 2&3 (2009): 203–21.

Liu An 劉安 (?–122 BC). *Huainanzi* 淮南子 [*Master Huainan*], in vol. 7 of *Zhuzi jicheng* 諸子集成 [*Collection of Masters Writings*].

Liu Baonan 劉寶楠 (1791–1855). *Lunyu zhengyi* 論語正義 [*The Correct Meaning of the Analects*], in vol. 1 of *Zhuzi jicheng* 諸子集成 [*Collection of Masters Writings*].

Liu, James J. Y. *The Art of Chinese Poetry*. Chicago: University of Chicago Press, 1962.

———. *Chinese Theories of Literature*. Chicago: University of Chicago Press, 1975.

Liu Xie 劉勰 (465?–522). *Wenxin diaolong zhu* 文心雕龍注 [*The Literary Mind or the Carving of Dragons with Annotations*]. 2 vols., annotated by Fan Wenlan 范文瀾. Beijing: Renmin wenxue, 1958.

Liu Xie (Liu Hsieh). *The Literary Mind and the Carving of Dragons: A Study of Thought and Pattern in Chinese Literature*, trans. Vincent Yu-chung Shih. New York: Columbia University Press, 1959.

Lloyd, G. E. R. *Demystifying Mentalities*. Cambridge: Cambridge University Press, 1990.

———. *Ancient Worlds, Modern Reflections: Philosophical Perspectives on Greek and Chinese Science and Culture*. Oxford: Clarendon Press, 2004.

———. *Cognitive Variations: Reflections on the Unity and Diversity of the Human Mind*. Oxford: Clarendon Press, 2007.

Lu Xun 魯迅 (1881–1936). *Lu Xun quanji* 魯迅全集 [*Lu Xun's Complete Works*], 16 vols. Beijing: Renmin wenxue, 1981.

Lu Xiangshan 陸象山 (1139–1193). *Lu Xiangshan quanji* 陸象山全集 [*Lu Xiangshan's Complete Works*]. Beijing: Zhongguo shudian, 1992.

Lucas, F. L. *Tragedy: Serious Drama in Relation to Aristotle's Poetics*, revised ed. London: the Hogarth Press, 1957.

Luo Guanzhong 羅貫中 (1330?–1400?). *San guo yanyi* 三國演義 [*The Romance of the Three Kingdoms*]. Beijing: Renmin wenxue, 1985.

———. *Three Kingdoms: A Historical Novel*, attributed to Luo Guanzhong, trans. Moss Roberts. Berkeley: University of California Press, 1991.

Marcus, George E. *Ethnography through Thick and Thin*. Princeton: Princeton University Press, 1998.

Marx, Karl, and Friedrich Engels. *The Communist Manifesto*. New York: The Seabury Press, 1967.

Merton, Robert K. *The Sociology of Science: Theoretical and Empirical Investigations*, ed. Norman W. Storer. Chicago: University of Chicago Press, 1973.

Miller, Barbara Stoler (ed.). *Masterworks of Asian Literature in Comparative Perspective: A Guide for Teaching*. Armonk, NY: M. E. Sharpe, 1994.

Miner, Earl. *Comparative Poetics: An Intercultural Essay on Theories of Literature*. Princeton, NJ: Princeton University Press, 1990.

Mirandola, Giovanni Pico della. *Oration on the Dignity of Man*, trans. A. Robert Caponigri. Washington, DC: Regnery Publishing, Inc., 1956.

More, Thomas. *Utopia: Latin Text and English Translation*, eds. George M. Logan, Robert M. Adams, and Clarence H. Miller. Cambridge: Cambridge University Press, 1995.

Moretti, Franco. "Conjectures on World Literature," *New Left Review* 1 (Jan.–Feb. 2000): 54–68.

Mueller-Vollmer, Kurt (ed.). *The Hermeneutics Reader: Texts of the German Tradition from the Enlightenment to the Present*. New York: Continuum, 1990.

Mufti, Aamir. "Orientalism and the Institution of World Literatures," *Critical Inquiry* 36:3 (Spring 2010): 458–93.

Nederman, Cary J., and Kate Langdon Forhan (eds.). *Medieval Political Theory—A Reader: The Quest for the Body Politic, 1100–1400*. London: Routledge, 1993.

Nelson, John S., Allan Megill, and Donald N. McCloskey (eds.). *The Rhetoric of the Human Sciences: Language and Argument in Scholarship and Public Affairs*. Madison: University of Wisconsin Press, 1987.

Newman, John Henry. *The Idea of a University*. New Have: Yale University Press, 1996 [1873].

Nisbett, Richard. *The Geography of Thought: How Asians and Westerners Think Differently . . . and Why*. New York: The Free Press, 2003.

Norman, Richard. *On Humanism*. London: Routledge, 2004.

Nussbaum, Martha C. "Human Functioning and Social Justice: In Defense of Aristotelian Essentialism." *Political Theory* 20: 2 (May 1992): 202–46.

———. *Cultivating Humanity: A Classical Defense of Reform in Liberal Education*. Cambridge, MA: Harvard University Press, 1997.

Owen, Stephen. "The Anxiety of Global Influence: What Is World Poetry?" *New Republic* (Nov. 19, 1990): 28–32.

———. "Stepping Forward and Back: Issues and Possibilities for 'World' Poetry," *Modern Philology* 100: 4 (May 2003): 532–48.

———. *Traditional Chinese Poetry and Poetics: Omen of the World*. Madison: University of Wisconsin Press, 1985.

Pagels, Elaine. *Adam, Eve, and the Serpent*. New York: Vintage Books, 1989.

Palumbo-Liu, David. "The Utopias of Discourse: On the Impossibility of Chinese Comparative Literature," *Chinese Literature: Essays, Articles, Reviews* 14 (December 1992): 165–76.

Pathak, R. S. *Comparative Poetics*. New Delhi: Creative Books, 1998.

Pizer, John. *The Idea of World Literature*. Baton Rouge: Louisiana State University Press, 2006.

Pollock, Sheldon (ed.). *Literary Cultures in History: Reconstructions from South Asia*. Berkeley: University of California Press, 2003.

Pope, Alexander. *Selected Poetry and Prose*. 2nd ed., ed. William K. Wimsatt. New York: Holt, Rinehart and Winston, 1972.

Putnam, Hilary. *Realism with a Human Face*, ed. James Conant. Cambridge, Mass.: Harvard University Press, 1990.

Qian Zhongshu 錢鍾書. *Guan zhui bian* 管錐編 [*Limited Views*], 2nd ed., 5 vols. Beijing: Zhonghua, 1986.

———. *Song shi xuan zhu* 宋詩選注 [*Selection of Song Dynasty Poetry with Annotations*]. Beijing: Renmin wenxue, 1958.

———. *Qi zhui ji* 七綴集 [*Collection of Seven Essays*]. Shanghai: Shanghai guji, 1985.

———. *Tan yi lu* 談藝錄 [*Discourses on the Art of Literature*], expanded ed. Beijing: Zhonghua, 1984.

Qiu Zhao'ao 仇兆鰲 (fl. 1685). *Du shi xiangzhu* 杜詩詳注 [*Du Fu's Poems with Detailed Annotations*], 5 vols. Beijing: Zhonghua, 1979.

Qu Yuan, et al. *The Songs of the South: An Ancient Chinese Anthology of Poems by Qu Yuan and Other Poets*, trans. David Hawkes. Harmondsworth, UK: Penguin, 1985.

Queen, Sarah A. *From Chronicle to Canon: The Hermeneutics of the Spring and Autumn, according to Tung Chung-shu*. Cambridge: Cambridge University Press, 1996.

Queiróz, Eça de. *The Mandarin and Other Stories*, trans. Margaret Jull Costa. Sawtry: Dedalus, 2009.

Rajendran, C. *Studies in Comparative Poetics*. Delhi: New Bharatiya Book Co., 2001.

Ruan Yuan 阮元 (ed.). *Shisan jing zhushu* 十三經注疏 [*The Thirteen Classics with Annotations*], 2 vols. Beijing: Zhonghua, 1980.

Ryckmans, Pierre. "Fou de chinois," *Le Monde*, June 10, 1983.

Said, Edward. *The World, the Text, and the Critic*. Cambridge, Mass.: Harvard University Press, 1983.

Sallis, John. *On Translation*. Bloomington: Indiana University Press, 2002.

Saussure, Ferdinand de. *Course in General Linguistics*, trans. Wade Baskin. New York: Philosophical Library, 1959.

Saussy, Haun. *The Problem of a Chinese Aesthetic*. Stanford: Stanford University Press, 1993.

———. *Great Walls of Discourse and Other Adventures in Cultural China*. Cambridge, Mass.: Harvard University Asia Center, 2001.

Schaer, Roland, Gregory Claeys, and Lyman Tower Sargent (eds.). *Utopia: The Search for the Ideal Society in the Western World*. New York: The New York Public Library, 2000.

Schauffler, Robert Haven. *Franz Schubert: The Ariel of Music*. New York: G. P. Putnam's Sons, 1949.

Schleiermacher, Friedrich. *Hermeneutics: The Handwritten Manuscripts*, trans. James Duke and Jack Forstman. Missoula, MT: Scholars Press, 1977.

Schwartz, Benjamin. *China and Other Matters*. Cambridge, MA: Harvard University Press, 1996.

Segalen, Victor. *Essai sur l'exotisme: une esthétique du divers*. Paris: Fata Morgana, 1978.

Sen, Amartya. *Identity and Violence: The Illusion of Destiny*. New York: W. W. Norton, 2006.

Sima Qian 司馬遷 (145?–90? BCE). *Shi ji* 史記 [*Record of History*]. Beijing: Zhonghua, 1959.

Smith, Adam. *The Theory of Moral Sentiments*, ed. Knud Haakonssen. Cambridge: Cambridge University Press, 2002.

Sophocles. *Theban Plays: Oedipus the King, Oedipus at Colonus, Antigone*, trans. Ruth Fainlight and Robert J. Littman. Baltimore, MD: Johns Hopkins University Press, 2009.

Spence, Jonathan D. *The Chan's Great Continent: China in Western Minds*. New York: W. W. Norton, 1998.

Spinoza, Benedict de. *Correspondence, The Chief Works of Benedict de Spinoza*, trans. R. H. M. Elwes, 2 vols. New York: Dover Publications, 1951.

Stein, Gertrude. *Everybody's Autobiography*. New York: 1971.

Stockwell, Peter. *Cognitive Poetics: An Introduction*. London: Routledge, 2002.

Sun Yirang 孫詒讓 (1848–1908). *Mozi jiangu* 墨子閒詁 [*Annotations on the Mozi*], in vol. 4 of *Zhuzi jicheng* 諸子集成 [*Collection of Masters Writings*].

Tang Yan 湯晏. *Minguo diyi caizi Qian Zhongshu* 民國第一才子錢鍾書 [*Ch'ien Chung-shu: Oppressed Genius*]. Taipei: Taipei Times, 2001.

Tao Yuanming 陶淵明 (365–427). *Tao Yuanming ji* 陶淵明集 [*Tao Yuanming's Works*], ed. Lu Qinli 逯欽立. Beijing: Zhonghua, 1979.

Thomsen, Mads Rosendahl. *Mapping World Literature: International Canonization and Transnational Literatures*. London: Continuum, 2008.

Thucydides. *The Peloponnesian War*, trans. Walter Blanco. New York: W. W. Norton, 1998.

Tillyard, E. M. W. *The Elizabethan World Picture*. New York: Vintage, 1959.

Tolstoy, Leo. *Anna Karenina*, trans. Louise Maude and Aylmer Maude. Oxford: Oxford University Press, 1998.

Ulmann, Stephen. *The Principles of Semantics*. Oxford: Basil Blackwell, 1963.

Vico, Giambattista. *The New Science of Giambattista Vico*, trans. Thomas Goddard Bergin and Max Harold Fisch. Ithaca, NY: Cornell University Press, 1968.

Wallerstein, Immanuel. *World-Systems Analysis: An Introduction*. Durham, NC: Duke University Press, 2004.

Wang Bi 王弼 (226–249). *Laozi zhu* 老子注 [*Laozi with Annotations*], in vol. 3 of *Zhuzi jicheng* 諸子集成 [*Collection of Masters Writings*].

Waters, Lindsay. "The Age of Incommensurability." *Boundary 2* 28:2 (Summer 2001): 134–72.

White, Hayden. *Tropics of Discourse: Essays in Cultural Criticism*. Baltimore, MD: Johns Hopkins University Press 1978.

Wilde, Oscar. *The Portable Oscar Wilde*, revised ed., eds. Richard Aldington and Stanley Weintraub. Harmondsworth, UK: Penguin, 1981.

———. *Plays, Prose Writings and Poems*, ed. Anthony Fothergill. London: J. M. Dent, 1996.

Wyschogrod, Edith. *An Ethics of Remembering: History, Heterology, and the Nameless Others*. Chicago: University of Chicago Press, 1998.

Yan Yu 嚴羽. *Canlang shihua jiaoshi* 滄浪詩話校釋 [*Canlang's Remarks on Poetry with Annotations*], ed. Guo Shaoyu 郭紹虞. Beijing: Renmin wenxue, 1983.

Yu, Anthony C. *Rereading the Stone: Desire and the Making of Fiction in Dream of the Red Chamber*. Princeton: Princeton University Press, 1997.

Yu Guanying 余冠英 (ed.). *San Cao shi xuan* 三曹詩選 [*Selected Poems of the Three Cao's*]. Beijing: Writers Press, 1956.

Zamyatin, Yevgeny. *We*, trans. Clarence Brown. Harmondsworth, UK: Penguin, 1993.

Żegleń, Urszula M. (ed.). *Donald Davidson: Truth, Meaning and Knowledge*. London: Routledge, 1999.

Zhang Longxi. *The Tao and the Logos: Literary Hermeneutics, East and West*. Durham, NC: Duke University Press, 1992.

———. *Mighty Opposites: From Dichotomies to Differences in the Comparative Study of China*. Stanford. CA: Stanford University Press, 1998.

———. *Allegoresis: Reading Canonical Literature East and West*. Ithaca, NY: Cornell University Press, 2005.

Zhou Guidian 周桂鈿. *Dong xue tan wei* 董學探微 [*Exploring the Intricacies of Dong Zhongshu's Doctrine*]. Beijing: Beijing Normal University Press, 1989.

Zhuzi jicheng 諸子集成 [*Collection of Masters Writings*]. 8 vols. Beijing: Zhonghua, 1954.

Index